Communications in Computer and Information Science 1383

Younghee Park · Divyesh Jadav ·
Thomas Austin (Eds.)

Silicon Valley Cybersecurity Conference

First Conference, SVCC 2020
San Jose, CA, USA, December 17–19, 2020
Revised Selected Papers

 Springer

Editors
Younghee Park 🆔
San Jose State University
San Jose, CA, USA

Divyesh Jadav 🆔
IBM Almaden Research Center
San Jose, CA, USA

Thomas Austin 🆔
San Jose State University
San Jose, CA, USA

ISSN 1865-0929   ISSN 1865-0937 (electronic)
Communications in Computer and Information Science
ISBN 978-3-030-72724-6   ISBN 978-3-030-72725-3 (eBook)
https://doi.org/10.1007/978-3-030-72725-3

This Springer imprint is published by the registered company Springer Nature Switzerland AG
The registered company address is: Gewerbestrasse 11, 6330 Cham, Switzerland

Preface

Silicon Valley Cybersecurity Conference (SVCC) facilitates research in dependability, reliability, and security to address cyber-attacks, vulnerabilities, faults, and errors in networks and systems. This conference provides a high-quality forum for participants to exchange their research in robustness and resilience in a wide spectrum of computing systems and networks. The conference discusses innovative system design, protocols, and algorithms for detecting and responding to malicious threats in dependable and secure systems and networks including experimentation and assessment.

The SVCC 2020 conference had five featured keynote speakers from academia and industry and six different research programs along with a distinguished research forum. The special research forum recognized three distinguished researchers in 2020 who presented their high-quality research in cybersecurity. The conference had 13 research papers and five poster papers this year, three of which were selected to be expanded into short papers. Papers were evaluated with a double-blind review process, with three reviews per paper.

In addition, the conference had a special session called UNiSEC (Underrepresented groups in Cybersecurity) with a poster session. We had two tutorial sessions: network security from Trend Micro and blockchain security. Finally, we hosted free student cybersecurity hackathons on December 19, 2020, supported by Cisco and San José State University.

In 2020, we had three conference sponsorships from well-known companies: Cisco, Intel, and Trend Micro.

December 2020

Younghee Park
Divyesh Jadav

Organization

Program Chairs

Divyesh Jadav   IBM Research, USA
Younghee Park   San José State University, USA

Local/Industry Organization Chairs

Michael Tjebben   Cybersecurity Consultant, USA
Sang-Soo Lee   San José State University, USA

Publicity Chair

Sara Tehranipoor   Santa Clara University, USA

Panel Chair

Sang-Yoon Chang   University of Colorado Colorado Springs, USA

Publication Chair

Thomas Austin   San José State University, USA

Registration Chair

Nima Karimian   San José State University, USA

Technical Program Committee

Andrea Visconti   Universit degli Studi di Milano, Italy
Samaneh Ghandali   Google, USA
Melike Erol-Kantarci   University of Ottawa, Canada
Qiong Zhang   Fujitsu Network Communications, USA
Hyoungshick Kim   Sungkyunkwan University, South Korea
Attila Altay Yavuz   University of South Florida, USA
Sunil K. Cheruvu   Intel, USA
Donghyun Kim   Georgia State University, USA
Hongxin Hu   University at Buffalo, USA
Hongda Li   Palo Alto Networks, USA

Contents

Machine Learning for Security

Application and Network Security

Dynamic Security Analysis of Zoom, Google Meet and Microsoft Teams

Nicholas Hunter Gauthier[1] and Mohammad Iftekhar Husain[2]([✉])

[1] Department of Computer Science, University of Houston, Houston, TX, USA
nhgauthier@uh.edu
[2] Department of Computer Science, Cal Poly Pomona, Pomona, CA, USA
mihusain@cpp.edu

Abstract. Videoconferencing platforms have received a large influx of traffic due to COVID-19 and the global pandemic it has caused. Professionals, students, politicians, and high-risk security individuals utilize these platforms to communicate with their colleagues. They blindly trust these platforms without understanding how secure they are, and their sensitive data may be vulnerable as it is transmitted through these third party platforms. Zoom, Google Meet, and Microsoft Teams are the most popular among the platforms, and they are examined in this paper. These platforms' security aspects were to be evaluated by simulating calls within a virtual environment, capturing the network traffic sent to/from the network, and analyzing the captured traffic to determine what information outside listeners had access to. It was discovered that these platforms utilized state-of-the-art encryption methods, but they did not provide end-to-end encryption since vendors as third parties have access to the end-user communication data. It was also discovered that some strange TCP connections were being established as well as unknown DNS communications. It also found TCP communications running in the background. This suggests that the platforms are not being transparent with users, and this could generate potential security concerns with users.

Keywords: Videoconferencing security · Videoconferencing privacy · Zoom · Meet · Teams vulnerabilities

1 Introduction

The COVID-19 pandemic resulted in an influx of traffic through videoconferencing platforms such as Zoom, Google Meet, and Microsoft Teams. Businessmen, doctors, lawyers, politicians, etc. are utilizing these applications to combat the spread of this virus. Thus, sensitive and non-sensitive data is being blindly

Thanks to the CyberCorps Scholarship For Service (SFS) Program and to the National Science Foundation (NSF) for funding this research.

© Springer Nature Switzerland AG 2021
Y. Park et al. (Eds.): SVCC 2020, CCIS 1383, pp. 3–24, 2021.
https://doi.org/10.1007/978-3-030-72725-3_1

entrusted to third parties. This has elevated security and privacy concerns for these platforms more than ever.

These concerns raise question like: "Is my data being encrypted/kept secure?", and "Who has access to my data?" Calls can be intercepted by outside listeners and past communications can be compromised if security protocols are not updated and maintained to industry standards or practices. An example of this is apparent in Marczak and Scott-Railton's work when they discovered that Zoom "rolled their own crypto" [10]. Data breaches at parliamentary levels would be catastrophic for governments, and should be avoided at all costs. So, how secure are these videoconferencing platforms?

This paper will answer those questions by simulating calls within a virtually created environment, and capture/analyze the network traffic with Wireshark. We chose to analyze Zoom, Google Meet, and Microsoft Teams because they appear to be a few of the most popular platforms for videoconferencing, and there is already established work based around these platforms. The Verge covered Zoom's, Teams', and Meet's average daily users [14]. In April 2020, Zoom approximated 300 million daily meeting participants, Teams with 75 million, and Meet with roughly 3 million. This work builds upon previous work from Marczak and Scott-Railton's research in which they detailed Zoom's recent vulnerabilities [10] and criteria similar to that of which was outlined from the Electronic Frontier Foundation [5].

Zoom, Google Meet, and Microsoft Teams were evaluated with the following modified criterion, which were taken as inspiration from the Electronic Frontier Foundation's electronic scorecard [5]:

1. Is the data encrypted in transit?
2. Is the data encrypted at rest?
3. Is the data encrypted so that the provider cannot read it?
4. Can the contact's identities be verified?
5. Are past communications secure if keys are stolen?
6. Is the code open source?
7. Is the platform's security design properly documented?
8. What Metadata can be obtained?

The paper is organized as follows: Sect. 2 provides an overview of the current literature, Sect. 3 outlines our experimental methodology, Sect. 4 details the evaluation of the platforms, Sect. 5 covers the research's results, Sect. 6 addresses the research's limitations, and Sect. 7 concludes and summarizes the paper.

2   Related Work

Marczak and Scott-Railton [10] discovered vulnerabilities involving privacy and security concerns in Zoom's infrastructure by capturing packets via "Wireshark" and "mitmproxy", analyzing the captured packets, and finding what type of cipher suites that Zoom utilized. They discovered that Zoom was communicating from servers in Beijing, China and that they had three companies on their payroll in China by tracing the IP addresses that established TCP connections with them during their call. Zoom is a US-based company, but it is developing and offering its services in China?

Zoom claimed to utilize TLSv1.2 AES-256 encryption as the cipher suite deployed during the call; however, Marczak and Scott-Railton discovered that Zoom implemented their own custom transport protocol along with AES-128 encryption with **ECB mode**. This was discovered through the analysis of the UDP packets. The UDP payloads begin with a specific hexadecimal sequence, and the RTP headers always had a specific value located within them. This lead to a discovery that the RTP payloads were fragmented, and this did not match a standard format. Thus, it was custom-formatted for Zoom.

Lastly, they discovered a large vulnerability in Zoom's waiting room feature. Public information about this vulnerability was not released, but directly reported to Zoom through an official process in early April, 2020. They provided enough conclusive evidence with their scans revealing the IP addresses, proof that AES-128 with ECB mode encryption was utilized[1], and that they launched an official process with Zoom to disclose their vulnerability with their waiting room feature to determine that not all of Zoom's security claims were accurate.

Zoom's security documentation [16] was informative for developing an explicit foundation of their security and privacy protocols on their platform. This document was utilized in this research to fully understand each feature deployed by the platform, and to confirm if their security claims were upheld. It was also utilized as a reference to determine if something that was discovered should be deemed as normal, recognized process by the platform or if it may be an intriguing discovery.

Google Meet's documentation for the security and privacy for administrators [6] was informative for its security protocols, transparency policies, features, and security/privacy protections for the available features. This information was utilized as a baseline in terms of what to expect from the platform as well as its normal functions. It offered more information pertaining to Meet's technical aspects such as encryption, anti-abuse measures, and telephony.

The documentation for users [7] was near analogous of the documentation for administrators. The difference between them was the lack thereof of the technical aspects and an emphasis on preventative measures that users can take to combat phishing and account hijacking.

Lakshminarayanan and Hashim [9] delves deeper into Google Meet's security protocols by discussing what Meet does to protect against abuse and hijacking attempts, how administrators and users have access and control over their data, and how the design of Meet's infrastructure provides a secure, compliant, and reliable videoconferencing space.

Meet is solely accessible in the browser, and this is a unique approach that separates them from platforms like Zoom and Teams. They claim that in doing so

---

[1] ECB mode is not a secure encryption as it preserves patterns in plaintext, and it is much easier to crack than the security standard: CBC or GCM. They were able to successfully identify and extract audio and video because ECB mode was used.

limits the attack surface of their platform as well as the need to push out security patches. Instead, they are able to immediately deploy changes to their platform. Google also requires that all users desiring to join meetings must perform a Single Sign-On (SSO) with their Google account. Google accounts are typically reinforced with two-step verification, so this creates a good layer of security in confirming user's identities. An Advanced Protection Program is also offered for all clients to further their protection on the platform. This program is primarily focused on preventing phishing and account hijacking.

Data security is a large concern for customers, and Meet prioritizes access transparency for G Suite Enterprise and Education customers. This feature logs all Meet/access recordings, and administrators may request access to this data along with their reason for desiring to access. This is also logged and can be viewed by other administrators. These customers also have the capability of storing their data in specific regions if they so desire. Google Meet also claims that they regularly undergo independent verification for security, privacy, and compliance controls.

Christensen [2] investigates how secure Microsoft Teams is given its claims and reputation. They specifically investigate Teams' ability to prevent phishing and account hijacking, account security, framework design, and data security(at transit and rest). Teams runs on Microsoft 365's enterprise-level cloud, and this provides several advantages: advanced security against phishing, malware and ransomware, and identity verification. Two-factor authentication is required, and data is encrypted at transit and rest within Microsoft 365. They store the data in multiple locations: Exchange, Stream, Groups, SharePoint, and OneDrive for Business. This approach is unique because the data is split between these locations, and not all of them belong to Microsoft. They are partnered with these companies, and thus have different types of encryption for Exchange, SharePoint, and OneDrive. This means that if only one of them is breached, then the rest of the data is still safe because that piece is meaningless without the entire message. This makes past communications difficult to attack, and thus more secure. Christensen concluded that these qualities make Teams as secure as they claim to be, and they encourage users to utilize this platform and that they must follow security best practices in order to ensure success with this platform.

Teams' documentation [11] provided analogous information to this research as Google's [6] and Zoom's [16] documentation. The more notable topics that were covered in Teams' documentation were their Advanced Threat Protection (ATP), the compliance policies that they follow, and their privacy protection policies. Their ATP feature automatically determines if content shown in the applications associated with them are malicious in nature, and then that content is blocked. Attachments are also scanned before being uploaded to determine if they are malicious. If they are, then they are not sent. This prevents other users from becoming infected.

Teams' compliance policies offer many features for administrators to prevent groups from mixing, preventing sensitive information from leaking by employing custom language filters, etc. Data loss prevention is also handled by Teams by keeping detailed audit logs, which are accessible by administrators. Legal Hold features are also offered.

Privacy is a concern for most users, and Teams claims to take that concern seriously. Their data storage framework is outlined in this section via diagrams, and Teams offers options for users to determine what location (such as region) they would like their data stored.

Paul Wagenseil [13] has up-kept an active blog post with Tom's guide about security issues with Zoom thus far. The list of updates includes current security issues, fixed issues, suggested settings to use on Zoom, etc. This blog can be informative about many security concerns with Zoom and its features.

Wagenseil organizes this post into the following categories: Zoom security tips, most recent unresolved issues, latest Zoom updates, known unresolved issues, and resolved issues. The overall conclusion in this post clarifies that Zoom is relatively safe to use for most cases, but he advises anyone discussing state, corporate, healthcare, etc. secrets on Zoom is unsafe. Wagenseil also suggests using two-factor authentication, joining Zoom meetings through your web browser, and signing in with a password. This is because Zoom has a large attack surface due to having desktop applications, mobile applications, and web browser applications. According to Wagenseil, the web browser is the most secure because it receives security enhancement quicker than the other applications [13].

Archibald et al. [1] contributed research pertaining to increasing awareness of methodology options for online data collection. The authors utilized Zoom for conducting one-on-one interviews with nurses across Australia. They collected demographic data via surveys and open-ended responses. Their results were analyzed with descriptive statistics, content analysis, and qualitative descriptions. Then, they were cross-compared with the interpretations.

Overall, the authors concluded that 69% of the participants preferred the interviews via Zoom over in-person, telephone, or other videoconferencing platforms because of the ability to generate more rapport, the convenience, and the platform being user-friendly.

This article contributes to the security aspect of Zoom because the authors mentioned that they were able to securely record Zoom interviews, with consent of the participants, and that Zoom does not record individual sessions unless specified otherwise. They were also given the option to store the recording on Zoom's cloud if they were a paying customer. Security issues were supposedly not experienced during these calls, and it was noted that Zoom was known to collect and store ranges of personal information about the users such as: personal data, ip address, user-generated information, and passive collection of data via cookies/tracking technologies [1].

Navid et al. [8] discusses some of the cybersecurity threats that are rampantly growing amid the COVID-19 pandemic. They address that several threats such as DDoS, malicious domains and websites, malware, ransomware, etc. have been increasingly growing at an alarming rate because people are stuck in quarantine, and thus more likely to be on the web whilst working from home.

The authors also addressed privacy concerns with platforms like Zoom, Google Meet, and Microsoft Teams becoming increasingly popular during the pandemic. They discovered that recent consumer reports found that these applications were collecting more data than they were being transparent about. This supposedly led security experts, FBI, and several others to suggest that Zoom's default settings are not secure [8].

3 Methodology

3.1 Materials

Virtual Machines (VMs) were deployed utilizing Oracle VM Virtualbox [12]. The following Operating Systems (OS) and application versions were deployed:

1. Kali Linux version 2020.2a-32bit
2. SEED Ubuntu version 16.04-32bit
3. Windows 10 version 10.0.17763 Build 17763
4. Zoom desktop application 5.1.3 (28656.0709)
5. Google Meet Web Browser application - version unavailable
6. Microsoft Teams Desktop Application 4.4.63.0

The VMs were configured to utilize NAT Networks for connecting to the open internet, and deployed on two hardware devices. They were connected to a private, secure network. Device one was connected via Ethernet, and device two was connected via 2.4GHz WiFi.

A TP-LINK AC1200 WiFi Router was used for these experiments. It was configured with default security settings, and it was secured with WPA2-PSK.

At the time that this research was conducted, the operating system versions used were the most up to date for the free versions, and the 32-bit versions were used due to resource constraints. The OS version should not impact the results of this research hardly at all because the research was mostly centered around the applications and web applications.

A diagram of the setup can be observed in the next section. See Fig. 1.

3.2 Experimental Setup

Experiments were setup with VMs to simulate one-on-one teleconferencing calls with two victims, and an outside listener on the network. See Fig. 1 for details.

The attacker was listening to the network via Wireshark on the SEED Ubuntu machine. Wireshark was utilized to capture all packets that traveled through the network. It was vital to capture packets sent for the call initiation, all messages sent during the call, and for the call's termination packets. This was because the client hellos, server hellos, and all types of Acknowledgment packets provide valuable information pertaining to the call.

Calls were initiated and recorded between VM 1 (host) and VM 2 (participant). The Attacker was capturing all traffic passing through the router's network via Wireshark. Audio, chat messages, and files/images were uploaded between the victims during the call. This was performed to check what the platforms were logging, sending, and to check if the plain-text was encrypted.

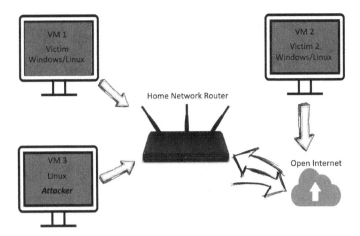

Fig. 1. An example of typical call setup for experimentation. VM 1 is the Host of the call, and VM 2 is represented as the participant. VM 3 is an outside listener listening in on the network.

3.3 Data Collected

Our own data was collected and utilized for these experiments. All packets were sent through the open internet via a private, secure network. Thus, all packets that traveled through the network were captured to create an interesting, and controlled environment for the experiment. Packets that were captured via Wireshark were saved in ".pcapng" files.

Files and logs that were available from the host machines were stored and included as part of the data collected for this experiment. These files were collected from the appropriate directories of each application as well as where each application stored temporary files.

Network information was also recorded via the "netstat" command before, during, and after each call on both host machines.

4 Results

4.1 Analysis

In this section, we take each of the proposed research questions and summarize our findings for each of the vendors.

4.2 End to End Encryption

In our experiment, we have found that none of the vendors: Zoom, Meet, and Teams provide end-to-end encryption. The client's communications can be decrypted by the vendors as they generate the session keys.

4.3   Call Setup and Cipher Suites

Two Zoom experimental calls were created:

a The first call was initialized between a Kali Linux machine (VM 1, host) and a SEED Ubuntu machine (VM 2, participant).
b The second call was initialized between a Kali Linux machine (VM 1, host) and a Windows 10 machine (VM 2, participant).

The captured packets were manually analyzed within Wireshark for both calls. The analysis revealed that Zoom has updated their cipher suites based on the previous work of Marczak and Scott-Railton [10]. They are no longer "rolling their own crypto", and have begun utilizing to be what is understood as the industry standard for cipher suites (Fig. 2).

```
∨ Cipher Suites (14 suites)
      Cipher Suite: TLS_AES_256_GCM_SHA384 (0x1302)
      Cipher Suite: TLS_CHACHA20_POLY1305_SHA256 (0x1303)
      Cipher Suite: TLS_AES_128_GCM_SHA256 (0x1301)
      Cipher Suite: TLS_ECDHE_RSA_WITH_AES_256_GCM_SHA384 (0xc030)
      Cipher Suite: TLS_DHE_RSA_WITH_AES_256_GCM_SHA384 (0x009f)
      Cipher Suite: TLS_ECDHE_RSA_WITH_CHACHA20_POLY1305_SHA256 (0xcca8)
      Cipher Suite: TLS_DHE_RSA_WITH_CHACHA20_POLY1305_SHA256 (0xccaa)
      Cipher Suite: TLS_ECDHE_RSA_WITH_AES_128_GCM_SHA256 (0xc02f)
      Cipher Suite: TLS_DHE_RSA_WITH_AES_128_GCM_SHA256 (0x009e)
      Cipher Suite: TLS_ECDHE_RSA_WITH_AES_256_CBC_SHA384 (0xc028)
      Cipher Suite: TLS_DHE_RSA_WITH_AES_256_CBC_SHA256 (0x006b)
      Cipher Suite: TLS_ECDHE_RSA_WITH_AES_128_CBC_SHA256 (0xc027)
      Cipher Suite: TLS_DHE_RSA_WITH_AES_128_CBC_SHA256 (0x0067)
      Cipher Suite: TLS_EMPTY_RENEGOTIATION_INFO_SCSV (0x00ff)
```

Fig. 2. Zoom's list of their offered cipher suites in the "Client Hello" packet.

The "Server Hello" packets indicated that the Cipher Suite: *TLS_ECDHE_RSA_WITH_AES_256_GCM_SHA384 (0xc030)* was used for both calls. This cipher suite is one of the stronger cipher suites available, and is certainly stronger than the AES-128-ECB cipher suite that Marczak and Scott-Railton [10] discovered Zoom was previously using.

An analogous experiment was performed with Google Meet. Two calls were created:

a The first call was initialized between a Kali Linux machine (VM 1, host) and a SEED Ubuntu machine (VM 2, participant).
b The second call was between a Kali Linux machine (VM 1, host) and a Windows 10 machine (VM 2, participant).

The analysis of the captured packets revealed that Google Meet offers a few more cipher suites than Zoom. Meet appears to use three types of cipher suites: GCM, CBC, and ChaCha20 Poly1305. This can be observed in Fig. 3.

```
∨ Cipher Suites (18 suites)
    Cipher Suite: TLS_AES_128_GCM_SHA256 (0x1301)
    Cipher Suite: TLS_CHACHA20_POLY1305_SHA256 (0x1303)
    Cipher Suite: TLS_AES_256_GCM_SHA384 (0x1302)
    Cipher Suite: TLS_ECDHE_ECDSA_WITH_AES_128_GCM_SHA256 (0xc02b)
    Cipher Suite: TLS_ECDHE_RSA_WITH_AES_128_GCM_SHA256 (0xc02f)
    Cipher Suite: TLS_ECDHE_ECDSA_WITH_CHACHA20_POLY1305_SHA256 (0xcca9)
    Cipher Suite: TLS_ECDHE_RSA_WITH_CHACHA20_POLY1305_SHA256 (0xcca8)
    Cipher Suite: TLS_ECDHE_ECDSA_WITH_AES_256_GCM_SHA384 (0xc02c)
    Cipher Suite: TLS_ECDHE_RSA_WITH_AES_256_GCM_SHA384 (0xc030)
    Cipher Suite: TLS_ECDHE_ECDSA_WITH_AES_256_CBC_SHA (0xc00a)
    Cipher Suite: TLS_ECDHE_ECDSA_WITH_AES_128_CBC_SHA (0xc009)
    Cipher Suite: TLS_ECDHE_RSA_WITH_AES_128_CBC_SHA (0xc013)
    Cipher Suite: TLS_ECDHE_RSA_WITH_AES_256_CBC_SHA (0xc014)
    Cipher Suite: TLS_DHE_RSA_WITH_AES_128_CBC_SHA (0x0033)
    Cipher Suite: TLS_DHE_RSA_WITH_AES_256_CBC_SHA (0x0039)
    Cipher Suite: TLS_RSA_WITH_AES_128_CBC_SHA (0x002f)
    Cipher Suite: TLS_RSA_WITH_AES_256_CBC_SHA (0x0035)
    Cipher Suite: TLS_RSA_WITH_3DES_EDE_CBC_SHA (0x000a)
```

Fig. 3. Google Meet's list of their offered cipher suites in the "Client Hello" packet between a Kali Linux VM (VM 1, Host) and Google Meet's servers.

For both experimental calls, Meet's server chose to utilize the *TLS_ECDHE_ECDSA_WITH_AES_128_GCM_SHA256 (0xc02b)* cipher suite. This was determined from the "Server Hello" packet made at the beginning of the connection between VM 1 and VM 2. Once again, the GCM cipher suite is being utilized; however, it should be noted that it is AES-128 encryption instead of AES-256. This is interesting because while it is a strong encryption, it is a slightly weaker encryption than Zoom.

Microsoft Teams required 64-bit machines to download the required browsers to run their web-browser application or their Teams application. Thus, VM 1 and VM 2 were limited to utilizing Windows 10 machines for these experiments based on the available resources for this research. 32-bit machines appear to be no longer supported for the Teams application. However, the outside listener remains on the SEED Ubuntu VM for capturing packets between the two victims. Two calls were setup for this experiment with Teams, and the packets for both calls were stored and analyzed analogous to Zoom and Meet.

Teams offered more cipher suites within the "Client Hello" packet than both Zoom and Google Meet at a total of 21 cipher suites offered.

Figure 4 shows that the cipher suites available are different variants of two types of cipher suites: CBC and GCM. Both the AES-128 and AES-256 encryption are offered with different methods. The "Server Hello" packets from both calls show that the server utilized the *TLS_ECDHE_RSA_WITH_AES_256_GCM_SHA384 (0xc030)* cipher suite. This matches the same cipher suite that Zoom utilizes, and it is a strong encryption.

```
v Cipher Suites (21 suites)
      Cipher Suite: TLS_ECDHE_ECDSA_WITH_AES_256_GCM_SHA384 (0xc02c)
      Cipher Suite: TLS_ECDHE_ECDSA_WITH_AES_128_GCM_SHA256 (0xc02b)
      Cipher Suite: TLS_ECDHE_RSA_WITH_AES_256_GCM_SHA384 (0xc030)
      Cipher Suite: TLS_ECDHE_RSA_WITH_AES_128_GCM_SHA256 (0xc02f)
      Cipher Suite: TLS_DHE_RSA_WITH_AES_256_GCM_SHA384 (0x009f)
      Cipher Suite: TLS_DHE_RSA_WITH_AES_128_GCM_SHA256 (0x009e)
      Cipher Suite: TLS_ECDHE_ECDSA_WITH_AES_256_CBC_SHA384 (0xc024)
      Cipher Suite: TLS_ECDHE_ECDSA_WITH_AES_128_CBC_SHA256 (0xc023)
      Cipher Suite: TLS_ECDHE_RSA_WITH_AES_256_CBC_SHA384 (0xc028)
      Cipher Suite: TLS_ECDHE_RSA_WITH_AES_128_CBC_SHA256 (0xc027)
      Cipher Suite: TLS_ECDHE_ECDSA_WITH_AES_256_CBC_SHA (0xc00a)
      Cipher Suite: TLS_ECDHE_ECDSA_WITH_AES_128_CBC_SHA (0xc009)
      Cipher Suite: TLS_ECDHE_RSA_WITH_AES_256_CBC_SHA (0xc014)
      Cipher Suite: TLS_ECDHE_RSA_WITH_AES_128_CBC_SHA (0xc013)
      Cipher Suite: TLS_RSA_WITH_AES_256_GCM_SHA384 (0x009d)
      Cipher Suite: TLS_RSA_WITH_AES_128_GCM_SHA256 (0x009c)
      Cipher Suite: TLS_RSA_WITH_AES_256_CBC_SHA256 (0x003d)
      Cipher Suite: TLS_RSA_WITH_AES_128_CBC_SHA256 (0x003c)
      Cipher Suite: TLS_RSA_WITH_AES_256_CBC_SHA (0x0035)
      Cipher Suite: TLS_RSA_WITH_AES_128_CBC_SHA (0x002f)
      Cipher Suite: TLS_RSA_WITH_3DES_EDE_CBC_SHA (0x000a)
```

Fig. 4. Packets from the first call with Microsoft Teams between a Windows 10 VM (VM 1, Host) and a Windows 10 VM (VM 2, participant) showing the available cipher suites offered by their servers.

4.4 Encrypted in Transit

Zoom encrypted all TCP and UDP packets throughout the call with the aforementioned GCM cipher suite. Transit between VM 1 and VM 2. This encryption is among the strongest in the industry, and it is a step-up from their previous encryption.

Meet encrypted all communication data in transit throughout the calls between VM 1 and VM 2. However, it was strange that the server used several protocols: DTLSv1.2, TLSv1.3, TCP, UDP, DNS and STUN. This was drastically different from either platform.

The analysis of Team's packets showed that all of the TCP and UDP packets communicated between VM 1 and VM 2 in transit was encrypted by the following cipher suite: *TLS_ECDHE_RSA_WITH_AES_256_GCM_SHA384 (0xc030)*.

Teams and Zoom utilized similar encryptions: AES-256-GCM. However, Meet only utilized AES-128-GCM. This is still a strong encryption, but it was the weakest encryption used in our experiments.

4.5 Encrypted at Rest

According to Zoom's documentation, recordings that are stored locally on the host's device *can* be encrypted [16]. The data that was collected for this experiment indicates that the data stored locally is not encrypted by default, and that this option must be selected. Thus, if the user's machine is compromised, then all recorded calls will be available to the attacker if they are not properly encrypted by the user themselves.

Meetings that are stored via their cloud are processed and stored after the call, and they can be protected via a pass-code. Files such as audio, video, chat messages, shared files, and meeting transcripts can be stored in Zoom's cloud. Zoom claims to encrypt all data in their cloud [16]. We did not test this as this is not available to free users.

Google claims to encrypt data at rest by default in Google Drive's cloud via their documentation [6]. It should be noted that this was not tested during this experiment due to Google Drive being an enterprise-grade cloud service. Further research is required for conclusive evidence to be determined if Meet encrypts data at rest.

Teams takes a unique approach compared to the other platforms in terms of storing data and encrypting at rest: All data stored for users/meetings are split between Exchange, Stream, Groups, SharePoint, and OneDrive for Business. This was outlined in Microsoft Teams documentation [11] and by Christensen [2]. Local files were checked to determine if the application logs anything locally outside of Team's advanced system, and it was discovered that logs were stored locally on both of the Windows 10 machines under "Teams/Local Storage/leveldb/#####log.txt", where the '#' represent dynamically generated numbers by Teams. The user's email address, and names of files uploaded on Teams were discovered in this log. This was an interesting discovery because it is not totally compromising. However, it is still concerning that this type of information is logged.

4.6   Past Communications Secure

Marczak and Scott-Railton [10] were able to uncover a key when decrypting the AES-128-ECB cipher suite that Zoom was using, and this allowed them to break past communications. However, A key for the Zoom calls were unable to be located since all TCP communications were heavily encrypted. Thus, an attacker is not able to break past communications unless the key is obtained by other means.

Similar to Zoom, Meet's key was unable to be determined due to the data being heavily encrypted. The same situation applies here for attackers as it did for Zoom. However, the difference is that Meet has a much smaller attack surface due to only being available via Web browser and mobile applications.

The key for Teams was also unable to be determined due to the data being heavily encrypted. It may also be significantly more difficult to break past communications due to the unique approach that Teams takes to store past communications that was mentioned in the previous segment.

4.7   Verifiable Contacts

Zoom meeting rooms were not examined for this experiment, but rather only scheduled meetings that were password protected and given session IDs. So, users will need that information to join the call, and they must be let in by the call's host. Users are able to join Zoom calls anonymously because they are not required to login before joining a call. However, Zoom has deployed a feature called Authentication profiles. If this feature is enabled by the host, then it allows the host to restrict participants to those whom are logged into Zoom [15]. This means that contacts are not always verifiable if this feature is disabled, but if the feature is enabled then identities are verifiable.

Meet's participant's identities are easily verifiable due to Meet requiring all users to sign in before being allowed to join meetings. This is required even if the user has already entered the meeting information. This means that anonymous users are not allowed to join meetings on this platform. Call administrators are also given options during the meeting to manually accept or decline users requesting to join as well as the option to remove unwanted users from the call.

Teams verifies all contact's identities by requiring users to be part of an institution or business to have access to their Teams/Groups. They could also be invited to the group/team. The user must also login after being invited and verified to be granted access. This experiment was limited in this aspect because both users were invited to a group as guests. These users were able to communicate and create calls amongst themselves, but they did not have access to administrative privileges. This also meant that these accounts were unable to enable recordings, audit logs, and other administrative privileges that Teams offers.

4.8   Open Source Code

Zoom's code is not open source, and thus not open to independent review. They currently only provide detailed documentation for their services and features that are offered on their platform.

Google Meet is not an open source platform, and thus their code is also not open to independent review. However, they do provide transparency reports to government according to their documentation [6].

Microsoft Team's code is not open source, and thus their code is not open to independent review.

4.9   Properly Documented Security Design

Zoom's security design is properly documented. They regularly release documentation on new patches, features, and when their security or privacy is updated or changed.

Meet's security design is also properly documented. They provide well-documented transparency, compliance policies, privacy policies, and outline their security protocols efficiently. Additional information for user best practices is also provided [6].

Their security documentation is vigorously thorough, and it covers their features as well as what access each administrator/user/guest has access to within their platform. They also heavily emphasize best security practices, and security protocols that are available to their clients.

4.10   Metadata

Metadata is present from the data captured as suspected in the Zoom calls. Attackers are able to learn several things from sniffing Zoom calls via the metadata available: Length of the call down to the 9th decimal place, IPv4 and IPv6 addresses from all users involved, timestamps of each packet, name of the network interface that the packets are being captured from, and MAC addresses from all machines involved. This is common metadata that is available from most packets; however, there is a vast amount of information that an attacker can learn from just sniffing. This also allows them to learn which cipher suite is being used if the data is encrypted, the initiation and termination of the TLS protocol, the location of the users, and they are able to build a time-line of the user if they have been sniffing the network. The attacker is hypothetically able to learn things like this, but are unable to determine exactly what the user is doing. These aspects are concerning, but still difficult to protect as this information is required in order to establish connections.

The same criteria can be observed in Meet as Zoom regarding metadata availability from Meet's captured packets: Length of the call, IPv4 and IPv6 addresses, timestamps of each packet, name of the network interface that the packets are being captured from, and MAC addresses from all machines involved. Much of this is common metadata; however, outside listeners can still gather quite a bit of information from this metadata as mentioned before.

The metadata available in Teams is analogous to the previous platforms: Length of the call, IPv4 and IPv6 addresses, timestamps of each packet, name of the network interface that the packets are being captured from, and MAC addresses from all machines involved.

4.11   Additional Findings

All criteria have been examined for Zoom; however, intriguing things were discovered during the analysis. An interesting packet sent via DNS was captured: notably "us04file.zoom.us" to the IP "3.80.20.197". These files were unable to be located on the local machine during and after the call. This can be observed in Fig. 5:

```
DNS          76 Standard query 0x6864 A us04file.zoom.us
DNS          76 Standard query 0x2e68 AAAA us04file.zoom.us
DNS         118 Standard query response 0x6864 A us04file.zoom.us CNAME us04file-va.zoom.us A 3.80.20.197
DNS         187 Standard query response 0x2e68 AAAA us04file.zoom.us CNAME us04file-va.zoom.us SOA ns-1137.awsdns-14.org
```

Zoom also established connections from 11 different IP addresses, and 13 different ports were utilized with these various IPs throughout the call. These IP addresses were traced with an IP WHOIS Lookup [4] tool to Amazon servers located in Seattle, WA and Oracle servers in Redwood Shores, CA. It should be noted that all connections were made with servers within the United States. This has changed from Marczak and Scott-Railton's data [10]. All data exchanged

| Wireshark · Endpoints · 7-29 Kali Win Zoom Call.pcapng   — □ × |

| Ethernet · 5 | IPv4 · 15 | IPv6 | TCP · 24 | UDP · 16 |

Address	Port	Packets	Bytes	Tx Packets	Tx Bytes	Rx Packets	Rx Bytes
3.80.20.178	443	7	470	4	265	3	205
3.80.20.197	443	17	11 k	7	5699	10	5721
3.235.72.198	443	21	1638	7	595	14	1043
3.235.82.186	443	35	5922	13	2449	22	3473
3.235.82.211	443	15	8526	6	5520	9	3006
3.235.82.214	443	44	16 k	22	11 k	22	5057
10.0.2.15	34836	21	1638	14	1043	7	595
10.0.2.15	39992	35	5922	22	3473	13	2449
10.0.2.15	36692	30	15 k	16	4647	14	10 k
10.0.2.15	44390	19	6482	11	1540	8	4942
10.0.2.15	33300	23	7767	13	2267	10	5500
10.0.2.15	39424	22	7707	14	2327	8	5380
10.0.2.15	58096	13	5757	8	1125	5	4632
10.0.2.15	57580	1,239	178 k	642	103 k	597	75 k
10.0.2.15	40902	7	470	3	205	4	265
10.0.2.15	36664	7	470	3	205	4	265
10.0.2.15	36662	7	470	3	205	4	265
10.0.2.15	50420	17	11 k	10	5721	7	5699
10.0.2.15	55760	15	8526	9	3006	6	5520
52.12.165.191	443	19	6482	8	4942	11	1540
54.188.100.69	443	13	5757	5	4632	8	1125
129.213.104.234	443	1,239	178 k	597	75 k	642	103 k
150.136.128.155	443	23	7767	10	5500	13	2267
150.136.199.138	443	22	7707	8	5380	14	2327

Fig. 5. List of all TCP connections established during the second call between a Kali Linux VM (VM 1, Host) and a Windows 10 VM (VM 2, participant).

between these IPs were encrypted with the same cipher suite aforementioned: *TLS_ECDHE_RSA_WITH_AES_256_GCM_SHA384 (0xc030)*. See Fig. 5.

A variety of IP addresses and ports were accessed throughout Google Meet's calls. These addresses were traced through the IP WHOIS Lookup tool [4]. In total, 33 IP addresses contacted VM 1, and 44 ports (all 443 based) were accessed. Most IP addresses were from Google LLC registered servers; however, one IP address stood out: "17.217.12.46" is an IP address registered to an Apple server in Cupertino, CA. Encrypted data packets were sent to this address with the same cipher suite aforementioned. Data was also being sent to: Akami Technologies, Inc. via the "23.66.52.197" IP address, sending data to "adservice.google.com", querying via DNS to hangouts clients, and uploading Wikimedia Foundation data: The data that is being sent to these locations is unknown, and has yet to be determined. Why is Google Adservices being contacted? What is being uploaded from Wikimedia? What do these have to do with a Google Meet call at all? This research is unable to provide conclusive evidence that answer these questions, and they will be addressed in a later section.

Address	Port	Packets	Bytes	Tx Packets	Tx Bytes	Rx Packets	Rx Bytes
10.0.2.15	51992	41	21 k	23	3417	18	17 k
10.0.2.15	44480	29	8835	17	3752	12	5083
23.66.52.197	443	59	35 k	27	32 k	32	2958
64.233.180.189	443	79	22 k	33	13 k	46	8478
74.125.198.189	443	22	2218	9	892	13	1326
142.250.30.189	443	221	37 k	100	22 k	121	15 k
172.217.1.129	443	20	7802	8	6310	12	1492
172.217.1.131	443	33	6250	13	4122	20	2128
172.217.1.142	443	922	288 k	391	101 k	531	186 k
172.217.1.227	443	521	563 k	309	536 k	212	27 k
172.217.1.238	443	29	5940	11	3971	18	1969
172.217.2.225	443	84	17 k	34	11 k	50	5750
172.217.2.227	443	15	4949	6	3637	9	1312
172.217.2.238	443	92	46 k	40	39 k	52	7191
172.217.6.131	443	50	23 k	20	20 k	30	2995
172.217.6.162	443	30	9028	11	5980	19	3048
172.217.6.174	443	48	9940	19	6388	29	3552
172.217.9.141	443	24	8654	10	5314	14	3340
172.217.9.163	443	62	16 k	23	11 k	39	5034
172.217.12.33	443	40	10 k	16	7702	24	2634
172.217.12.36	443	34	8240	13	4990	21	3250
172.217.12.42	443	72	17 k	31	12 k	41	5050
172.217.12.46	443	2,382	2781 k	1,414	2545 k	968	236 k
172.217.12.67	443	27	6750	11	4474	16	2276
172.217.12.78	443	312	190 k	152	174 k	160	16 k
172.217.14.170	443	31	13 k	13	10 k	18	3130
208.80.153.240	443	455	772 k	227	757 k	228	15 k
216.58.193.132	443	798	658 k	391	600 k	407	58 k
216.58.193.142	443	29	5938	11	3969	18	1969
216.58.194.33	443	47	12 k	19	9903	28	3084
216.58.194.42	443	1,983	624 k	883	248 k	1,100	375 k
216.58.194.67	443	211	162 k	115	154 k	96	8113
216.58.194.68	443	119	72 k	63	63 k	56	8692
216.58.194.110	443	16	4976	6	3604	10	1372
216.58.194.132	443	36	9090	14	4996	22	4094

Meet has also been discovered to be writing local logs within the browser. These files were found on my local machine under "/AppData/Local Storage/leveldb/....log.txt". Some call initialization data was discovered in this file, but nothing else appears compromising. However, this data raises the question: What is being sent to Google that the customers are unaware of?

Fig. 6. Packets from the second Meet call showing Meet querying adservices and uploading Wikimedia.

Teams has been the most intricate in its communication out of the three platforms. 49 different IPv4 addresses established TCP connections with the host machine throughout the call, and 92 different ports (all 443 based) were utilized. Many of the IP addresses and ports were adjacent to each other in their ranges (Fig. 6).

These IP addresses were traced utilizing the same resource, the IP WHOIS Lookup tool [4], and some interesting locations outside of Microsoft were discovered transmitting encrypted information. MCI communications, Inc. (Verizon) in Ashburn, VA, Akami Technologies, Inc. (a known partner with Microsoft), LinkedIn in Sunnyvale, CA, Skype, and Highlands Network Group Dallas, TX were all of the locations outside of Microsoft's server registration. The primary IP that made the most contact by far was the Highlands data center location. The amount of packets sent between each IP can be observed in the images below.

5   Evaluation

Zoom, Google Meet, and Microsoft Teams were evaluated by the following criterion:

1. Is the data encrypted in transit?
2. Is the data encrypted at rest?
3. Is the data encrypted so that the provider cannot read it?
4. Can the contact's identities be verified?
5. Past communications secure if keys are stolen? (I.e., forward secrecy)
6. Is the code open source?
7. Is the platform's security design properly documented?
8. What Metadata can be obtained?

A scorecard has been created to roughly breakdown the evaluation for each of these platforms. This scorecard is a modified version of EFF's scorecard matrix [5] (Figs. 7, 8 and 9).

Metadata has been removed from the scorecard for usability. The metadata available from each platform is as follows: Length of the call, IPv4 and IPv6 addresses, Timestamps of each packet, Name of the network interface that the packets are being captured from, and MAC addresses from all machines involved (Fig. 10).

The scorecard is not as clear cut as desired, and will be broken down here to ensure that its meaning is clear. Each platform, Zoom, Google Meet, and Microsoft Teams encrypt all data in transit with a version of AES-128 or AES-256 GCM cipher suites. Zoom is misleading with its encryption at rest. The host has the option to record a meeting, and that recording is typically stored locally and potentially on Zoom's cloud if specified. If it is stored locally, it is *not encrypted by default*. The host must specify when setting up the recording options that it should be encrypted. If the meeting is stored in Zoom's cloud, then it is encrypted by default with what they claim to be AES-128-GCM. Thus,

Wireshark · Endpoints · 7-29 Teams call.pcapng   —   □   ×

| Ethernet · 10 | IPv4 · 61 | IPv6 · 4 | TCP · 140 | UDP · 83 |

Address	Port	Packets	Bytes	Tx Packets	Tx Bytes	Rx Packets	Rx Bytes
10.0.2.5	49725	6	627	0	0	6	627
10.0.2.5	50530	8	555	5	375	3	180
10.0.2.5	50531	67	62 k	30	20 k	37	42 k
10.0.2.5	50532	216	48 k	122	18 k	94	30 k
10.0.2.5	50533	56	89 k	18	79 k	38	9259
10.0.2.5	49711	188	71 k	88	20 k	100	51 k
10.0.2.5	50534	20	7868	10	2854	10	5014
10.0.2.5	50535	34	19 k	17	12 k	17	7108
10.0.2.5	50536	21	8457	10	3383	11	5074
10.0.2.5	50537	142	113 k	65	83 k	77	30 k
10.0.2.5	50538	55	23 k	27	9893	28	13 k
10.0.2.5	50053	9	667	5	350	4	317
10.0.2.5	50539	127	28 k	71	14 k	56	14 k
10.0.2.5	50540	63	26 k	31	13 k	32	13 k
10.0.2.5	50541	20	8226	10	3211	10	5015
10.0.2.5	49715	50	18 k	27	4124	23	14 k
10.0.2.5	50542	20	8832	9	1195	11	7637
10.0.2.5	50543	21	4897	11	1246	10	3651
10.0.2.5	50544	19	9272	9	1445	10	7827
10.0.2.5	50545	9	1586	5	655	4	931
10.0.2.5	50546	9	1253	6	683	3	570
10.0.2.5	50547	1,424	4278 k	599	37 k	825	4240 k
10.0.2.5	50548	19	7847	9	2833	10	5014
10.0.2.5	50528	6	385	3	180	3	205
10.0.2.5	50549	270	886 k	106	6695	164	880 k
10.0.2.5	50550	25	11 k	14	5595	11	5426
10.0.2.5	49756	6	435	0	0	6	435
10.0.2.5	50551	8	555	5	375	3	180
10.0.2.5	50552	65	92 k	22	82 k	43	9967
10.0.2.5	50553	18	10 k	9	5164	9	5260
10.0.2.5	50554	20	10 k	9	5212	11	5379
10.0.2.5	51987	4	290	0	0	4	290
10.0.2.5	50555	16	8571	8	1454	8	7117
10.0.2.5	50556	16	8508	8	1484	8	7024
10.0.2.5	50557	19	12 k	9	4012	10	7990
10.0.2.5	50558	22	15 k	9	7854	13	8099
10.0.2.5	50559	18	10 k	9	5164	9	5260
10.0.2.5	50560	8	555	5	375	3	180
10.0.2.5	50561	18	10 k	9	5212	9	5260
10.0.2.5	50562	18	7996	9	3041	9	4955
10.0.2.5	50563	19	10 k	9	5164	10	5320
10.0.2.5	50523	1	60	0	0	1	60
10.0.2.5	50529	1	60	0	0	1	60
10.0.2.5	50525	1	60	0	0	1	60
10.0.2.5	50524	1	60	0	0	1	60
10.0.2.5	50564	19	10 k	9	5164	10	5320
10.0.2.5	50527	1	60	0	0	1	60
10.0.2.5	50522	1	60	0	0	1	60
10.0.2.5	50526	1	60	0	0	1	60
10.0.2.5	50565	19	10 k	9	5164	10	5320
10.0.2.5	50566	19	10 k	9	5204	10	5320

Fig. 7. Shows established TCP connections made with VM 1 and Microsoft Teams servers from the first call with Microsoft Teams between a Windows 10 VM (VM 1, Host) and a Windows 10 VM (VM 2, participant) part 1/3.

Address	Port	Packets	Bytes	Tx Packets	Tx Bytes	Rx Packets	Rx Bytes
10.0.2.5	50567	19	10 k	9	5164	10	5319
10.0.2.5	50568	20	10 k	9	5204	11	5374
10.0.2.5	50569	20	14 k	9	9172	11	5380
10.0.2.5	50570	44	32 k	19	2231	25	29 k
10.0.2.5	50571	53	48 k	25	4146	28	44 k
10.0.2.5	50572	25	8045	13	1858	12	6187
10.0.2.5	50573	24	5858	13	1856	11	4002
10.0.2.5	50574	13	1513	7	982	6	531
10.0.2.5	50575	29	14 k	15	1980	14	12 k
10.0.2.5	50576	13	1513	7	982	6	531
10.0.2.5	50577	8	555	5	375	3	180
10.0.2.5	50578	168	350 k	55	336 k	113	13 k
10.0.2.5	51996	2	120	0	0	2	120
10.0.2.5	50579	31	14 k	17	13 k	14	1366
10.0.2.5	50580	21	3911	13	2676	8	1235
10.0.2.5	50581	28	7536	17	1786	11	5750
10.0.2.5	50582	10	2654	6	828	4	1826
10.0.2.5	50583	27	10 k	15	2014	12	8184
10.0.2.5	50584	25	9785	15	1722	10	8063
10.0.2.5	50585	18	2876	11	1974	7	902
10.0.2.5	49751	2	410	0	0	2	410
10.0.2.5	50586	8	555	5	375	3	180
10.0.2.5	49799	1	60	0	0	1	60
10.0.2.5	49798	1	60	0	0	1	60
10.0.2.5	50587	8	555	5	375	3	180
10.0.2.5	50588	58	58 k	25	47 k	33	10 k
10.0.2.5	50589	8	486	4	246	4	240
10.0.2.5	50590	8	555	5	375	3	180
10.0.2.5	50591	8	555	5	375	3	180
10.0.2.5	50592	18	7796	9	2843	9	4953
10.0.2.5	50593	18	7812	9	2857	9	4955
10.0.2.5	50594	20	11 k	10	6256	10	5055
10.0.2.5	50595	40	37 k	17	29 k	23	7719
10.0.2.5	50596	18	8181	9	3226	9	4955
10.0.2.5	50597	8	555	5	375	3	180
10.0.2.5	50598	21	13 k	12	4115	9	9639
10.0.2.5	50599	8	555	5	375	3	180
10.0.2.5	50600	8	555	5	375	3	180
10.0.2.5	50601	30	31 k	12	25 k	18	6250
10.0.2.5	50602	18	9495	9	6719	9	2776
13.86.124.174	443	67	62 k	37	42 k	30	20 k
13.107.3.254	443	1	60	1	60	0	0
13.107.6.158	443	22	3971	9	1295	13	2676
13.107.6.254	443	25	9785	10	8063	15	1722
13.107.18.254	443	1	60	1	60	0	0
13.107.21.200	443	32	14 k	15	1426	17	13 k
13.107.42.254	443	1	60	1	60	0	0
13.107.246.254	443	28	10 k	13	8244	15	2014
23.35.172.68	443	39	18 k	21	15 k	18	2640
23.193.22.68	443	6	435	6	435	0	0
23.216.55.17	80	9	1586	4	931	5	655

Fig. 8. Shows established TCP connections made with VM 1 and Microsoft Teams servers from the first call with Microsoft Teams between a Windows 10 VM (VM 1, Host) and a Windows 10 VM (VM 2, participant) part 2/3.

23.216.55.17	80	9	1586	4	931	5	655
23.216.55.90	443	6	385	3	205	3	180
40.126.0.73	443	21	13 k	9	9639	12	4115
51.140.157.153	443	40	25 k	22	10 k	18	14 k
52.113.194.132	443	160	123 k	86	32 k	74	90 k
52.113.206.1	443	50	18 k	23	14 k	27	4124
52.113.206.3	443	216	48 k	94	30 k	122	18 k
52.114.7.36	443	41	16 k	21	10 k	20	6237
52.114.74.44	443	95	52 k	50	26 k	45	25 k
52.114.75.79	443	168	350 k	113	13 k	55	336 k
52.114.75.149	443	66	59 k	37	10 k	29	48 k
52.114.76.34	443	121	182 k	81	19 k	40	162 k
52.114.77.33	443	36	15 k	18	9908	18	5700
52.114.77.34	443	39	16 k	20	10 k	19	6044
52.114.88.28	443	55	42 k	29	11 k	26	30 k
52.114.128.33	443	35	20 k	18	15 k	17	5466
52.114.128.34	443	38	24 k	21	15 k	17	9338
52.114.128.70	443	18	7996	9	4955	9	3041
52.114.128.74	443	20	10 k	11	5379	9	5212
52.114.132.73	443	36	18 k	18	10 k	18	8390
52.114.142.144	443	127	28 k	56	14 k	71	14 k
52.114.144.98	443	118	50 k	60	27 k	58	23 k
52.114.168.24	443	188	71 k	100	51 k	88	20 k
52.115.62.6	443	9	667	4	317	5	350
52.184.217.20	443	21	4897	10	3651	11	1246
52.184.221.185	443	20	11 k	10	5055	10	6256
52.242.211.89	443	2	410	2	410	0	0
72.21.81.200	443	6	627	6	627	0	0
72.21.91.29	80	10	2654	4	1826	6	828
104.69.125.175	80	2	120	2	120	0	0
104.97.205.13	443	4	290	4	290	0	0
104.124.58.147	443	201	112 k	102	98 k	99	14 k
108.174.10.10	443	28	7536	11	5750	17	1786
168.62.57.154	443	36	20 k	18	10 k	18	10 k
191.232.139.2	443	74	56 k	40	14 k	34	41 k
192.168.0.100	7680	88	6105	33	1980	55	4125
204.79.197.222	443	19	2936	8	962	11	1974
205.185.216.10	80	279	888 k	167	880 k	112	7378
205.185.216.42	80	1,426	4278 k	827	4241 k	599	37 k

Fig. 9. Shows established TCP connections made with VM 1 and Microsoft Teams servers from the first call with Microsoft Teams between a Windows 10 VM (VM 1, Host) and a Windows 10 VM (VM 2, participant) part 3/3.

Platform	Encrypted In Transit?	Encrypted at Rest?		Encrypted so provider can't read it?	Are contact's identities verifiable?		Code open source?	Security design properly documented?
		By default	Feature available		Required sign in before joining by default?	Features available to require sign in before joining?		
zoom	✓	✗	✓	✗	✗	✓	✗	✓
Google Meet	✓	✓	✓	✗	✓	✓	✗	✓
Microsoft Teams	✓	✓	✓	✗	✓	✓	✗	✓

Fig. 10. Scorecard, similar to EFF's scorecard matrix [5], showing which values are true or false for Zoom, Google Meet, and Microsoft Teams.

by default, the host has to specify whether they want the local storage to be encrypted or not. If the platform would like to be safe, then they should encrypt it by default to ensure that the user cannot make this mistake by accident. The other two platforms, Google Meet and Microsoft Teams *do encrypt all data at rest by default*. This appears to be the best course of action to limit user mistakes.

Due to the nature of the videoconferencing platforms being third-party and how each of their infrastructures are designed, none of them encrypt in such a way that the providers themselves do not have access to your data. Nor are they true end-to-end encrypted. A basic definition of end-to-end encryption is that the messages are encrypted by the sender, and decrypted by the receiver. The third party *should not* have the means to decrypt the messages. This is a vital distinction. Each of the users are consistently communicating with each other between servers utilized by the platform providers. This does not satisfy the definition of true end-to-end encryption. Each of the platforms explicitly has a feature dealing with encrypting user storage, and logs for each user. Thus, this means that they have the means to read the data that is sent between the users from current and past communications.

Verifying contact's identities is extremely important when establishing secure communications, and the distinction needs to be broken down further than "Can it be verified?" Once again, Zoom does not require users to sign in by default when joining a meeting. If they have the meeting details, then they can request to join. The host must have a feature enabled to allow or deny users to join the call or to enable an authentication feature that requires users to sign in before requesting to join the meeting. Thus, by default, Zoom does allow anonymous users. However, since they have the authentication feature, then contact's *are verifiable* if that feature is utilized. Meet and Teams both require users to sign in by default, and add that extra layer of security to ensure that contact's identities are verifiable.

None of the aforementioned videoconferencing platforms have open source code.

Each platform has well-documented security design, and they explicitly cover their compliance policies, threat protection, transparency policies, privacy policies, security features, etc. Most of the information an administrator needs is within the documentations.

6   Limitations and Future Work

Video was not recorded during any of the calls for Zoom, Google Meet, and Microsoft Teams due to lack of hardware for the experiment. Recordings and audit logs were turned on if they were available. In this case, recordings and audit logs were only stored with Zoom. Recordings and audit logs were not available to the guest accounts created for Teams nor Meet due to lack of access to member accounts. To create a more realistic simulation of a personal meeting it would be ideal for all user accounts involved to have full member permissions, and one of them to potentially have administrator privileges in order to utilize all of the data storage features to their fullest extent.

The temporary log files that were being sent were also unable to be located. The time frame for this research project was also quite short, so the scope was very limited to accommodate for that.

Marczak and Scott-Railton [10] discussed Zoom's custom crypto because it was less secure due to using ECB mode. ECB mode, by design, preserves patterns in plain text. This can lead to vulnerabilities in the encryption, and thus in the platform. Customized crypto can definitely be more secure if designed properly, but it is not in this case as the authors mentioned. This could be expanded upon in a future topic as there could be much more depth explored here.

7 Conclusion

This research could be taken further by looking into what else is being sent, logged, or processes being executed in the background whilst the call is running. There appears to be something going on that these third party platforms are not telling the public, and this should be public information if its the case. Several "bread crumbs" have been left, but due to the scope of the project not all of them were able to be investigated thoroughly.

Zoom seems to leave a lot of options up to the user in terms of security. Many users may overlook these features, and this could leave them vulnerable. This could pose more of a problem than it seems, and may be worth examining.

Lastly, we would like to outline an ideal framework for a videoconferencing platform after thoroughly investigating a few of the top contenders for this area. None of these platforms provide true end-to-end encryption, and they certainly have the means to do so. The reason why they may not provide end-to-end encryption could be either surveillance friendly or they may use the information to boost their ad revenue. Zoom has been caught in the past sending data to Facebook [3].

The direct connection could potentially be created after the server initially connects them both. The encrypted data from the two users could then be sent to the server, and re-encrypted upon storage to ensure encryption at rest. Thus far, it would provide end-to-end encryption, encryption in transit, and encryption at rest. Another key to the solution would be to let the client device generate the session keys that will be used to encrypt the communication instead of the vendor servers generating those keys. The platform would still be generating the connection, but no longer being able to eavesdrop on the conversation.

Security protocols should be enabled by default, and up to the user if they would like to disable them. In our opinion, Google Meet and Microsoft Teams are doing things correct in that regard. The less work that the user has to put into security, then the more secure it will be. Many vulnerabilities are created through user error. So, eliminating those possibilities ultimately raises security.

Verifying contact's identities is vital to ensuring a secure conversation. Using features like Single-Sign On (SSO), two-factor authentication, and manual call admission are all great features to ensure security is top priority for a meeting.

Having open source code allows for a more secure, diverse, and community-based platform. It allows independent reviewers to quickly investigate potential vulnerabilities. By design, this creates a more secure platform. However, there are trade-offs with open source. This could slow development if there are not enough contributors, and new features could take longer to deploy.

The security design must also be properly documented in order for the users and administrators to easily use the platform. User friendly features are an important aspect for many users. All of the platforms have successfully executed this as well.

Acknowledgment. This work is supported in part by NSF Award 1504526. We are also grateful for the support from the Scholarship For Services (SFS) program.

References

1. Archibald, M.M., Ambagtsheer, R.C., Casey, M.G., Lawless, M.: Using zoom videoconferencing for qualitative data collection: perceptions and experiences of researchers and participants. Int. J. Qual. Methods **18**, 1609406919874596 (2019)
2. Christensen, R.: Microsoft teams - how secure is it really? A rundown. Brainstorm Inc., pp. 1–7 (2020)
3. Cox, J.: Zoom ios app sends data to facebook even if you don't have a facebook account (2020). https://www.vice.com/en/article/k7e599/zoom-ios-app-sends-data-to-facebook-even-if-you-dont-have-a-facebook-account
4. Dnschecker.org: Ip who is lookup (2020). https://dnschecker.org/ip-whois-lookup.php
5. Electronic Frontier Foundation: Secure messaging scorecard (2020). https://www.eff.org/node/101713
6. Google: Google meet security & privacy for admins. Google LLC, pp. 1–6 (2020)
7. Google: Google meet security & privacy for users. Google LLC, pp. 1–4 (2020)
8. Khan, N.A., Brohi, S.N., Zaman, N.: Ten deadly cyber security threats amid covid-19 pandemic (2020). https://doi.org/10.36227/techrxiv.12278792.v1. https://www.techrxiv.org/articles/preprint/Ten_Deadly_Cyber_Security_Threats_Amid_COVID-19_Pandemic/12278792/1
9. Lakshminarayanan, K., Hashim, S.: Secure connections: how google meet keeps your video conferences protected. Google LLC, pp. 1–5 (2019)
10. Marczak, B., Scott-Railton, J.: Move fast and roll your own crypto. Report, The Citizen Lab (2020)
11. Microsoft: Security and compliance in microsoft teams. Microsoft Corporation, pp. 1–10 (2020)
12. Oracle: Oracle vm virtualbox (version 6.1.10), 17 January 2007. https://www.virtualbox.org/
13. Wagenseil, P.: Zoom security issues: here's everything that's gone wrong (sofar) (2020). https://www.tomsguide.com/news/zoom-security-privacy-woes
14. Warren, T.: Zoom admits it doesn't have 300 million users, corrects misleading claims (2020). https://www.theverge.com/2020/4/30/21242421/zoom-300-million-users-incorrect-meeting-participants-statement
15. Zoom: Authentication profiles for meetings and webinars (2020). https://support.zoom.us/hc/en-us/articles/360037117472-Authentication-Profiles-for-meetings-and-webinars
16. Zoom: Security guide. Report, Zoom Video Communications, Inc. (2020)

A Secure Encapsulation Schemes Based on Key Recovery System

Tae-Hoon Kim[1], Won-Bin Kim[1], Daehee Seo[2], and Im-Yeong Lee[1]([✉])

[1] Soonchunhyang University, Asan 31538, Republic of Korea
{20134101,wbkim29,imylee}@sch.ac.kr
[2] Sangmyung University, Seoul 03016, Republic of Korea
daehseo@smu.ac.kr

Abstract. Network users apply encryption to send and receive data securely. Since ciphertext can be encrypted and decrypted only by lawful users, third parties do not have the ability to know the content of an encrypted message. However, a secret key is uesed for encryption, and if the secret key is lost or corrupted, there is a problem that the encrypted text cannot be decrypted. Additionally, malicious use of this encryption will cause problems. If encryption is used maliciously, the government cannot prevent criminal activity. Because of this law enforcement agencies need support for lawful interception to decrypt criminals or suspect's ciphertexts. We need a key recovery system that can safely recover these secret keys or decrypt messages for lawful interception. There are two types of key recovery systems, a key escrow method and a key encapsulation method. This paper proposes secure schemes using key encapsulation. The key encapsulation method requires the key information used in the ciphertext, and the key information can be obtained from the KRF (Key Recovery Field). The obtained key can be used to decrypt the ciphertext. however, various security threats exist in key recovery system. Such as forgery and alteration of KRF, single point of failure, inability to recover keys, and collusion attacks. To solve these problems, we propose secure encapsulation schemes based on key recovery system.

Keywords: CL-PKC · Key encapsulation · Key recovery system · Signcryption · Proxy re-encryption

1 Introduction

Encryption is essential in Information Technology (IT). However, it is impossible to decrypt ciphertext if keys are accidentally lost or corrupted, and criminals may exploit cryptography, triggering financial loss and embarrassment. Therefore, key recovery system is very important in IT.

A key recovery system is a technology that recovers the secret key used for encryption. If certain conditions are satisfied, it helps the authorized user to decrypt the ciphertext [1]. However, there are various security threats that exist in key recovery system. Such as forgery and alteration of Key Recovery Field

© Springer Nature Switzerland AG 2021
Y. Park et al. (Eds.): SVCC 2020, CCIS 1383, pp. 25–37, 2021.
https://doi.org/10.1007/978-3-030-72725-3_2

(KRF), single point of failure, inability to recover keys, and collusion attacks. To solve this, we propose two secure key recovery systems.

This paper proposes two schemes using an encapsulation based key recovery system. The key recovery system using signcryption is that a lawful user who has lost or corrupted key requests a Law Enforcement Agency (LEA) to recover the key. The requested LEA proceeds with a key recovery request to the Key Recovery Center (KRC) and later recovers the complete key [2]. Multi-Key Recovery Agent (M-KRA) work to reduce the KRC's key recovery burden. In this case, KRC assists in some operations of key recovery. Also, KRA works to reduce the computational burden of key recovery. After receiving the partially calculated KRF from KRC, the LEA generates a session key to decrypt the criminal or suspect's ciphertext.

The contributions of this paper are as follows.

– This paper analyzes the security requirements for a key recovery system based on encapsulation that is safe from various attacks. Provides the ability to safely recover a key when the user is lost or corrupted the key or when the LEA wants to intercept it from a criminal or a suspect.
– The encrypted session key can be recovered according to the procedures of LEA, KRC, and KRA when the key is lost or corrupted. So, when a user requests key recovery from the LEA, the KRC and KRA, the LEA, the KRC and KRA can recover and send the complete session key.
– The encrypted session key is recoverable following a procedure determined by an LEA as needed to intercept the encrypted message. So, if the LEA requests the KRC and KRA recover the key, the KRC and KRA can recover and send the complete session key.

2   Related Work

This section defines of a key recovery system, and discusses existing key recovery, and encryption schemes.

2.1   Encapsulation Key Recovery System

A key recovery system is the most important part of an encryption system. If a private key or session key used for the ciphertext is lost and corrupted, or an LEA wants to lawfully intercept a suspicious ciphertext, then the key must be recovered. Many studies have been conducted and are developing such important key recovery systems.

Kanyamee et al. [3] proposed a highly available distributed session key recovery system. It provides high availability and attack detection for secure session key management and group authentication while using M-KRA to solve the single point of failure problem encountered in the traditional KRA approach. However, problems such as forgery, counterfeiting, and collusion attacks for user generated KRFs occur, causing problems in the key recovery service.

Lim et al. [4] proposed an encapsulation based on M-KRA key recovery system. This study was conducted to solve the problem that the M-KRA must communicate directly with one or more KRAs in the existing M-KRA method, and the user must directly perform a complex key recovery process. To solve this problem, this scheme provides secure session key management and recovery while using a new type of M-KRA. However, problems arise in the key recovery service due to forgery or modulation of KRFs, and non-repudiation problems for user generated KRFs.

Kyusuk et al. [5] proposed an ID based key escrow scheme to prevent malicious use of keys by LEA. Here, the malicious use of the key by an LEA can expose the encrypted data from the wanted user, therefore by providing the key does not change once the key of the user who requested the interception is known. To solve this problem, this scheme generates a user's key pair using a master key generated by KGC and the user's ID. However, since it is a single KRA, problems such as a single point of failure and collusion attacks occur, it causes problems with the key recovery service.

2.2 Multi-agent Key Recovery

The use of a single key recovery system is associated with service overload and security problems. We thus use a multi-agent (at least two agents) key recovery system. The multi-agent receives encrypted key ciphertext from the user or the KRC. Then KRA sends pieces of the key to the KRC to allow the KRC to recover the complete key. However, various attacks and security breaches are possible; efforts have been made to deal with these [6]. In the key recovery system using signcryption, we enhance security by increasing availability and security.

2.3 Signcryption

Zheng [7] proposed a signcryption scheme. It is a public key based scheme simultaneously performing digital signature and encryption while traditional schemes digitally sign messages and then encrypt them. Signcryption ensures data integrity, non-repudiation, and encryption, effectively reducing computational costs and communication overheads compared to those of post-signature encryption schemes.

2.4 Proxy Re-Encryption

A Proxy Re-Encryption (PRE) scheme is a scheme that converts the ciphertext so that the Proxy Server can decrypt the ciphertext encrypted with user A public key by using user B's private key. Proxy re-encryption is a technology that converts a ciphertext encrypted with Alice's public key into a ciphertext that the proxy server can decrypt with Bob's private key without decrypting or exposing Alice's private key. When using proxy re-encryption, data owners can entrust the proxy so that the contents of his/her data or his/her private keys can be converted into ciphertext that can be decrypted by a third party user without revealing to the proxy [8].

3   System Models

This section describes the system models and security requirements of the scheme proposed in this paper.

3.1   Key Recovery System Using Signcryption

Design Goals. The model of the key recovery system using signcryption is a key recovery system that is used when a user is lost or corrupted a key as shown in Fig. 1. b. User requests key recovery from LEA and sends KRF. The LEA receiving the KRF verifies that it is a lawful user of the KRF. If it is a legitimate user, it requests KRC to recover the key and sends KRF. Upon receiving the KRF, the KRA decodes the KRF and sends the obtained KRF pieces to the M-KRA. Upon receiving the fragments of KRF, M-KRA decrypts each and sends the session key fragments to KRC. It collects the session key pieces, generates a complete session key, and sends it to the user.

This section describes the system structure and each component accordingly and sets security requirements.

Security Requirements. The security requirements of the key recovery system using signcryption are as follows.

- **KRF integrity:** No participant in key recovery can maliciously transform KRF information from the sender, and KRF information required for key recovery cannot be changed.
- **Non-repudiation:** The sender shouldn't be able to reject the fact that they created the KRF. Also, the fact that the sender generated the KRF must be clear after transmission, exchange, communication, and processing.
- **Attack on group authentication detection:** If a malicious third-party KRA pretends to be a lawful member of the key recovery group, this KRA should be detected through group verification.
- **Single point of failure protection:** In M-KRA, some KRAs should be able to recover session keys even if another fails.

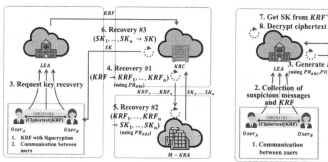 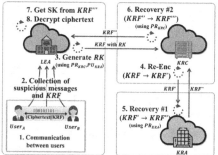

a. Key recovery system using signcryption   **b.** Key recovery system using proxy re-encryption

Fig. 1. System models

3.2   Key Recovery System Using Proxy Re-Encryption

Design Goals. The model of the key recovery system using proxy re-encryption is a key recovery system used when an LEA wants to intercept ciphertext from criminals or suspects as shown in Fig. 1b. The LEA obtains the passphrase and KRF of the criminals or suspects. And it generates a re-encryption key. Requests key recovery from KRC and send the obtained KRF and re-encryption key. After receiving the KRF and the re-encryption key, the KRA partially calculates the KRF and transmits the partially calculated KRF to the KRA. After receiving the partially calculated KRF, the KRA performs some calculations and sends the partially calculated KRF to KRC. Upon receiving the KRF, the KRC sends it to the LEA. The LEA decrypts it, generates a session key, and decrypts the ciphertext.

This section describes the system structure and each component accordingly and sets security requirements.

Security Requirements. The security requirements of the key recovery system using proxy re-encryption are as follows.

- **KRF integrity:** No participant in key recovery can maliciously transform KRF information from the sender, and KRF information required for key recovery cannot be changed.
- **Law enforcement support:** The session key used for communication must be encrypted and stored in a key recovery field. The encrypted session key must be recoverable according to a procedure determined by an LEA as necessary to enable interception of encrypted messages.
- **Collusion attack resistance:** Between the LEA, KRC and KRA, two or fewer participants should not be allowed to obtain keys even if they are maliciously colluding.

4   Proposed Schemes

In this section describes a key recovery system using signcryption and a key recovery system using proxy re-encryption, and the designs of the protocols in detail.

4.1   Key Recovery System Using Signcryption

This is a scheme for recovering a user's key after loss or corruption. This is mainly composed of a signcryption phase, a KRF generation phase, and a session key recovery phase as shown in Fig. 2.

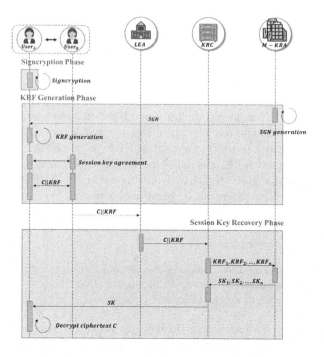

Fig. 2. Scenario of the key recovery system using signcryption

System Parameters. The system parameters used in the proposed scheme are shown in Table 1.

Signcryption Phase. In this phase, the key recovery system using signcryption ensures integrity, and non-repudiation, and performs the encryption of the session key all at once.

- **Step 1:** $User_A$ selects $User_A$'s private key X_A at random from $1, 2, \ldots, q$ and generates k Then, the generated k is divided in half into k_1 and k_2.
- **Step 2:** $User_A$ selects session key SK at random from $1, 2, \ldots, q$.
- **Step 3:** c, r and s are generated using k_1, k_2, X_A and SK.
- **Step 4:** Distribute c, r and s according to the number of agents ($1 \leq n \leq x$).
- **Step 5:** The divided c_i, r_i and s_i pieces are used to produce KRF_i and are stored.

KRF Generation Phase. This phase describes how to generate a KRF.

- **Step 1:** $User_A$ requests SGN from $M - KRA$.
- **Step 2:** $M - KRA$ received SGN request from $User_A$, $M - KRA$ choose random values $R_1, R_2, \ldots, R_n$. Then $M - KRA$ generate SGN.
- **Step 3:** The generated SGN is transmitted to the $User_A$.

Table 1. System parameters of the key recovery system using signcryption

Notation	Description
H	Hash function
q	Prime number
X_A, X_{KRC}	Private key of $User_A$, KRC
Y_A, Y_{KRC}	Public key of $User_A$, KRC
SK	Session key
nag_i	Neighbor agent of KRA_i
R_i	Random number of KRA_i, $R_i \in Z_q^*$
SGN	Group authentication values assigned to agents (Shared Group Number), $SGN = R_1 \oplus R_2 \oplus, \ldots, \oplus R_n$
Tc_i	ith signcryption pieces, $Tc_i = c_i \oplus SGN$
Tr_i	ith signcryption pieces, $Tr_i = r_i \oplus SGN$
Ts_i	ith signcryption pieces, $Ts_i = s_i \oplus SGN$
TT_i	Value that contains the value to recover when an agent fails service, $TT_i = Tc_i \oplus Tr_i \oplus Ts_i$
KRF	Key recovery field, $E_{pk_{KRC}}(KRF_1 \| KRF_2 \| \ldots \| KRF_n \| H(SGN))$
KRF_i	ith key recovery field piece, $E_{pk_{ag_i}}(c_i \| r_i \| s_i \| SGN \| TT_i)$

- **Step 4:** $User_A$ generates TT_i.
- **Step 5:** The generated TT_i distributes TT_i.
- **Step 6:** After creating the KRF_i pieces, we generates KRF. Then $User_A$ attaches the generated KRF to the ciphertext.

Session Key Recovery Phase. This phase, describes how to recover a key if the requestor requests key recovery.

- **Step 1:** When $User_B$ requests KRF decryption from KRC to recover SK, send KRF.
- **Step 2:** The KRC recovers KRF with own private key and obtains KRF_i pieces. Then the obtained KRF_i pieces are sent to each $M - KRA$ to request decryption.
- **Step 3:** The $M - KRA$ acquire c_i, r_i, s_i, SGN, TT_i values with their private key. Among the obtained values, c_i, r_i, s_i, SGN values are encrypted with the public key of KRC and sent to the KRC.
- **Step 4:** KRC compares SGN obtained by decrypting the received ciphertext with KRC's private key and $H(SGN)$. If they match, collect c_i, r_i, s_i pieces and recover c, r, s.
- **Step 5:** Recover the k value using the received ciphertext, public parameters, and recovered c, r, s. Then divide into k by k_1, k_2.

– **Step 6:** Recover the session key using the obtained k_1 and c. Then compare the calculated $H_{k_2}(SK)$ and r values using the obtained k_2.
– **Step 7:** If it matches, the recovered SK is sent to $User_B$ and the message is decrypted using the received SK.

4.2   Key Recovery System Using Proxy Re-Encryption

The key recovery system using proxy re-encryption is a scheme for recovering a key when a government agency intercepting an offender's ciphertext message as shown in Fig. 3.

System Parameters. The system parameters used in the proposed scheme are shown in Table 2.

Setup Phase. In this phase, the KGC takes as input the security parameter 1^λ and generates public parameters.

– **Step 1:** The KGC choose λ-bit large prime q and group G of prime order q. Also, a random generator g is chosen.
– **Step 2:** Randomly select a master private key s and compute master public key S.
– **Step 3:** Choose hash functions.
– **Step 4:** Public parameters $params = (G, n, q, g, S, H_1, H_2, H_3)$ are published.

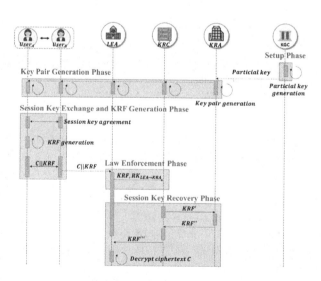

Fig. 3. Scenario of the key recovery system using proxy re-encryption

Table 2. System parameters of the key recovery system using proxy re-encryption

Notation	Description
G	Group generator
q	Prime number
H_1	Hash function, $H_1 : \{0,1\}^* \times G \to Z_q^*$
H_2	Hash function, $H_2 : G \to \{0,1\}^n \, for \, some \, n \in N$
H_3	Hash function, $H_3 : \{0,1\}^* \to Z_q^*$
s	Master private key, $s \in Z_q^*$
S	Master publci key, $S = g^s$
g	Random parameters, $g \in G$
$Part_j$	Participant j in the network, $(User_i, LEA, KRC, KRA \in Part_j)$
w_j, t_j, j_j, v_j	Random parameters, $w_j, t_j, j_j, v_j \in Z_q^*$
sk_j	$User_j$'s private key
SK	Session key
M	Message space, $\{0,1\}^n$
KRF	Key recovery field, $KRF = (g_{KRC}^Z, SK \oplus H_2(Y_A^r))$
KRF'	Some calculated key recovery field, $KRF' = (g^{Z_{KRA} \cdot r}, SK \oplus H_2(Y_A^r))$
KRF''	Some calculated key recovery field, $KRF'' = (g^r, SK \oplus H_2(Y_A^r))$
KRF'''	Some calculated key recovery field, $KRF''' = (KRF''^{1/T_{KRC \to LEA}}, SK \oplus H_2(Y_A^r))$

Key Pair Generation Phase. In this phase, $Part_j$ receives a partial private key from KGC and uses it to generate full private key sk_j and public key pk_j.

- **Step 1:** KGC generates parameters w_j, t_j for participant $Part_j$ and transmits them to $Part_j$ through a secure channel.
- **Step 2:** Participant $Part_j$ who receives X_j, d_j from KGC, selects random values z_j, v_j and sets $Part_j$'s private key sk_j.
- **Step 3:** Participant $Part_j$ generates Z_j, V_j and sets (X_j, Z_j, V_j) as the public key pk_j.

Session Key Exchange and KRF Generation Phase. In this phase, a session key is exchanged between $User_A$ and $User_B$, and a KRF is generated.

- **Step 1:** $User_A$ and $User_B$ respectively select a_i and b_i, and generate A_i, B_i.
- **Step 2:** Both users exchange A_i and B_i.
- **Step 3:** The session key SK is generated using the received A_i and B_i.
- **Step 4:** $User_U$ ($User_A$ or $User_B$) generates the ciphertext message C using the generated session key SK.
- **Step 5:** After that, $User_U$ select a random value r and generates KRF.
- **Step 6:** The generated encrypted message C and the key recovery field KRF are connected and transmitted to the other users.

Law Enforcement Phase. In this phase, the LEA attempts to recover the key to view suspicious communication between $User_A$ and $User_B$.

- **Step 1:** The LEA selects the KRF and ciphertext C of the suspected communication.
- **Step 2:** The LEA generates the re-encryption key $rk_{LEA \rightarrow KRA}$ using the obtained KRF, its own private key, and KRA public key.
- **Step 3:** The LEA requests the key recovery by transmitting the KRF of the message to be recovered and the generated re-encryption key $rk_{LEA \rightarrow KRA}$ to the KRC.

Session Key Recovery Phase. This phase, after receiving a request for key recovery from the LEA, KRC starts the key recovery process using the re-encryption key and KRF received from the LEA.

- **Step 1:** After receiving KRF, KRC re-encrypts using the re-encryption key and KRF to obtain KRF'.
- **Step 2:** The KRC sends the generated KRF' to the KRA.
- **Step 3:** KRA obtains KRF'' by decrypting the received KRA' with the private key. And then send KRF'' to the KRC
- **Step 4:** KRC calculates KRF''' using KRF' received from KRA.
- **Step 5:** KRC sends the KRF''' to LEA.
- **Step 6:** The LEA decrypts KRF''' to obtain SK, and decrypts the message M using the acquired SK.

5   Analysis of the Proposed Schemes

This section explores whether the security requirements described above are satisfied by the two schemes as shown in Table 3 and Table 4.

5.1   Key Recovery System Using Signcryption (Proposed Scheme1)

- **KRF integrity:** The receiver, LEA, KRA, and KRC participating in key recovery should not be able to maliciously transform a sender key that generates a KRF. We thus include the session key hash in parameter r of the KRF. KRF data thus cannot be forged. No-one but the sender can access the KRF session key generated by that sender.
- **Non-repudiation:** If the sender creates and uses the wrong KRF, KRC cannot recover the key. To solve this, the sender shouldn't be able to reject the fact that they created KRF. We thus include the private key X_A of a sender in parameter s of the KRF. The sender cannot deny that he created the KRF.
- **Attack on group authentication detection:** Third-party KRAs should not be maliciously involved in key recovery. So, a lawful KRA group member XOR operation the values from R_1 to R_n to generate a shared group value

Table 3. Comparison of key recovery system using signcryption

	[3]	[4]	[5]	Proposed Scheme1
KRF integrity	×	×	×	V
Non-repudiation	×	×	×	V
Attack on group authentication detection	V	×	×	V
Single point of failure protection	V	V	×	V

V: Provided/×: Not provided

of SGN between groups. The sender receives it from a lawful group member and hashes the SGN to include $H(SGN)$ in the KRF. When KRC recovers the complete key, it hashes and compares the SGN sent by the M-KRA with the SGN contained in the KRF to ensure it was received from a lawful KRA.

– **Single point of failure protection:** As both the KRC and all KRAs engage in session key recovery, it should be possible to recover the key even if some KRAs fail. Thus, a special value TT is generated. If some KRAs fail to recover session key pieces, a neighboring KRA generates a piece and transmits it to the KRC rather than the corresponding KRA. TT is defined as TT_i, which includes all c_i, r_i, s_i pieces and the SGN that XOR operated. The neighboring KRA (not the corresponding KRA) generates TT_i and sends it to the KRC, allowing the KRC to recover the complete session key.

5.2   Key Recovery System Using Proxy Re-Encryption (Proposed Scheme2)

– **KRF integrity:** In this proposed scheme, the KRF is encrypted with the LEA's public key. Therefore, during the key recovery process, KRC and KRA cannot forge or change KRF without knowing the LEA's private key.

– **Law enforcement support:** LEAs must be able to eavesdrop on suspect encrypted messages. Thus, the LEA transmits a KRF and re-encryption key $rk_{LEA \rightarrow KRA}$ to the KRC, and when requested, the KRC generates a re-encrypted ciphertext using the KRF. $rk_{LEA \rightarrow KRA}$. That re-encrypted ciphertext is sent to the KRA for decryption using a private key; the KRA then generates some session keys using the acquired parameters and sends them back to the KRC, which then recovers the complete session key and transmits it to the LEA, allowing message decryption.

– **Collusion attack resistance:** Among the LEA, KRC, and KRA, any two or more entities must be prevented from acting together and maliciously, preventing the recovery of the key, and unauthorized entities must be prevented from obtaining the key. Therefore, the LEA requires the cooperation of the KRC and KRA in order to decrypt KRF. Thus, even if an LEA has colluded with a single participant among the KRC and KRA, complete key recovery cannot be achieved without the assistance of the third participant.

Table 4. Comparison of key recovery system using proxy re-encryption

	[3]	[4]	[5]	Proposed Scheme2
KRF integrity	×	×	×	∨
Law enforcement support	∨	×	∨	∨
Collusion attacks resistance	×	×	×	∨

∨: Provided/×: Not provided

6   Conclusions

Encryption is essential in IT. However, it is impossible to decrypt ciphertext if keys are accidentally lost or corrupted, and criminals may exploit cryptography, triggering financial loss and embarrassment.

The key recovery system operates when users are lost or corrupted their keys. And the key recovery system allows government agencies to intercept ciphertext messages of suspicious users. In this paper, key information in ciphertext is decrypted by the KRF and used to recover both the message and the decrypted key. However, a KRF can be forged or changed, and KRF access by multiple agents poses security threats.

To solve this, this paper ensures the security requirements mentioned in Sect. 3, including KRF integrity and non-repudiation related to a secure multi-agent key recovery system and proxy re-encryption.

In the case of a key recovery system using signcryption, it is safe against various security requirements such as forgery and alteration of KRF, non-repudiation, and single point of failure. And it efficiently provides encryption and signature using signcryption. In addition, since KRC decrypts the complete session key and transmits it to the user, it reduces the user's computational load.

In the case of a key recovery system using proxy re-encryption, it is safe against various security requirements such as forgery and alteration of KRF, LEA support, and collusion attacks. Therefore, you need the help of all objects to do key recovery.

Future studies should investigate whether this recovery system can resolve security threats and achieve key recovery when it is implemented in real-world environments. Further research is also needed to determine whether the system is safe from other types of security threats.

Acknowledgment. This research was supported by the MSIT (Ministry of Science, ICT), Korea, under the High-Potential Individuals Global Training Program) (2020-0-01596) supervised by the IITP (Institute for Information & Communications Technology Planning & Evaluation) and was supported by the Soonchunhyang University Research Fund.

References

1. NIST: Escrowed Encryption Standard. Federal Information Processing Standards Publication (1994)

2. Denning, D.E., Branstad, D.K.: A taxonomy for key recovery encryption systems (1997)
3. Kanyamee, K., Chanboon, S.: High-availability decentralized cryptographic multi-agent key recovery. Int. Arab J. Inf. Technol. **11**(1), 52–58 (2014)
4. Lim, S., Kang, S., Sohn, J.: Modeling of multiple agent based cryptographic key recovery protocol. In: 19th Annual Computer Security Applications Conference, Proceedings. IEEE (2003)
5. Han, K., Yeun, C.Y., Kim, K.: New key escrow model for the lawful interception in 3GPP. In: 2009 Digest of Technical Papers International Conference on Consumer Electronics (2009)
6. Gennaro, R., et al.: Two-phase cryptographic key recovery system. Patent no. 5 (1999)
7. Zheng, Y.: Digital signcryption or how to achieve cost (signature & encryption) $\ll$ cost(signature) + cost(encryption). In: Kaliski, B.S. (ed.) CRYPTO 1997. LNCS, vol. 1294, pp. 165–179. Springer, Heidelberg (1997). https://doi.org/10.1007/BFb0052234
8. Blaze, M., Bleumer, G., Strauss, M.: Divertible protocols and atomic proxy cryptography. In: Nyberg, K. (ed.) EUROCRYPT 1998. LNCS, vol. 1403, pp. 127–144. Springer, Heidelberg (1998). https://doi.org/10.1007/BFb0054122

Path Authentication Protocol: Based on a Lightweight MAC and a Nonlinear Filter Generator

Yuki Taketa$^{(\boxtimes)}$ (ID), Yuta Kodera (ID), Takuya Kusaka (ID), and Yasuyuki Nogami (ID)

Graduate School of Natural Science and Technology, Okayama University,
Okayama, Japan
yuki_taketa@s.okayama-u.ac.jp,
{yuta_kodera,kusaka-t,yasuyuki.nogami}@okayama-u.ac.jp

Abstract. In this research, the authors propose a functionality based on message authentication code (MAC) to ensure the correctness of its path from a source to a destination. It aims to use a controller area network (CAN) over driving system. In the construction, MAC and a pseudorandom number generator having an intentional group structure are employed so that the correct user can authenticate a message and its path. The proposed method is experimentally evaluated by observing the computational time over IoT devices. As a result, it is found that the results show that it is possible to implement as an additional function that gives path authentication with additional time at most 3 times for the corresponding computation.

Keywords: Message authentication code (MAC) · Path authentication · Chaskey · Non-linear filter generator · Controller area network

1 Introduction

The recent innovation of artificial intelligence (AI) technology enables us to realize a high-quality recognition system and various industries have begun to build a framework utilizing IoT (Internet of Things). For example, an autonomous vehicle is a representative system (or a product) of such industrial products. Concretely, it detects and identifies objects with a camera and controls each driving device via a local area network on the vehicle, so-called CAN (controller area network) [1]. In addition, the current automobile system equips wireless communication modules such as Wi-Fi and Bluetooth so as to control an application by communicating with external servers. In these circumstances, instructions handled in the network in the car must be trustable enough to guarantee the integrity of the system.

As one of the cryptographic primitives to address this possible falsification, a MAC (message authentication code) [2] is known and adopted. It allows us to prevent an attacker from falsifying the data by evaluating the MAC.

© Springer Nature Switzerland AG 2021
Y. Park et al. (Eds.): SVCC 2020, CCIS 1383, pp. 38–48, 2021.
https://doi.org/10.1007/978-3-030-72725-3_3

In this research, the authors attempt to give additional functionality to a MAC that aims to prevent devices from spoofing. The function is referred to as path authentication in this paper and it verifies the nodes that went through.

In the path authentication, we use a pseudorandom number generator (PRNG) [3] that has a special structure. In detail, the authors design a PRNG which inherently has a group structure under a certain operation, and each node chains their respective sequence generated by the PRNG. As a result, the path authentication enables us to validate the message if the user is authorized and the message comes through the correct nodes. Moreover, since the sequences are applied by masking over the MAC of a message, it is expected to stir the output of the MAC.

The proposed method is implemented by employing Chaskey [4] as a lightweight MAC as with the conventional research [5] conducted by Carel et al. In addition, the authors use non-linear filter generators (NLFG) [6] to enable the generation of pseudorandom numbers that have a group structure. Then, the time for a single verification is estimated by measuring 100,000-times executions over CAN on IoT devices. As a result, it is shown that the protocol can be executed on a 32-bit microcontroller with a shorter computation time than the transmission delay of CAN communication. Thus, it is estimated that the path verification can be added without affecting the processing of CAN communication. On the other hand, the computation time on an 8-bit microcontroller is longer than the transmission delay. Therefore, the incremental time from the time taken to calculate generating a MAC digest is expected to have a significant impact on the process.

2   Preliminaries

This section briefly reviews the fundamentals of MAC and PRNGs.

2.1   Message Authentication Code

Typical MAC is a symmetric key cryptographic technique that verifies the consistency of messages in two devices to exchange messages reducing the risk of forgery. Essentially, a MAC is an encrypted checksum generated by combining a plain message and a common key that is a set along with the message to ensure message authentication. Since it generates a unique checksum, a sender and a receiver can generate the same checksum themselves from the message and the common key. The sender transmits the message and its MAC digest. Then, the receiver compares the received MAC digest and the regenerated MAC digest, if they are the same the receiver regards that the message is correct. Therefore, the sender needs to know the secret key to produce the correct MAC digest, so as long as the key management is secure no attacker would not be available a valid message.

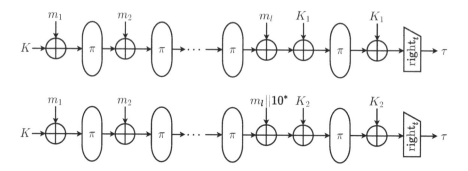

Fig. 1. Chaskey mode of operation

2.2   Chaskey

Chaskey is an efficient lightweight MAC proposed by Nickey Mouha in [4] and Chaskey is included in ISO/IEC 29192-6 standard [2]. It is designed for 32-bit microcontrollers and it mainly uses additions, permutations, and XOR to provide low-cost computation and strong security. The entire process of Chaskey is shown in Fig. 1. The inputs are a message M of arbitrary size and a common key K of 128-bit. The message M is divided l blocks $m_1, \cdots, m_l$ of 128-bits each. Also, two sub-keys K_1 and K_2 of 128-bit are generated from the common key K. In addition, a new 128-bit output is obtained from the 128-bit input by the permutation π that performs multiple rounds of the operation represented in Fig. 2. The permutation π is built by using an addition modulo 2^{32}, bit rotation, and an XOR. Finally the function right_t selects the last t significant bits of the last permutation. In this research, the authors use the Chaskey-12, which carries out 12 rounds permutation.

2.3   Controller Area Network

CAN [1] is a multi-master serial bus system developed for an in-vehicle network to make the communication between ECUs. The main characteristics of CAN protocol are real-time messages, broadcast communication, and resilient channel. As shown in Fig. 3, the CAN standard message format is consisting of seven-part. The message is stored in the data part and in this research, the authors assume that the MAC digest is stored in a part of the data part or in the data part of the next transmission frame.

In addition, CAN FD is an extension and improvement of the original CAN protocol. A notable difference is that the length of the payload is increased from 8 bytes to 64 bytes as shown in Fig. 4. This research assumes the data part of these two protocols and considers three cases of 32, 64, and 128-bit as the size of the MAC digest sent.

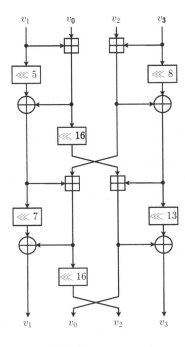

Fig. 2. Chaskey permutation π

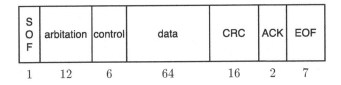

S O F	arbitation	control	data	CRC	ACK	EOF
1	12	6	64	16	2	7

Fig. 3. CAN 2.0A standard frame (inbits).

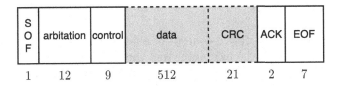

S O F	arbitation	control	data	CRC	ACK	EOF
1	12	9	512	21	2	7

Fig. 4. CAN FD standard frame (inbits).

2.4   Pseudorandom Number Generator

PRNGs generate a random number sequence that has reproducibility. It is used for simulations and for sharing the random number sequence obtained from the same initial values. One of the well-known PRNGs is a maximum length sequence (M-sequence) [7]. It is a sequence having a maximum period and can be generated based on the linear recurrence relation. This research uses binary M-sequence

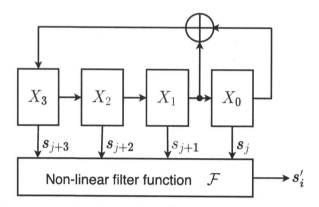

Fig. 5. The NLFG with 4-stages LFSR and 4-tuple input

which is generated by using a Linear Feedback Shift Register (LFSR) [8] with n stages as shown in Fig. 5, where X_i is a bit of 0 or 1.

In this research, the authors mainly use NLFG [6] to generate a set of random number sequences that form a group. An NLFG generates a pseudorandom binary sequence by applying a non-linear operation to d-tuples extracting from an M-sequence as follows:

$$S' = \{s'_i\}, s'_i = \mathcal{F}(s_j, s_{j+1}, \cdots, s_{j+d-1}), i = 1, 2, \cdots, \tag{1}$$

where $\mathcal{F}$ is a boolean function, which is referred to as non-linear filter function, and s_j is j-th output of an M-sequence. The NLFG is constructed by applying non-linear filter function to the internal state of LFSR that generates the M-sequence as shown in Fig. 5.

3   A New Protocol

This section introduces the basic concept of a new path authentication protocol to verify a message where the message is sent through a predetermined path and transit point. In addition, a method of generating pseudorandom numbers to be a group is also introduced. It is an essential factor for accomplishing to realize the proposed path authentication protocol.

3.1   Conditions of NLFG

By using the set of random numbers $\mathbb{G}_r = \{E, r_A, r_B, r_C\}$ that forms a group $\langle \mathbb{G}_r, \oplus \rangle$, the equation is established as follows:

$$r_A \oplus r_B = r_C, \tag{2}$$

$$r_A \oplus r_B \oplus r_C = E, \tag{3}$$

Table 1. The group table of $\mathbb{G}_S$

$\oplus$	S_E	S_1	S_2	S_3
S_E	S_E	S_1	S_2	S_3
S_1	S_1	S_E	S_3	S_2
S_2	S_2	S_3	S_E	S_1
S_3	S_3	S_2	S_1	S_E

where E is an all zero element as the unit element of $\mathbb{G}_r$. In this research, a random number, which is the element of $\mathbb{G}_r$, is assigned to each transit point. Then, it enables to verify the path by comparing the random number of the verifier with the result of the XOR operation at each transit point.

The NLFG is employed to allow the generation of pseudorandom numbers that are a group at each transit point when using the same initial values. In order to accomplish our idea, nonlinear filter functions are intentionally designed so that the sequences are being a group. Let us consider the combination of NLFGs with the same configuration of the LFSR. If the initial values of the internal states are the same, the inputs of the nonlinear filter functions are the same. Then, if the outputs of the nonlinear filter functions have a closure concerning XOR operation, then the output sequences will be a group since the inputs will always be the same. In order to reduce the bias in the appearance bits of the output sequences, the 0s and 1s of the output of each function are uniformed.

As an example, let the length of tapping bits from the M-sequence to the nonlinear filter be 3. First, let us consider three nonlinear filter functions $\mathcal{F}_1, \mathcal{F}_2$, and $\mathcal{F}_3$ and the all-zero element E, which is the unit element, shown as follows:

$$E = \{0,\ 0,\ 0,\ 0,\ 0,\ 0,\ 0,\ 0\},$$
$$\mathcal{F}_1 = \{1,\ 1,\ 0,\ 1,\ 1,\ 0,\ 0,\ 0\},$$
$$\mathcal{F}_2 = \{1,\ 0,\ 0,\ 0,\ 1,\ 0,\ 1,\ 1\},$$
$$\mathcal{F}_3 = \{0,\ 1,\ 0,\ 1,\ 0,\ 0,\ 1,\ 1\}.$$

In this case, the set $\langle \mathbb{G}_{\mathcal{F}} = \{E, \mathcal{F}_1, \mathcal{F}_2, \mathcal{F}_3\},\ \oplus \rangle$ is a group. Secondly, we generate pseudorandom sequences S_1, S_2, and S_3 by using $\mathcal{F}_1, \mathcal{F}_2$, and $\mathcal{F}_3$, respectively. Then, the set $\mathbb{G}_S$ consisting of all zero sequence S_E and S_1, S_2, and S_3 also forms a group when the input sequence of $\mathcal{F}_1, \mathcal{F}_2$, and $\mathcal{F}_3$ is the same. Furthermore, a group table of $\langle \mathbb{G}_S,\ \oplus \rangle$ is shown in Table 1. Note that the inverse of S_i is S_i itself. Furthermore, the above is an example of a case where the order is 4. In the same way, it is possible to form a group whose order is a power of 2, and to set up a large number of transit points.

3.2   The Flow of Protocol

This section introduces the flow of the proposed path authentication protocol. The illustration of the overview of the protocol is shown in Fig. 6. Let $C(M, K)$

be a function to calculate the MAC of a message M by using a common key K. Let $R(\cdot)$ be a function to generate a random number and let $H(\cdot)$ be a hash function. Firstly, the sender (client) calculates the MAC from a message M and generates the initial value of NLFG by applying a hash function $H(\cdot)$ to M. In addition, the random number generated from $H(M)$ is masked to the value of MAC by using XOR operation as follows:

$$W_s = C(M, K) \oplus R_s(H(M)), \tag{4}$$

where W_s is the data for the path authentication sent by the sender and $R_s(\cdot)$ is NLFG in the sender. Then, the message M and the generated W_s are sent from the sender.

Similarly, the transit point (Gateway) generates the random number from the message M sent by the sender, and performs XOR operation on W_s as follows:

$$W_t = W_s \oplus R_t(H(M)), \tag{5}$$

where W_t is the data for the path authentication sent by the transit point and $R_t(\cdot)$ is NLFG in the transit point.

After the receiver (Device) receives the message M and W_t, the random number is generated from M as the same as the above, and XOR operations are performed on W_t as follows:

$$W_r = W_t \oplus R_r(H(M)), \tag{6}$$

where W_r is the data for the path authentication and $R_r(\cdot)$ is NLFG in the receiver. Finally, the receiver compares $C(M, K)$ generated from the message M and the common key K with W_r calculated in Eq. (6). If $C(M, K) \neq W_r$, then the message is rejected since the random numbers generated at each point have the relationship as follows:

$$R_s(H(M)) \oplus R_t(H(M)) = R_r(H(M)). \tag{7}$$

Since the receiver knows the result of the passage through the path, it can be verified.

3.3   Security Analysis

The security of the proposed protocol is based on that of the hash function, the MAC and the NLFG. Especially, the key management of MAC is an essential factor of a practical application. It needs to be careful about compromising the common key to preventing attackers from creating valid messages. In the proposed protocol, the security expected to be improved rather than the conventional MAC protocol due to the masking procedure by a pseudorandom number. In other words, the security concerning the masking is relying on the sufficiency of the use of a one time pad. Therefore, it is essential to regularly update the common key. Also, if the same message is sent many times, random numbers are generated many times with the same initial value. As a countermeasure, it is considered to add a counter to the hash calculation to change the initial value. The analysis of occurring collisions of MAC and pseudorandom numbers is the future work.

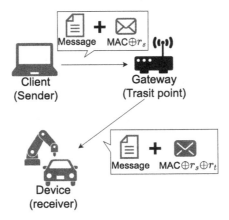

Fig. 6. The illustration of the proposed protocol

4 Experiment and Result

This section describes experimental results by focusing on the computation time. The authors select CAN communication which is expected to be feasible by employing the proposed protocol, and measurements using IoT devices are conducted.

4.1 Assumption and Experimental Enviroments

In this research, the experiment is conducted assuming the CAN and CAN FD data formats are shown in Fig. 3 and 4, respectively. Arduino Uno [9] and Raspberry Pi 3A+ [10] are used to measure the computation time as a representative of IoT devices to evaluate the proposed protocol. The specifications of Arduino Uno and Raspberry Pi 3A+ are shown in Tables 2 and 3, respectively. It is assumed to send 32-bit, 64-bit, 128-bit, and 256-bit messages. Correspondingly, it generates 32-bit, 64-bit, 128-bit, and 128-bit MACs and random numbers, respectively. As the MAC algorithm, Chaskey-12, known as the lightweight MAC, is employed. The configuration of the NLFG is a nonlinear filter function that takes 8-bits as its input, and an M-sequence is generated based on the recurrence relation $s_{31} = s_3 \oplus s_0$ as shown in Fig. 7. Then, the authors implement the NLFG to generate pseudorandom numbers by using a lookup table that works in the same manner as $\mathcal{F}$.

The Hash function, which generates the initial value of NLFG, uses Chaskey-12 by using a key as a countermeasure for considering the transmission of the same message. In addition, a single computation time is estimated by measuring 100,000-times executions.

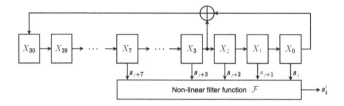

Fig. 7. The NLFG with 31-stages LFSR and 8-tuple input

Table 2. Arduino Uno main characteristics

Processor	ATmega328P (8-bit)
Clock Speed	16 MHz
SRAM	2 KB
Flash Memory	32 KB

Table 3. Raspberry Pi 3A+ main characteristics

Processor	ARM Cortex-A53 (64-bit)
Clock Speed	1.4 GHz
SDRAM	512 MB
OS	Raspbian-buster (32-bit)

4.2   Experimental Result and Consideration

Tables 4 and 5 show the computation time on Arduino Uno and Raspberry Pi, respectively. As a result, the calculation time increased by a maximum of 3.08 times compared to the calculation time for the conventional MAC protocol, Chaskey alone. The reason why the calculation time of Chaskey-12 on Raspberry Pi is closer to that of the NLFG than on Arduino is thought to be due to the fact that Chaskey-12 is designed to be optimized for 32-bit microcontrollers. Note that since the output of Chaskey-12 is 128-bit, the length of random numbers is restricted to 128-bit. In the case that the length of a MAC is 32-bits or 64-bits, the digest is generated by folding 128-bits MAC into the corresponding length via XOR. Therefore, though there is a slight computational difference between them, the difference would be negligible in this computational experiment. Also, as shown in Fig. 1, Chaskey-12 performs permutation on every 128-bit block. Therefore, the computation time is considered to be increased in proportion to the message size per 128-bits. In other words, it is found that the increased computation time from the traditional protocol is at most 3.08 times since the size of the MAC does not change even if the message size is further increased.

However, according to the Arduino Crypto Library [11], widely used Hash functions, such as SHA-256, take longer to compute than the computation time in Table 4. Therefore, we need to take into account the impact of the choice of a Hash function.

Table 4. Computation time of the proposed protocol on Arduino Uno

Message size	MAC size	Computation time [μs]		
		Chaskey	NLFG	Total
32-bit	32-bit	675	99	1449
64-bit	64-bit	675	194	1544
128-bit	128-bit	669	392	1730
256-bit	128-bit	1247	392	2886

Table 5. Computation time of the proposed protocol on Raspberry Pi 3A+

Message size	MAC size	Computation time [μs]		
		Chaskey	NLFG	Total
32-bit	32-bit	3.79	0.94	8.52
64-bit	64-bit	3.88	1.90	9.66
128-bit	128-bit	3.67	3.95	11.29
256-bit	128-bit	6.41	3.96	16.78

Finally, considering the original CAN transmit rate, it takes 222 μs per frame. The computation time on Raspberry Pi is fast enough for that time to be feasible for the proposed protocol. On the other hand, it is slower than the CAN transmit rate on Arduino Uno. Therefore, it is necessary to take countermeasures such as making the communication interval 10 ms. In addition, the calculation of the initial value by the hash function takes more time in the increased time. Therefore, one of countermeasure against the above is that the initial value is shared in advance by using a secret key and synchronize it with a counter.

5   Conclusion

In this research, the authors proposed a new path authentication protocol based on MAC for ensuring the correctness of the path from a source to a destination. This functionality targets a local area network and is composed by getting the concepts of MAC and one-time pad together. In short, our method takes a mask, which is an element in a special group, for a MAC digest in each transit point and we can confirm the correctness of the path.

The authors measure the computation time required for the proposed protocol using CAN communication. As a result, Raspberry Pi 3A+, which is a 32-bit microcontroller, is expected to operate without any problems when embedded in the CAN communication protocol. On the other hand, the computation time on Arduino Uno, which is an 8-bit microcontroller, increases to 2.5 times of generating MAC digest, and further reduction of computation time is required.

The future work is to improve the security and efficiency of PRNGs, which are used to generate random numbers to form a group structure. In addition, the investigation of the collision of pseudorandom numbers and masked MAC is necessary for a security analysis. Furthermore, the PRNGs may be applied as a countermeasure against man-in-the-middle attacks of key-sharing protocols.

Acknowledgment. This work was partially supported by the JSPS KAKENHI Grant-in-Aid for Challenging Research (Pioneering) JP20K20484 and Grant-in-Aid for Research Activity Start-up JP20K23327.

References

1. ISO 11898–1:2015: Road vehicles - Controller area network (CAN) - Part 1: Data link layer and physical signalling. ISO, Geneva, Switzerland
2. ISO/IEC DIS 29192–6:2019: Information technology - Security techniques - Lightweight cryptography - Part 6: Message authentication codes (MACs). ISO, Geneva, Switzerland
3. Barker, E., Kelsey, J.: Recommendation for random number generation using deterministic random bit generators. NIST, SP 800–90A, Revision 1 (2015). https://csrc.nist.gov/publications/detail/sp/800-90a/rev-1/final. Accessed 22 Apr 2019
4. Mouha, N., Mennink, B., Herrewege, A.V., Watanabe, D., Preneel, B., Verbauwhede, I.: Chaskey: an efficient MAC algorithm for 32-bit microcontrollers. Cryptology ePrint Archive, Report 2014/386. https://eprint.iacr.org/2014/386. Accessed 23 Aug 2020
5. Carel, G., Isshiki, R., Kusaka, T., Nogami, Y.: Design of a message authentication protocol for CAN FD based on chaskey lightweight MAC. In: Sixth International Symposium on Computing and Networking Workshops (CANDARW), pp. 267–271. CPS, Hida Takayama (2018)
6. Golić, J.D.: On the security of nonlinear filter generators. In: Gollmann, D. (ed.) FSE 1996. LNCS, vol. 1039, pp. 173–188. Springer, Heidelberg (1996). https://doi.org/10.1007/3-540-60865-6_52
7. Golomb, S.W.: Shift Register Sequences. Holden-Day, San Francisco (1967)
8. Murase, M.: Linear Feedback Shift Register. European Patent Application (1991)
9. Arduino. https://www.arduino.cc. Accessed 23 Aug 2020
10. Raspberry Pi 3A+. https://www.raspberrypi.org/products. Accessed 23 Aug 2020
11. Weatherley, R.: Arduino Cryptography Library. https://rweather.github.io/arduinolibs. Accessed 23 Aug 2020

STRISA: A New Regulation Architecture to Enforce Travel Rule

Wei-Tek Tsai[1,2,3,4,5], Dong Yang[1], Rong Wang[1(✉)], Kangmin Wang[1], Weijing Xiang[1], and Enyan Deng[3]

[1] Digital Society and Blockchain Laborator, Beihang University, Beijing, China
{yangdong2019,wangrong,drw1997,xwj9712}@buaa.edu.cn
[2] Arizona State University, Tempe, AZ 85287, USA
[3] Beijing Tiande Technologies, Beijing, China
{tsai,deng}@tiandetech.com
[4] Andrew International Sandbox Institute, Qingdao, China
[5] IOB Laboratory, National Big Data Comprehensive Experimental Area, Guizhou, China

Abstract. FATF introduces a new regulation framework with Travel Rule in 2019, many crypto exchanges have incorporated the TRISA (Travel rule information sharing architecture) system as a part of their compliance mechanisms. However, the TRISA system may not meet the regulation requirements for all the countries. This paper proposes another version of TRISA, STRISA, that is compatible with the TRISA, but with four new features: 1) track individual digital wallets; 2) support a BDL (Blockchain Data Lake) platform that can interoperate with various blockchain (BC) systems for analysis; 3) supply a regulation enforcement framework using smart contracts with automated machine learning techniques; 4) Most of data are stored in associated BCs to ensure that no one including regulators should try to alter the data stored to protect the integrity of entire regulation compliance process. This paper also discusses other design and protocols to support these new features including unique storage scheme, double-interlocking mechanism. STRISA has been implemented and is available for research and experimentation.

Keywords: STRISA · Blockchain · Smart contracts · Regulation · Travel Rule

1 Introduction

This paper proposes a new version of TRISA (Travel Rule Information Sharing Architecture) called STRISA. The TRISA framework was proposed to regulate current cryptocurrency transactions by Financial Action Task Force (FATF). The regulation is with respect to Virtual Asset Service Providers (VASPs) and other crypto entities as increasingly crypto or digital assets are used for money laundering and/or terrorist financing. The updated guidance proposes "Travel Rule", and this rule requires VASPs to share sender (originator) and receiver

© Springer Nature Switzerland AG 2021
Y. Park et al. (Eds.): SVCC 2020, CCIS 1383, pp. 49–67, 2021.
https://doi.org/10.1007/978-3-030-72725-3_4

(beneficiary) information for digital asset transactions [1]. This is similar to previous Travel Rules that require financial institutions to share this information when executing bank wire transfers and SWIFT funds transfers [2].

The TRISA framework has the following features:

- Regulators or authorities can identity information without modifying the current blockchain (BC) protocols, and without incurring increased transaction costs or modifying current cryptocurrency transaction processes.
- Protecting user privacy.
- Remaining open source and decentralized.
- Having an open governance body.
- Maintaining interoperability with other approaches.

In other words, the TRISA framework strikes a balance between regulation and privacy protection, and TRISA monitors transactions between VASPs only, and it will not monitor individuals or enterprises that interact with VASPs.

While the TRISA framework satisfies the FATF regulation recommendation, it does not meet the requirements of existing regulations in some countries. For example, it is necessary to trace all the transactions, not just those transactions between VASPs. This paper proposes an updated STRISA as it adds four new features:

- It monitors and tracks individual digital wallets.
- It has a bigdata platform BC Data Lake (BDL) that interconnects with participating BCs and exchanges, and the BDL support AML analysis.
- It has a regulation compliance system developed using smart contracts (SCs) for automated detection and actions. The system also deploys machine learning tools to detect potential new frauds.
- Most data except those stored at the BDL will be stored in related BCs, even those BDL data are also interlocked with associated BCs to ensure that even regulators will not try to alter these data, and this protects the integrity of regulators and entire regulation process.

However, these changes require significant new system designs because STRISA also needs to meet the same requirements as TRISA, i.e., it will not modify the current BC protocols, without increasing transaction costs, or modify existing transaction flows. Furthermore, the STRISA has additional requirements:

- The system should do so in an efficient manner, as most crypto transactions will settle in real time without the possibility of rollback, thus compliance technology will be in real time.
- The system should operate in a reliable and secure manner. Particularly regulators should not be able to modify the data stored unilaterally. If so, this will create a significant legal challenge to the system.
- The system should be scalable so that it can process hundreds of thousands of VASPs with millions of transactions that may happen at the same time.

This paper is organized as follows: Sect. 2 introduces TRISA; Sect. 3 presents STRISA including its transaction management, the BDL system that has been implemented; Sect. 4 discusses related work; and Sect. 5 concludes this paper.

2 TRISA Introduction

While the TRISA system specifies design and various trade-offs are still being discussed today, e.g., whether to use a BC or not in tracking participants and whether a centralized approach should be adopted, but most of its features are clear at this time. The TRISA system will not store data in BCs, possibly due to privacy issues, and it will operate in a decentralized manner, like a BC, not it is not a BC.

The TRISA framework involves several important steps, the first is the certification of VASPs, each VASP needs to authenticate with fellow trading VASP partners, and each VASP needs to deal with their clients including their authentication and transaction records. As the TRISA deals with transactions between VASPs, those transactions that are performed within a VASP will not appear in the TRISA database.

2.1 VASP Certificate

The first process is for VASPs to register in the TRISA network, and this process is shown in Fig. 1.

One or more third parties verify the identity of a VASP via email identification, domain name ownership identification, phone call verification, and business paperwork verification. The regulators can then issue a digital certificate signed by the regulators and the VASP to serve as identification and a way to establish secure encrypted communications with the verified VASP. These certificates have expiration dates [7]. They should also be subject to revocation by the regulators through an Online Certificate Status Protocol (OCSP) mechanism or revocation list.

A validated certificate X.509 from the regulators protects communications between two VASPs by encrypting the connection between them [8]. In this model, a VASP applies for certification through a registered VASP and the regulators. The regulators would then verify that all legal requirements have been met before the VASP can send a certificate signing request (CSR) and the TVASP regulators (Trusted VASP regulators) can produce the signed certificate.

2.2 Authentication Between VASPs

The second step requires each VASP to authenticate with each trading VASP partner in both ways as shown in Fig. 2.

When a transaction is initiated, authentication needs to be performed first, VASP certificates need to be issued, trading VASPs need to authenticate with each other, via the public key certificate show trading receiver VASP, receiver

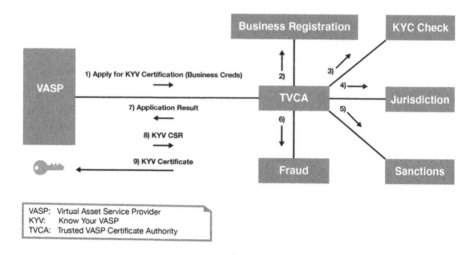

Fig. 1. A VASP registers the TRISA network.

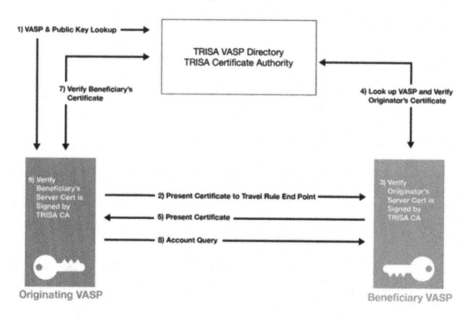

Fig. 2. Authentication between VASPs.

verify sponsors certificate and certificate by regulators to find their own show sponsors, sponsors an account after verification certificate query, confirm the transaction after the receiver account belongs to the VASP, continue to trade.

The TRISA framework does not include personal wallets and trace only those transactions in-between VASPs, and thus many transaction will not be visible to regulators. Some even suggest using DEX (Decentralized Exchange systems) for maximum privacy.

3   STRISA Framework

The STRISA framework consists of three major components:

- The STRISA network.
- The STRISA BDL system.
- Associated BDL system, an AML processing system with machine learning tools.

The STRISA network is an open network where BCs, SCs, BDLs, and related systems can participate in the system via secure registration. In this way, hundreds of thousands of BCs, SCs, and BDLs can participate in this regulation enforcement network. The STRISA BDL system is a data-lake system that interconnect with BCs to sore their transaction data; The AML detection system associated with each BDL is used to detect potential money-laundering events.

Comparing to the TRISA, the STRISA framework monitors more transactions, thus the number of transactions that will be tracked increases significantly. However, as data in a database system can be altered, there is a need to ensure that the data stored in the database system cannot be easily modified without being noticed. Recently, IBM has proposed a BC database approach, and the system uses Kafka to direct messages, and if the Kafka server is compromised, the entire regulation framework is compromised. Essentially, the IBM approach is a simulation approach, and it is a good strategy for research and experimentation. But for regulation, as numerous legal issues may be at stake, data stored must have high integrity. Thus a simulation approach may not protect sufficient protection.

Similarly, the BlockchainDB approach proposed by Microsft was not taken, as not every node will be involved in consensus voting. But for regulators, they must have complete information, and they must be able to find information quickly.

Scalable Data Storage Schemes of STRISA. Instead, a BDL approach is taken where data are first stored in their original trading BCs, and the same data with their associated hash information are written into the BDL. The BDL system also has its own BCs, and first stores all the data into the associated BC, and obtain a new hash, send the same data with the new hash back to the original trading BCs. In this way, the same data are stored at in four places:

- Original trading BCs, and the data are stored at least twice, the first time the associated trades are made, the second time when the BDL sends back the data. The original trading BC can verify that these two sets of data are consistent, if not, it will alert the BDL that something is wrong.

– BDL, the data are stored with their corresponding hash values. After obtaining the hash, the same data with their hash values are sent to the original trading BCs and the associated BC with the BDL.
– The BDL BC.

Both the BDL and associated BDL BC will be a bigdata platform, and the BDL will interact with many trading BCs. Thus both the BDL and the BDL BC must be scalable.

The BDL is scalable because it is a traditional bigdata platform with scalability; the BDL BC is also scalable because this BC is essentially an ABC(account BC). An ABC does not trade, but stores account information, thus it is scalable by horizontal extension, and different workloads can be sent to different processors for execution.

Data Validation. Transaction data are stored in at least three systems: the trading BCs, the BDL, and BDL BC. As original trading BCs and BDL BC are BC systems, data cannot be easily altered. But data stored in the BDL can be altered. When a regulator uses the BDL to perform analysis, she will have the following choices:

– Use the data stored in the BDL directly without any validation. This has the worst dependability, but this is most efficient.
– Use the data stored in the BDL, but verify the data with the corresponding hash values, also in the BDL. This has the 2nd least dependability, and it is also fast.
– In addition to the previous step, this will also verify the data and corresponding hash values in the BDL BC.
– In addition, the previous step, this will also verify the data stored in the original trading BC, this is to verify that the data and the corresponding hash values are consistent with the ones stored in the original trading BC. This has the highest dependability, but this is the most expensive way.

Depending on specific issues that need to be addressed, the system may decide the options to exercise. If transaction values are small, and clients involved have high reputation, lighter versions can be used. For large-value transactions as well as for risky clients, a conservative approach should be taken.

3.1   STRISA Network

The STRISA network is a network protocol that runs on top of the Internet or ChainNet. The Network mainly supports the registration of BCs, SCs, and BDLs so to work coherently in the STRISA framework. This STRISA network follows the LSO (Ledgers, Smart contracts, Oracles) framework [30] (Fig. 3).

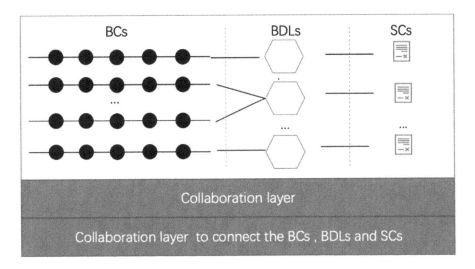

Fig. 3. STRISA network.

In this network, a BDL system has a set of associated SCs, possibly supplied from different service providers, e.g., central banks or regulators can supply their own SCs for regulation as Bank of England has hinted in their March 2020 CBDC report, or from third-party vendors so that different vendors can supply their algorithms to different regulators.

Different jurisdictions may choose to have their own BDLs so that they have better control and management of transaction data, and different service providers may offer their BDL services.

Similarly, different VASPs such as exchanges or payment systems have their own BCs (with their own SCs), and they need to interconnect with various BDL for regulation compliance.

For a given country, there may be multiple BDLs with many associated SCs from different service providers, and numerous VASPs with their own BCs and SCs.

Thus, the STRISA will be an international framework that has open interface and software. Furthermore, each jurisdiction can have its own customization and the customization can be realized by different set of SCs that will be deployed.

If a VASP needs to trade digital assets with another VASP, these two VASPs need to make sure that both talk to the same BDL system, and this requires a registration process. These STRISA registration processes are shown in Fig. 4. The initiating individual will alert its VASP, the VASP will send an alert to the corresponding VASP. These VASPs need to authenticate with each other if they have not done so before. Once these two VASPs authenticate with each other, the transaction can then proceed.

These two VASPs will exchange all relevant information with each other. Once both VASPs confirms the validity of the transaction, the transaction is made, and transaction data are stored in relevant BCs.

Then the current transaction data are sent to the BDL for regulation compliance.

STRISA needs to synchronize all account information to the BDL including account information; furthermore, all transactions information will be stored, not just those across VASPs. shall be written into the BDL.

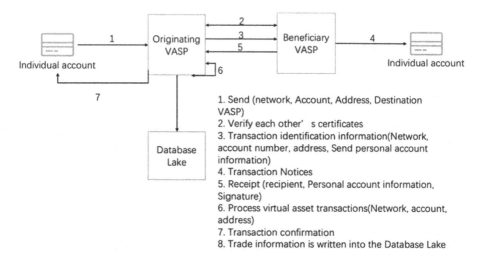

1. Send (network, Account, Address, Destination VASP)
2. Verify each other' s certificates
3. Transaction identification information(Network, account number, address, Send personal account information)
4. Transaction Notices
5. Receipt (recipient, Personal account information, Signature)
6. Process virtual asset transactions(Network, account, address)
7. Transaction confirmation
8. Trade information is written into the Database Lake

Fig. 4. Transaction processes.

To speed up trading, STRISA stores the mapping from BC addresses to VASP addresses in the BDL. This will facilitate efficient query processing. Currently, the TRISA system uses a cache system to store active trading information. But the size of cache is limited, it is possible that the cache does not contain the needed information, if the information is not available, the TRISA will broadcast its need so that participating VASPs will respond. STRISA is different, as it uses the BDL saves all data BC address to the VASP mapping, the BDL contains all the relevant information. If there is a change in a VASP, it will alert the BDL so that they can be synchronized. The BDL is a data-lake system with sufficient redundancy so that no single failures will cripple the system. The STRISA method is shown in Fig. 5.

3.2   BDL System

The BDL system will contain enormous amount of data as it needs to store all the transaction information from all the participating VASPs including their client information.

A data lake is a centralized repository or database system that store all structured and unstructured data at any scale. A BDL is a data lake that contains BC data. Like a BC, the BDL will keep on adding more data without deleting them, and old data may move to the storage systems. As the database system is not a BC system, potentially data stored in the BDL can be modified. To

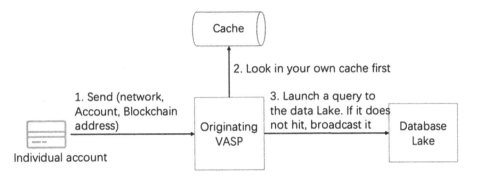

Fig. 5. The STRISA method lookup.

over this problem, the BDL has an associated BC that store all the information that enters into the BDL. In this case, if there is an attempt to modify the data in the BDL, the BDL BC will detect that. A data-lake system rather than a data warehouse is chosen because the BDL needs to process all the transactions from all the participating BCs with different formats and protocols, and until the world has a unified data format, a data-lake system is preferred. A data-lake system does not unify the data stored.

Microsoft's BlockchainDB system has a consensus protocol but not all the nodes will participate in this process. Only selected nodes, e.g., those nodes that contain relevant data, will participate in this process. This design is not used because in regulation compliance, regulators need to access information quickly, and they should not need to search on nodes to find relevant information. IBM BC database is a centralized system.

The STRISA architecture requires a large platform to database across the BC to process all VASP transaction data and store all account information, as well as providing a mapping of VASP addresses to BC addresses.

The BDL system as shown in Fig. 6 is a bigdata platform interconnecting with various BCs for regulation compliance and monitoring. The interconnection is through a Collaboration Layer (CL), and this supports complex query, data mining and data analysis functions.

The CL system is a dynamic registration service for BCs, and it acts like a DNS in Internet, except the CL system stores participating BC information. Furthermore, the CL system is also a BC system so that data cannot be easily changed without being noticed.

The system includes: 1) Mirror BC data module, including data acquisition and transmission modules; 2) BCDP (BC data pipeline) that supports BC data transfer, data conversion and processing; 3) BDL core, including BC database, data analysis component, data security and access component, and BDL BC.

The mirror BC data module collects data from different BCs and sends the data to the BC data pipeline. The BCDP is responsible for the connection between BCs and the BDL, including data transmission and reception of BCs and BDL, and data conversion and processing.

The platform can be scaled by adding more servers and communication links. As regulators can see all the transactions done in participating BCs, they can perform KYC, AML and other analysis easily as all the data are gathered and stored at the platform. The data stored in the BDL platform are also written back to participating BCs so that these BCs can verify that the data stored have not been altered by regulators. In this manner, regulators can monitor all the related transactions, and all participating BCs can be assurance that data reported are stored at the BDL without any modifications.

The system architecture of BDL is shown below:

BDL stores information into three major segments: 1) account information; 2) transaction data; 3) mapping information from BCs to VASPs. All BC data will be stored in the BDL sequentially with the following features:

(1) No BC data structures are changed.
(2) Storing BC data in the BDL will facilitate efficient query, search.

Account information is synchronized when the VASP access to the BDL, and deposited in the BC, all the account information changes are recorded and cannot be changed, it is more conducive to regulation. The blocks in the BC are stored in the database for easy query, trading information after dealing with the big data platform generated settlement information and cash flow data, the data will be stored in the BC and written to the database to ensure that the transaction data cannot be changed, VASP addresses to chain address mapping information also needs to be stored in the block chain, In this way, some BC addresses can be prevented from changing their VASP addresses, all information is stored in the BC and written to the database as blocks, and has the advantage of facilitating supervision and improving system efficiency (Figs. 7, 8, 9 and 10).

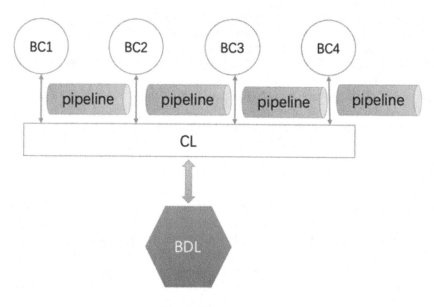

Fig. 6. BDL system.

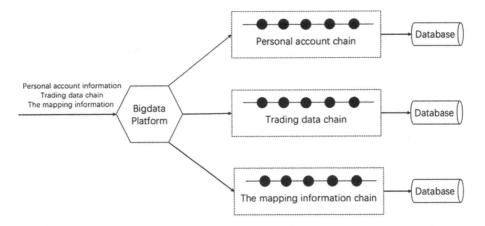

Fig. 7. BDL system architecture.

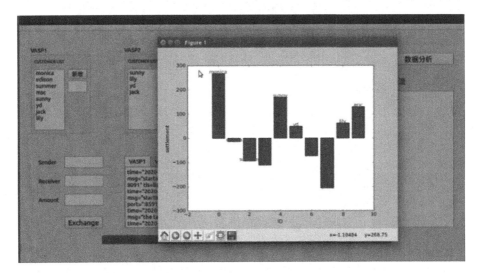

Fig. 8. Using BDL system to analyze capital flow.

VASPs will need to be approved by regulators to verify and issue the certificate, the certificate has timeliness. VASP will need to report related information of individual accounts such as user name, ID, BC address, physical address, and the information will uploaded to BDL, when a new individual account, need to access authentication to the regulator, and the account information data synchronization to the BDL, for each transaction record their trading information, will be the information of both parties and transaction data uploaded to the BDL. Regulators are responsible for issuing certificates to compliant VASP and allowing transactions, while the BDL keeps all account information under VASP and all transaction information, thus achieving penetrating supervision.

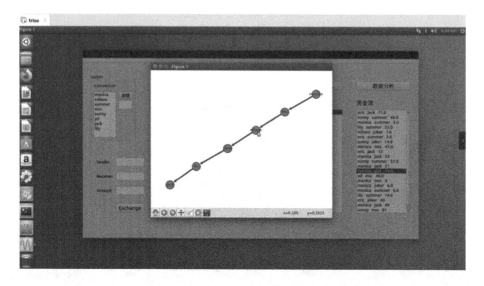

Fig. 9. Transaction analysis using BDL system.

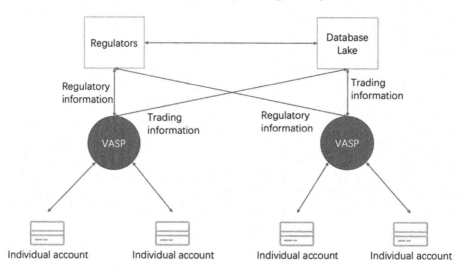

Fig. 10. STRISA architecture.

The main functions of BDL are as follows:

1. Store All VASP's Account Information. When all VASPs access BDL, they need to upload all account information in their system. The data format is as follows:

All personal information is stored in the database in the form of blocks. If there are changes, all the change records will be recorded, which is more conducive to supervision and prevent account information from being tampered with.

2. Store All Transaction Information. VASP will upload all the transaction information to the big data platform at regular intervals. The format of the transaction information is as follows:

- Transaction originator name: Sender (the name in the corresponding user information).
- Address of initiator: Snd_addr (address of user).
- Transaction amount: Amount.
- Beneficiary name: Receiver (name of the receiver in the user information).
- Beneficiary account address: Rcv_addr (address of user) (Fig. 11).

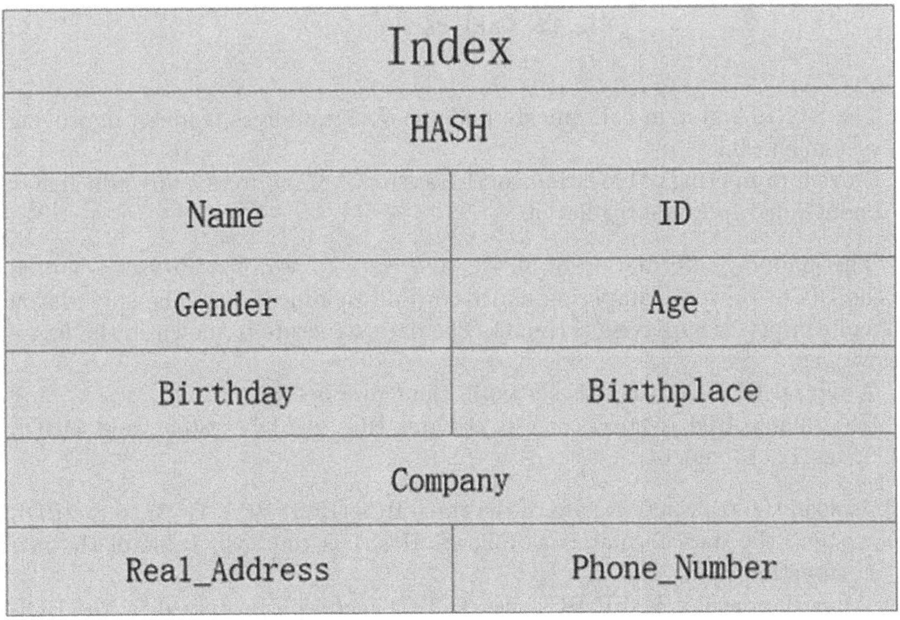

Index	
HASH	
Name	ID
Gender	Age
Birthday	Birthplace
Company	
Real_Address	Phone_Number

Fig. 11. BDL data format.

BDL's big data platform generates account clearing and settlement information and capital flow information based on transaction information, Regulators have a clear idea of what happens to the money in individual accounts and where it goes, This allows for better monitoring of AML.

3. Provide the Mapping of VASP Address to Blockchain Address. A BDL system that stores mapping information from VASP addresses to blockchain addresses has two benefits:

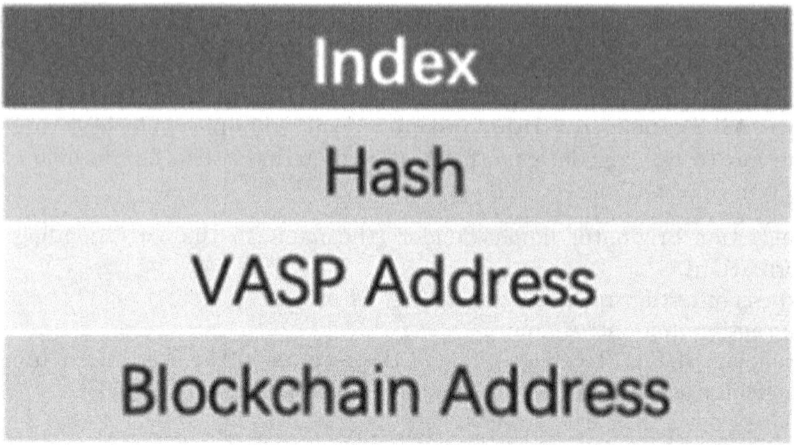

Fig. 12. VASP data format.

– The STRISA system can quickly find the VASP address trading, improving system efficiency.
– Prevent tampering of blockchain addresses to VASP address maps, which may be intended to evade regulation.

The mapping information of all BC addresses to VASP addresses is stored in the BC to prevent tampering and record all modifications. The supervision system can better supervise accounts. The data structure is shown in the figure below:

A typical BDL data flow is shown in the figure below:

The sample BDL system consists of three BCs, a BDL system, and a BDL BC (Figs. 12, 13 and 14).

(1) Upload the transaction data of the three BCs (BC1, BC2, BC3) to the BDL system, the data format is as follows, Hash1 is the hash value of the raw transaction data.
(2) After the data of VASP BCs such as BC1 has been processed by the BDL system, clearing and settlement information is generated, and the new data is processed to produce a new hash value Hash2. The Hash2 contains all the previous data as shown in Fig. 15.

Write the data from the BDL back to the VASP BC (in this case BC1) to generate Hash3, and at the same time write data from the BDL to the BDL BC to generate Hash4 as shown in Fig. 16.

This double-interlocking mechanism ensures that data will not be altered without being noticed. First, data stored in various BCs are ensured by their BC mechanism, the data stored in the BDL are ensured by the data in the original trading BC as well as the BDL BC.

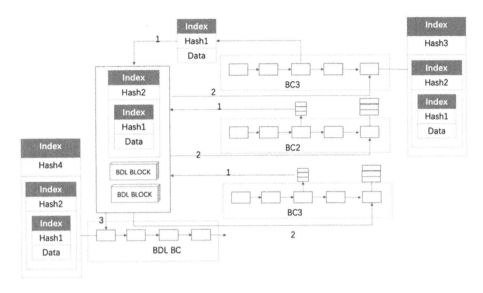

Fig. 13. BDL data flow.

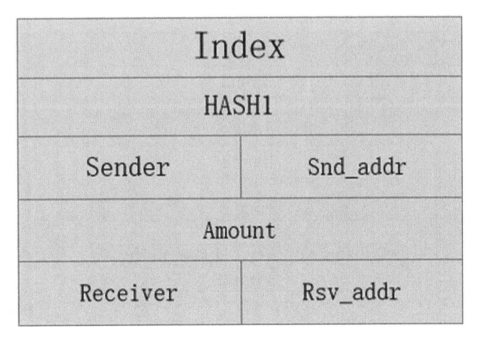

Fig. 14. Raw transaction data.

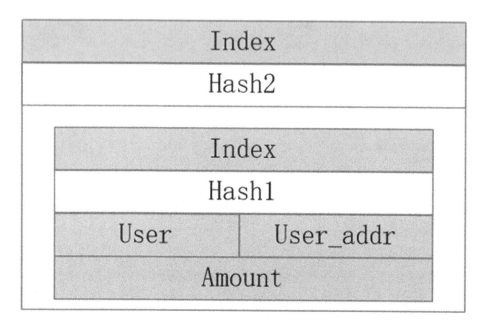

Fig. 15. Previous data.

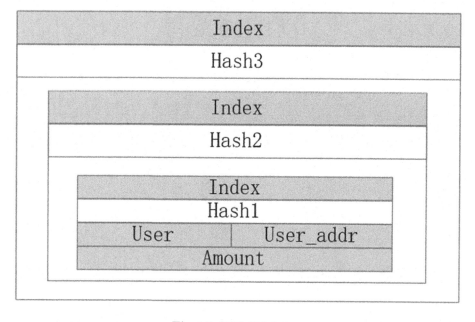

Fig. 16. BDL BC data.

3.3 Blockchain-Based AML Regulation System

Money laundering activities help criminals evade legal sanctions, encourage illegal and criminal activities, disrupt economic and financial order, and undermine social justice. This paper applies BC, SC (smart contract) and AI technology to anti-money laundering activities (AML).

We use semi-supervised machine learning based on graph convolution, using behavioral data and a small number of feature tags to complete the identification of group suspicious transactions, thereby restoring money laundering scenarios and effectively identifying complex money laundering transactions. This greatly improves the timeliness and accuracy of reporting suspicious money-laundering transactions, and reduces the compliance costs of financial institutions' AML work.

4 Related Work

4.1 CFTC

CFTC has published a report on smart contracts (SCs) in 2018, and SCs can be used to implement parts of transactions as well as for regulation compliance. This has implications to BC application architecture as SCs should be written in a standard manner and each SC will execute only a portion of transaction process. This will standardize SCs, e.g., some SCs will be responsible for KYC, other SCs responsible for AML, others for ID verification, others for compliance reporting. STRISA adopts this approach by applying SCs to monitor and regulate trades.

4.2 Blockchain Databases

To perform regulation, it is necessary to have a database to store and evaluate transaction data and identify potential frauds. Thus, BC database has been a hot topic recently. One example database BlockchainDB is developed by Microsoft and Darmstadt University of Technology.

BlockChainDB implements a database layer on top of the existing BC. To improve system performance, not all the nodes will be involved in consensus. This improves efficiency, it also uses sharding for file sharing.

The system uses partial consensus, and only shared nodes involved in the transaction participate in this process. This is to improve efficiency but not all the nodes contain the same data. Regulators may need to search all the nodes to identify the data.

Another BC database is proposed by IBM, and the goal is to add BC features into the database systems. As many fast and reliable database systems are already available, if they can perform parts of BC operations, they will be more efficient than current BC systems.

The system uses atomic broadcast as the consensus mechanism. Atomic broadcast can be implemented by Kafka, a messaging system, and all the receiving nodes receive the same data in the same order. However, Kafka is a centralized process where a center is responsible to keep message streaming consistent and in the right order. If the central server is compromised, the system may be under the control of external parties.

4.3   ABC/TBC Architecture

This is a protocol designed for scalability and privacy protection for financial application. This approach allows BCs to scale in two dimensions, one way is horizontal scaling by adding resources into account BCs (ABCs), the other way is by adding new trading BCs (TBCs). This approach is used because scaling an account system and a trading system require two different scalability mechanisms. By providing two different scaling mechanism, a BC system can be scaled. This protocol has been used to process trade clearing in a commodity trading firm in 2017 with a BC system with bigdata capabilities. The STRISA framework uses the approach as the BDL BC is an ABC and thus can be scaled out, i.e., horizontal scalability.

5   Conclusion

This paper proposes a new system STRISA to enforce Travel Rule proposed by FATF. However, the new system monitors more activities and entities, and thus is larger and more complex than the TRISA system. To overcome these challenges, this paper proposes many new concepts and design to address the problems encountered, and these include a dynamic and secure registration network to support the ever increasing complex regulation structure; a BC BDL system that support large data processing and at the same time ensures that data cannot be altered without being noticed; and a built-in SC-based AML system with machine learning capabilities. The system has been developed and will be available for research and experimentation.

Acknowledgment. This work is supported by National Key Laboratory of Software Environment at Beihang University, National 973 Program (Grant No. 2013CB329601) and National Natural Science Foundation of China (Grant No. 61672075) and (Grant No. 61690202). This work was also supported by Chinese Ministry of Science and Technology (Grant No. 2018YFB1402700). This is also supported by LaoShan government. This is also supported by Major Science and Technology Innovation Projects in Shandong Province (Grant No. 2018CXGC0703).

References

1. FATF, Virtual Asset and Virtual Asset Service Providers (2019). http://www.fatf-gafi.org/media/fatf/documents/recommendations/RBA-VA-VASPs.pdf
2. Reis, G.A., et al.: SWIFT: software implemented fault tolerance. In: International Symposium on Code Generation and Optimization. IEEE (2005)
3. Travel Rule Information Sharing Architecture for Virtual Asset Service Providers (2020). https://TRISA.io/TRISA-whitepaper/
4. Yves Mersch (2019). https://www.bis.org/review/r190902a.htm
5. Libra White Paper (2020). https://libra.org/zh-CN/white-paper/?noredirect=zh-Hans-CN
6. Tsai, W.T., Deng, E., Ding, X., Li, J.: Application of blockchain to trade clearing. In: QRS Companion, pp. 154–163 (2018)

7. ISO: Information Technology - Open Systems Interconnection - The Directory - Part 8: Public-key and Attribute Certificate Frameworks. International Organization for Standardization, ISO/IEC 9594–8:2017, February 2017

8. Housley, R., Ford, W., Polk, W., Solo, D.: Internet X.509 public key infrastructure certificate and CRL profile, RFC2459, January 1999. http://tools.ietf.org/rfc/rfc2459.txt

9. Tsai, W.T.: ChainNet: A New Approach for Structuring System Architecture and Applications. Keynote Presentation on August 6, 2020 with video recording

10. Financial Conduct Authority (FCA): Call for Input: Using Technology to Achieve Smarter Regulatory Reporting, February 2018

11. Brastrad, J., Stendahl, P.A.: Blockchain in Financial Markets and Intermediation - A Qualitative Exploratory Study of the Impact of Blockchain Technology on the Financial Market Infrastructure and Financial Services. Master thesis. Norwegian School of Economics, Bergen (2018)

12. Casey, M.J.: The Revolutionary Power of Digital Currency, January 2015

13. Harper, C.: Audits and quality assurance: patching the holes in smart contracts security. BitCoin Magazine, 2 August 2018

14. Merle-Huet, A.: Overview of the U.S. Payments, Clearing and Settlement Landscape. Payment System Policy and Oversight Course, 11 May 2015

15. Mills, D., et al.: Distributed leger technology in payments, clearing, and settlement. Finance and Economics Discussion Series (2016)

16. Orcutt, M.: Ethereum's Smart Contracts Are Full of Holes. MIT Technology Review, 1 March 2018

17. Pinna, A., Ruttenberg, W.: Distributed Ledger Technologies in Securities Post-Tading: Revolution or Evolution?, April 2016

18. Tsai, W.T., Blower, R., Zhu, Y., Yu, L.: A system view of financial blockchains. In: Proceedings of IEEE SOSE (2016)

19. Tsai, W.T., Yu, L.: Blockchain application development techniques. J. Softw. (2017). (in Chinese)

20. Tsai, W.T., Bai, X., Yu, L.: Design issues in permissioned BCs for trusted computing. In: Proceedings of IEEE SOSE, pp. 153–159 (2017)

21. Tsai, W.T., Yu, L.: Lessons learned from developing permissioned blockchains. In: QRS Companion, pp. 1–10 (2018)

22. Tsai, W.T., et al.: Big data-oriented blockchain for clearing system. Big Data Res. **4**, 22–34 (2018). (in Chinese)

23. Tsai, W.T., Jiang, X.: The PFMI Viewpoint of BC, 16 August 2018. (in Chinese)

24. Tsai, W.T., Bai, X.: PFMI and System Requirements of Financial BCs, 24 December 2018. (in Chinese)

25. Bai, X., Tsai, W.T., Jiang, X.: Blockchain design - a PFMI viewpoint. In: Proceedings of IEEE SOSE (2019)

26. Tsai, W.T., Jiang, X.: The Design Principles for Clearing and Settlement Blockchains, 5 January 2019. (in Chinese)

27. Zamani, M., Movahedi, M., Raykova, M.: RapidChain: Scaling BC via Full Sharding (2018). https://eprint.iacr.org/2018/460.pdf

28. CPSS and IOSCO: Principles for Financial Market Infrastructures: Disclosure Framework and Assessment Methodology (2012)

29. CPMI: Distributed Ledger Technology in Payment, Clearing and Settlement: An Analytical Framework, February 2017

30. Tsai, W.T., et al.: LSO: A Dynamic and Scalable Blockchain Structuring Framework (2020)

System Security

Post-quantum Hash-Based Signatures
for Secure Boot

Panos Kampanakis[(⊠)], Peter Panburana[(⊠)], Michael Curcio[(⊠)],
and Chirag Shroff[(⊠)]

Security and Trust Organization, Cisco Systems, San Jose, USA
{pkampana,pepanbur,micurcio,cshroff}@cisco.com

Abstract. The potential development of large-scale quantum computers is raising concerns among IT and security research professionals due
to their ability to solve (elliptic curve) discrete logarithm and integer
factorization problems in polynomial time. All currently used, public-key
cryptography algorithms would be deemed insecure in a Post-quantum
setting. In response, the United States National Institute of Standards
and Technology has initiated a process to standardize quantum-resistant
cryptographic algorithms, focusing primarily on their security guarantees. Additionally, the Internet Engineering Task Force has published
two quantum-secure signature schemes and has been looking into adding
quantum-resistant algorithms in protocols. In this work, we investigate
two post-quantum, hash-based signature schemes published by the Internet Engineering Task Force and submitted to the National Institute of
Standards and Technology for use in secure boot. We evaluate various
parameter sets for the use-cases in question and we prove that Post-
quantum signatures would not have material impact on image signing.
We also study the hierarchical design of these signatures in different
scenarios of hardware secure boot.

Keywords: HBS signatures · PQ image signing · PQ root of trust ·
Post-quantum secure boot.

1 Introduction

Digital communications have completely penetrated everyday life as enablers
of numerous critical services including telemedicine, online banking, massive e-
commerce, machine-to-machine automation, mobile and cloud computing. As
part of guaranteeing that the software on digital devices is genuine, vendors have
implemented several security features that validate the authenticity of software.
When starting the booting process, a device's firmware is initially booted from
a tamper-resistant ROM or flash memory. Then the boot process is passed onto
a bootloader that is responsible for further loading the operating system (OS).
Software verification takes place at every step of the process. Before being loaded,
a bootloader signature is verified by boot 0 code, namely Unified Extensible

© Springer Nature Switzerland AG 2021
Y. Park et al. (Eds.): SVCC 2020, CCIS 1383, pp. 71–86, 2021.
https://doi.org/10.1007/978-3-030-72725-3_5

Firmware Interface (UEFI) on x86 based systems. The OS signature is verified by the bootloader before loading the OS. This verification process is often referred to as secure boot and ensures that there is a chain of trust that is passed from the very first step until the operating system comes live [8]. In virtual environments, vendors often follow a similar paradigm.

The signatures that are validated in each step of the secure boot process are usually classical RSA signatures. While the security of these signatures cannot effectively be challenged by conventional computer systems, this would not be the case in a Post-quantum (PQ) world where a large scale quantum computer is a reality [27]. Shor's quantum algorithm [30,33], assuming a practical quantum computer (QC) becomes available, would solve elliptic curve discrete logarithm (ECDL) and integer factorization (IF) problems in polynomial time rendering the algorithms insecure. In this scenario a QC-equipped attacker would be able to sign any specially crafted malicious software in the secure trust chain and boot non-genuine, malicious software.

The cryptographic community has been researching quantum-secure public key algorithms for some time in order to address the QC threat, and the US National Institute of Standards and Technology (NIST) has started a public project to standardize quantum-resistant public key encapsulation and digital signature algorithms. At the time of this writing, NIST's evaluation process has moved to Round 3 with 15 PQ algorithms remaining. Similarly, the European Telecommunications Standards Institute (ETSI) has formed a Quantum-Safe Working Group [9] that aims to make assessments and recommendations on the various proposals from industry and academia regarding real-world deployments of quantum-safe cryptography. In addition, the Internet Engineering Task Force (IETF) has seen multiple proposals that attempt to introduce PQ algorithms in protocols like TLS and IKE [12,15,28,35,37]. The integration of PQ algorithms in today's technologies presents challenges that pertain to (a) bigger keys, ciphertexts and signatures, (b) slower performance, (c) backwards compatibility, and (d) lack of hardware acceleration. The IETF has also published two PQ signature algorithms in Informational RFCs [16,25].

Our focus for this work is on Post-quantum secure boot signatures. We chose to evaluate two well-established hash-based signature (HBS) schemes, namely LMS [25] and SPHINCS$^+$ [2], which are based on mature, quantum-secure primitives. We compare their verification time against classical RSA signatures used today. Verification happens every time booting takes place, thus its performance is important. We also study the signing time; even though signing takes place once per image, we still need to maintain relatively fast signing for high-rate signers. We also investigate the signatures and public key sizes which would affect the verification process, especially for resource-constrained verifiers. We finally study the code footprint and stack used at the verifier in order to estimate the impact on resource-limited verifiers.

The **key contributions of our work** are summarized as follows:

(i) We formalize and propose Post-quantum HBS signature hierarchies for secure boot software signing.

(ii) We establish parameter sets suitable for different software signing use-cases for two PQ security levels.

(iii) We analyze the impact of two well-studied HBS algorithms (one stateful, one stateless) when they are used for image signing in hardware secure boot and FPGAs, and compare them to classical RSA.

(iv) We show that trusted Post-quantum signatures are possible with immaterial impact on the verifier, and an acceptable impact on the signer.

The rest of the paper is organized as follows: Section 2 summarizes related work. Section 3 lays out the signature schemes, the proposed hierarchy and parameter sets for our investigation and Sect. 4 presents our experimental results and analysis in various platforms. Section 5 concludes the paper.

2   Related Work

There has been a large body of research on PQ cryptography [4,18,22,39]. Recently, more works are exploring NIST's PQ candidate schemes focusing mainly on their security and computational performance.

More closely related to this work which focuses on PQ signatures for secure boot, is the potential for using quantum-secure, HBS schemes on constrained processors that was first demonstrated in [31]. What is more, a variant of a stateful HBS scheme, called XMSS [6], was implemented on a 16-bit smart-card in [17] which showed the practicality of stateful HBS in constrained devices. [13] also demonstrated an efficient implementation of XMSS in constrained IoT motes. [23] integrated XMSS in a SoC platform around RISC-V cores and evaluated on an FPGA to show that it is very efficient. XMSS shares similarities with LMS investigated in this work, but with worse performance and a tighter security proof [29]. What's more, [1] investigated the practicality of stateful HBS (LDWM, a predecessor of LMS studied here) in TPMs without studying real time, performance or memory footprint or stateless HBS schemes and HBS parameters specific to the secure boot use-case.

Boneh and Gueron proposed stateful HBS signatures using various one-way functions for signing Intel SGX enclaves in [5]. They concluded that HBS verification can be faster than RSA3072 and QVRSA. Additionally, Hülsing et al. implemented stateless HBS SPHINCS signatures in an ARM Cortex M3 with only 16 KB of memory [19]. They also compared SPHINCS with stateful XMSS in an ARM Cortex M3 and showed that stateless HBS verification is acceptable but its signing is 30 times slower. The authors in [3,34] conducted a comparison of NIST Round 2 candidate algorithm hardware implementations with a focus on algorithm operations and impact on hardware design. In [21], Kannwischer et al. benchmarked Round 2 algorithms on ARM Cortex-M4 and evaluated the more suitable ones for embedded devices. [32] studied the energy consumption of the NIST algorithm candidates and identified the most expensive ones in terms of energy. The SPHINCS$^+$ variants were found to be one of the most energy-intensive ones compared to their competitors at the same security level.

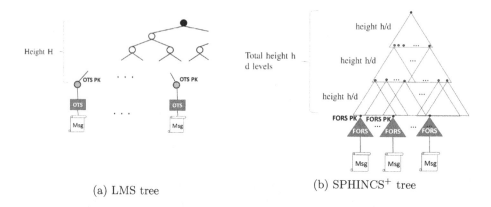

(a) LMS tree

(b) SPHINCS⁺ tree

Fig. 1. HBS trees

3   HBS for Secure Boot

3.1   Intro to HBS

The HBS family of PQ signature algorithms is considered mature, well-understood, and significantly reliable. The first scheme in the family, the Merkle signature scheme (MSS), was presented in the late 1970s [7]. HBS signatures rely on Merkle trees and few or one-time-signature (FTS/OTS) used with secure cryptographic hash functions.

HBS schemes generate keypairs for the FTS/OTS. The FTS/OTS signs a message and the corresponding public key is a leaf in the Merkle tree, whose root is the public key that is expected to be pre-trusted by the verifier. An HBS signature consists of the OTS/FTS signature and the path to the root of the tree. The signature is verified using the public key inside it, and by using the authentication path to construct the root of the hash tree. Currently, the most mature members of the HBS family are the stateful LMS [25] and XMSS [16], and stateless SPHINCS⁺, one of the NIST signature candidates [2]. Figure 1a shows an LMS tree. The message is signed by an OTS (LMS-OTS or WOTS+) and the OTS public key forms a binary tree leaf that is aggregated all the way to the Merkle tree root. The parameters of the tree include the hash function, the tree height, and the Winternitz parameter of the OTS. Multi-level tree variants are also available and consist of smaller subtrees that form a big HBS tree. Readers should note that stateless XMSS [6], which was also published by IETF [16], shares similarities with LMS, but with worse performance and a tighter security proof [29].

Figure 1b shows a SPHINCS⁺ tree which consists of an FTS, namely a FORS tree, that signs a message, and a multi-level Merkle tree. The FORS tree root is signed by an OTS (i.e., WOTS+). The corresponding WOTS+ public key forms the Merkle tree leaf that is aggregated all the way to the bottom subtree root. That root is signed by WOTS+ and the WOTS+ public key is aggregated to the root of the subtree above. Subtree roots are signed by subtrees above until we reach the top subtree. Going forward we focus only on LMS and SPHINCS⁺.

Excluding their architectural differences, the most significant difference between a stateful and stateless HBS is state. Stateful schemes (i.e., LMS, XMSS) include a four-byte index value in their signature which represents the state. The state is used when signing a message and should never be reused as that could allow for forgeries. The state management requirement is considered an important disadvantage which has been often brought up in IETF and NIST fora [14,24]. Stateless HBS (i.e., SPHINCS$^+$), on the other hand, have no state requirement. Hence, messages are signed by an HBS hypertree without having to keep state with every signature. While stateless SPHINCS$^+$ eliminates the need for proper state management, it also leads to a significant increase in signature size and slower performance because of the FORS structure. Section 4 shows the performance comparison between LMS and SPHINCS$^+$.

3.2 Hierarchy

An HBS hierarchy would be needed to provide signatures for multiple platforms or chips and firmware/software versions, and comply with existing secure boot standards. Typically, these hierarchies would include multiple tree levels. Each multi-level tree would serve as a different UEFI signing structure, namely the PK, Firmware Update Key or KEK. The root of each tree would become the key included in the UEFI db/dbx databases pre-trusted by the verifier. Each tree would be responsible for signing firmware, firmware packages, PK updates, or software images. Figure 2 shows such a hierarchy with a three-level tree architecture. The hypertree structurally consists of smaller trees in order to limit the key generation and signing times.

In such architectures, the height of the trees should be chosen so they can provide enough signatures for the use-case. A typical top tree could sign 2^{15} bottom trees. A bottom tree that can sign one million images (2^{20}) would probably suffice for most use-cases. Most vendors' portfolio would never exceed 2^{35} total images. As an example, in 2020, major IT vendors with thousands of products in their portfolio were signing less than 250 million ($\sim 2^{28}$) images annually which would lead to $\sim 2^{33}$ signatures over a 30 year signing root's lifetime.

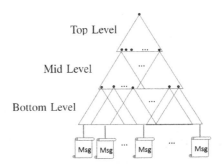

Fig. 2. HBS hierarchy

Table 1. HBS parameters

Parameter name	Scheme	Parameters	PQ Sec level
LMS256H5W4	LMS	LMS_SHA256_M32_H5 with LMOTS_SHA256_N32_W4	128-bits
LMS256H5W8	LMS	LMS_SHA256_M32_H5 with LMOTS_SHA256_N32_W8	128-bits
LMS256H10W4	LMS	LMS_SHA256_M32_H10 with LMOTS_SHA256_N32_W4	128-bits
LMS256H10W8	LMS	LMS_SHA256_M32_H10 with LMOTS_SHA256_N32_W8	128-bits
LMS256H15W4	LMS	LMS_SHA256_M32_H15 with LMOTS_SHA256_N32_W4	128-bits
LMS256H15W8	LMS	LMS_SHA256_M32_H15 with LMOTS_SHA256_N32_W8	128-bits
LMS256H20W4	LMS	LMS_SHA256_M32_H20 with LMOTS_SHA256_N32_W4	128-bits
LMS256H20W8	LMS	LMS_SHA256_M32_H20 with LMOTS_SHA256_N32_W8	128-bits
HSS256L2W4	HSS	$L = 2$ w. top LMS256H20W4 and bottom LMS256H15W4	128-bits
HSS256L2W8	HSS	$L = 2$ w. top LMS256H20W8 and bottom LMS256H15W8	128-bits
HSS256L3oW4	HSS	$L = 3$ w. LMS256H15W4, LMS256H10W4 and LMS256H10W4	128-bits
HSS256L3oW8	HSS	$L = 3$ w. LMS256H15W8, LMS256H10W8 and LMS256H10W8	128-bits
SPX192H15w16	SPHINCS$^+$	$n = 24$, $H = 15$, $d = 3$, $k = 18$, $a = 13$ $w = 16$	96-bits
SPX192H15w256	SPHINCS$^+$	$n = 24$, $H = 15$, $d = 3$, $k = 18$, $a = 13$ $w = 256$	96-bits
SPX192H20w16	SPHINCS$^+$	$n = 24$, $H = 20$, $d = 4$, $k = 18$, $a = 13$ $w = 16$	96-bits
SPX192H20w256	SPHINCS$^+$	$n = 24$, $H = 20$, $d = 4$, $k = 18$, $a = 13$ $w = 256$	96-bits
SPX192H35w16	SPHINCS$^+$	$n = 24$, $H = 35$, $d = 5$, $k = 20$, $a = 12$ $w = 16$	96-bits
SPX192H35w256	SPHINCS$^+$	$n = 24$, $H = 35$, $d = 5$, $k = 20$, $a = 12$ $w = 256$	96-bits
SPX256H15w16	SPHINCS$^+$	$n = 32$, $H = 15$, $d = 3$, $k = 19$, $a = 16$ $w = 16$	128-bits
SPX256H15w256	SPHINCS$^+$	$n = 32$, $H = 15$, $d = 3$, $k = 19$, $a = 16$ $w = 256$	128-bits
SPX256H20w16	SPHINCS$^+$	$n = 32$, $H = 20$, $d = 4$, $k = 19$, $a = 16$ $w = 16$	128-bits
SPX256H20w256	SPHINCS$^+$	$n = 32$, $H = 20$, $d = 4$, $k = 19$, $a = 16$ $w = 256$	128-bits
SPX256H35w16	SPHINCS$^+$	$n = 32$, $H = 35$, $d = 5$, $k = 21$, $a = 15$ $w = 16$	128-bits
SPX256H35w256	SPHINCS$^+$	$n = 32$, $H = 35$, $d = 5$, $k = 21$, $a = 15$ $w = 256$	128-bits

Key Revocation is an important concept for HBS multi-level tree hierarchies. Revoking a tree root, a signature or any of the lower level trees is essential to providing a way to eliminate trust in roots that have been compromised, broken or replaced. In secure boot, the trusted certificate/key and revocation list exist in the UEFI db and dbx respectively [26]. Often the UEFI db/dbx is stored in a Trust Anchor module. Updating these lists takes place with messages authenticated by a KEK tree. The KEK HBS tree would be used to sign UEFI db/dbx updates or sign revocation images.

3.3 Parameters

In the process of evaluating HBS for secure boot and image signing, we had to come up with parameters that would satisfy most use-cases. We experimented with many parameters in order to find the most suitable ones. LMS offers many options up to 2^{25} signed messages which would suffice for the multi-level architecture described in Sect. 3.2. The PQ security level of all LMS parameters is 128 bits. Note that all LMS/HSS parameters could be adjusted to provide 96-bit PQ security by truncating the SHA256 outputs to 192 bits [11]. On the other hand, SPHINCS$^+$, as proposed to NIST, offers three PQ security levels of 64, 96 and 128 bits. For our evaluation we chose to be conservative and use the latter two. The SPHINCS$^+$ variants submitted to NIST can sign up to 2^{64} messages, as required by NIST. We generated new parameters for our maximum signature count which does not exceed a total of 34 trillion (2^{35}) signatures. In preliminary investigations, we found that the equivalent NIST-submitted SPHINCS$^+$ parameter sets (2^{64} signatures) would perform much slower verification which would lead to significant delays in the booting process. We also chose to only evaluate the 'simple' variants of SPHINCS$^+$ because of their superior performance. What's more, we only used SHA256 SPHINCS$^+$ variants because of its superiority in SPHINCS$^+$ benchmarks and its prevalence in hardware implementations.

Table 1 summarizes all the LMS and SPHINCS$^+$ parameter sets we used in our evaluation. LMS256H5W4, LMS256H5W8, LMS256H10W4 and LMS256H10W8 are not included as single tree LMS variants in our analysis. We just list them because they are used in multi-level HSS variants. Additionally, LMS256H20W4 and LMS256H20W8 could be tested as an HSS with two levels of height 10, which would speed up key generation and key loading, at the expense of increased signature sizes. Key generation and loading can be considered offline operations for the secure boot use-cases and thus we chose to use height 20 LMS trees. HSS256L3oW4 and HSS256L3oW8 offer a balance between key generation and key load time.

4   Experiments

4.1   RSA vs. LMS vs. SPHINCS$^+$

In order to compare our options. We initially experimented and measured the performance of RSA and all the LMS and SPHINCS$^+$ parameters of interest. We ran all these tests in a Google Cloud instance with an Intel Xeon CPU 2.20 GHz with 2 cores and 7.68 GB RAM. To compile our code we used gcc version 7.4.0. The tests were run 1000 times for each parameter set.

To measure RSA performance, we used OpenSSL 1.1.1c with OPENSSL_BN_ ASM_MONT enabled. Our LMS testing code was based on [10], dynamically linked to OpenSSL's SHA256 implementation and properly instrumented with various performance optimizations and memory speed trade-offs. Our SPHINCS$^+$ testing code was based on [20] which is a fork of the original code [36] from the SPHINCS$^+$ NIST submission. The SPHINCS$^+$ verification was dynamically linked to the OpenSSL 1.1.1c library for its SHA256 implementation which proved to provide the best verification performance. For SPHINCS$^+$ signing, we found that the AVX2 optimized code in [36] provided the best results possible and thus we didn't link SPHINCS$^+$ signing to OpenSSL. Multi-threading was disabled for both implementations. We also measured the memory footprint (code and stack) of LMS/HSS and SPHINCS$^+$ verification in order to assess their practicality in constrained verifier chips. Both verifiers used OpenSSL's

SHA256 implementation which was not counted against the reported code size. As in [21], we measured the stack usage by writing a random canary to a big chunk of the available stack space, then running the verification, and finally checking which parts of the memory have been overwritten.

Table 2 shows the results from our testing. We can see that all the private and public keys are of negligible size. It is also clear that the verifier code and stack size of a few KB would not practically impact most secure boot verifiers. The heap used by the verifier was always zero. What's more, LMS/HSS signing was less costly in CPU cycles than SPHINCS+. SPHINCS+ verification was worse than LMS/HSS but not as significantly as signing. The standard deviation for both signing and verification CPU cycles was insignificant. Our results are in agreement with the ARM Cortex M3 results in [19]. In terms of key generation, LMS/HSS took much longer mainly because LMS generates trees at every level which is counted against key generation; in SPHINCS+ only the top tree is counted as part of the key generation and all the other tree generations are part of the signature operation. Thus, LMS is optimized by taking longer to generate keys but performs signing faster by using auxiliary data and pre-loaded private keys, whereas SPHINCS+ includes part of this work in the signature generation itself.

Figure 3 demonstrates the signature sizes of all parameter sets. As expected, parameter sets with $W = 8$ and $w = 256$ have smaller signatures. We also see that LMS/HSS offers signatures that stay below 8 KB. Note that all LMS/HSS parameters could be adjusted to provide 96-bit PQ security by truncating the SHA256 outputs to 192 bits [11] which would shrink all reported LMS/HSS signatures by 25%. SPHINCS+ signatures exceed 10 KB and grow to almost 23 KB for 128-bit PQ security level parameters with $w = 16$. 23 KB signatures are small enough for most secure boot use-cases. In rare scenarios where small signatures are required, LMS/HSS would be preferable.

Figure 4 shows the absolute signing times for all parameter sets measured on our testing platform. We can see that all signatures take less than one second which would suffice for almost all software signing use-cases where signing does not take place live. Signing is performed offline, only once and thus is immaterial to the booting process. The standard deviation was insignificant. LMS/HSS and SPHINCS+ with $W = 8$ and $w = 256$ perform worse than with $W = 4$ and $w = 16$ respectively, but their time is still acceptable. SPHINCS+ performs orders of magnitude worse than LMS/HSS, but still at an acceptable level. Note that signing performance would increase even further if multi-threading was enabled.

Figure 5 shows the HBS verification times. None of the proposed parameter sets perform verification slower than 7 ms which is satisfactory. Verification times would still be acceptable even at 100 or 200 ms with slower processors than in our testbed. The standard deviation was insignificant. Parameters with $W = 4$ (LMS) or $w = 16$ (SPHINCS+) verify signatures significantly faster than with $W = 8$ or $w = 256$ respectively.

Table 2. HBS key, signature sizes, memory footprint and performance

Parameter	Keys (B)		Verifier (KB)		Keygen (s)	Sign (Mcycles)		Verify (Mcycles)	
	Priv.	Pub.	Code	Stack		Mean	Stdv.	Mean	Stdv.
LMS256H15W4	48	60	2.57	1.81	2.519	1.145	0.051	0.370	0.033
LMS256H15W8	48	60	2.15	1.81	13.720	6.237	0.302	2.855	0.290
LMS256H20W4	48	60	2.57	1.81	3.222	1.465	0.037	0.373	0.026
LMS256H20W8	48	60	2.15	1.81	19.373	8.807	0.555	2.857	0.274
HSS256L2W4	48	60	3.15	1.81	350.2	3.945	0.041	0.716	0.026
HSS256L2W8	48	60	2.51	1.81	2712	19.351	0.288	5.771	0.271
HSS256L3oW4	48	60	3.15	1.81	10.86	3.771	0.024	1.050	0.022
HSS256L3oW8	48	60	2.51	1.81	84.5	13.084	0.261	8.187	0.254
SPX192H15w16	96	48	4.46	4.98	0.003	176.049	1.170	1.022	0.020
SPX192H15w256	96	48	4.41	2.87	0.026	332.180	1.860	7.045	0.094
SPX192H20w16	96	48	4.46	4.39	0.003	183.444	1.154	1.382	0.024
SPX192H20w256	96	48	4.41	3.24	0.026	391.554	2.219	10.193	0.189
SPX192H35w16	96	48	4.50	4.97	0.012	212.532	1.374	1.591	0.027
SPX192H35w256	96	48	4.43	2.87	0.103	1,218.257	4.139	11.711	0.151
SPX256H15w16	128	64	4.54	6.14	0.004	1,297.180	5.589	1.385	0.024
SPX256H15w256	128	64	4.47	4.68	0.032	1,491.183	5.405	9.219	0.163
SPX256H20w16	128	64	4.54	6.70	0.004	1,310.393	5.480	1.768	0.046
SPX256H20w256	128	64	4.47	4.25	0.032	1,566.816	4.856	11.599	0.139
SPX256H35w16	128	64	4.53	6.58	0.016	814.356	3.697	2.080	0.031
SPX256H35w256	128	64	4.46	4.52	0.128	2,057.650	6.223	15.341	0.214

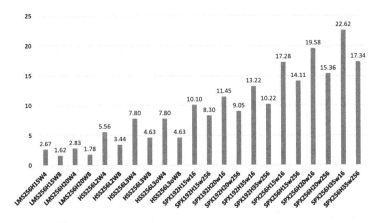

Fig. 3. HBS signature size (KB)

To give some perspective, today's status-quo with secure boot and image signing is classical RSA2048. An **RSA2048** signature offers 112 bits of classical security, 0.26 KB private, public key and signature, and was measured to take 1.657Mcycles/0.753 ms per signature and 0.049Mcycles/0.022 ms per verification in our testbed. **RSA4096** offers over 128-bits of classical security, 0.52 KB private, public key and signature, and was measured to take 11.241Mcycles/5.11 ms

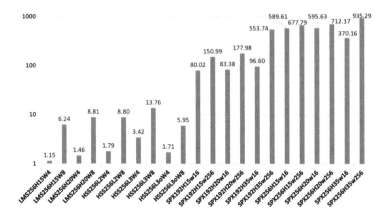

Fig. 4. HBS signing time (log-scale in ms)

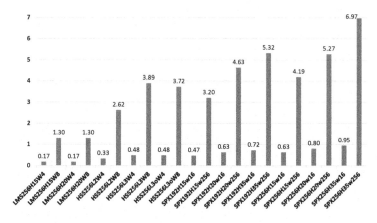

Fig. 5. HBS verification time (ms)

per signature and 0.173Mcycles/0.078 ms per verification. Thus, RSA has smaller signatures and performs faster than HBS, but within the same order of magnitude which makes HBS appealing. Note that all RSA variants are considered to offer ∼0 bits of PQ security.

By combining all of the collected data, we can conclude that the best LMS parameters are with $W = 8$ where verification takes immaterially longer but signature sizes are a few Kilobytes smaller. The best HSS parameter is HSS256L3oW4 which offers a balance of fast signing and verification with slightly bigger signature sizes. Regarding SPHINCS+, parameters with $w = 256$ seem more favorable as they keep signature sizes smaller with acceptable signing and verification performance. Adopters could of course make different signature, signing and verification performance trade-off decisions and pick different parameters.

Table 3. Verification in Xilinx UltraScale chips

Parameter	Time (ms)	Clock (MHz)	FFs	LUTs	BRAM	DSP	CLB
RSA2048 [38]	–	~300	94455	28668	0	128	3428
RSA4096-Verilog*	~60	200	316	818	1	1	–
RSA4096-VHDL†	~10	200	484	346	1	3	–
LMS256H5W8 (HSS L=2)#	~10						
LMS256H20W4#	~0.8	250	468#	811#	1	1	97#
LMS256H20W8#	~5						

* Measurements from example Verilog design provided by Xilinx.
† Measurements from example VHDL design provided by Xilinx.
# SHA256 logic excluded. SHA256 accounted for 1117 FFs, 1852 LUTs and 374 CLBs.
The hashing of the image is limited by the Serial Peripheral Interface (SPI) speed
when reading the image from flash at just a few MiB/s. Our SHA256 implementation
was hashing data ~184 MiB/s. The Xilinx Vitis Libraries documentation reports 296
MiB/s respectively (64 bytes per 68 cycles at 330.25 MHz). Thus, the image hash
calculation was excluded from our evaluation so that our results are not dominated
by the amount of time it takes to read the signature into on-chip memory.

4.2 FPGA-Based Signature Verification

Modern embedded systems, use FPGAs to perform variety of functions. While
this can be facilitated by custom ASICs, FPGAs can also be used. FPGA configuration bitstreams exist at the lowest level of user-programmable functionality
in the system. FPGAs provide greater logic density than circuits composed of
discrete gates or most CPLDs, and they do so at a lower development cost
than a custom ASIC. Custom ASICs also do not provide the same degree of
flexibility and upgradability. An FPGA device often plays a fundamental role
in the functioning of the system, capable of implementing basic "glue logic"
that manages separate design domains and their components. In more advanced
applications, FPGAs may also be customizable hardware acceleration resources.
When implementing signature verification functions or system critical functions,
it is essential that the system only use authentic FPGA images.

Vendors of FPGAs have included various technologies in their devices to
protect the confidentiality of bitstream configuration data and integrity assurances to ensure correct hardware functionality. However, these technologies are
not equivalent among all vendors, nor are the same levels of security shared
among different device families from the same vendor. Often times, the built-
in bitstream integrity functions are not available to user logic. Furthermore,
it is not uncommon for an FPGA design to implement user logic that emu-
lates a microcontroller or even a full-fledged "soft" CPU core that itself runs
user-defined microcode or firmware. Using Post-quantum signatures in upgrade
images, microcontroller code or code for other parts of the system would improve
the security of the system in a quantum computing future.

To evaluate the practicality of HBS verification in FPGAs, we developed an
FPGA core capable of verifying a subset of the LMS parameters. We implemented verifiers for HSS with two (L=2) LMS256H5W8 subtrees. We also implemented single-level LMS LMS256H20W4 and LMS256H20W8 verifiers. We tested

these parameters through functional simulation. We chose to focus on the LMS algorithms for this evaluation as their smaller signature size relative to SPHINCS$^+$ requires fewer Block RAM resources to store a signature on-chip for verification. This concern is particularly relevant to lower power, lower density, and less costly devices that are more likely to be used in embedded and IoT-type applications. We did not implement SPHINCS$^+$ verification in FPGAs. We expect their required resources to be higher but in-line with the resources observed in our FPGA-based LMS verifier. To support this claim, [3] evaluated SPHINCS$^+$ verification with Xilinx Vivado HLS and Xilinx Virtex-7 FPGA as the target devices and showed that SPHINCS$^+$ verification would perform acceptably even in constrained devices.

To provide a more direct comparison of LMS with an RSA implementation, we implemented our design in an FPGA from the Xilinx UltraScale architecture family. Testing assumed that a short message and its signature were preloaded into a known location of FPGA Block RAM dedicated to the LMS verifier logic. The LMS algorithm would run to completion and provide a pass/fail indication via a top-level interface port. The messages were very short (less than 256 bytes) to ensure time measurements also predominantly represented signature verification time. Table 3 shows our results. The stateful HBS data points were collected from Xilinx Vivado 2018.2, targeting a mid-speed, industrial temperature grade Kintex UltraScale device (`xcku025-ffva1156-2-i`). Vivado was set to use the default options for the `Flow_PerfOptimized_high` Synthesis Strategy and the `Performance_Explore` Implementation Strategy. Timing constraints defining a 4ns logic clock period were successfully met. The RSA4096 results were kindly provided by Xilinx from an example design that was optimized for low logic area or high clock rate. The RSA2048 results were taken from [38]. The latter design is optimized for speed and compatibility with the new Vitis development platform and therefore has a significantly higher logic footprint. All RSA data points exclude the image hash calculations that would precede an image verification, which would increase the footprint significantly.

Given this approach, we observe that the performance of our LMS implementation, in terms of clock rate, exceeds that of comparative cores implementing RSA4096 signature verification. It does not attain the speed of the Vitis library module (RSA2048) though. Total verification time between the classical and PQ signature algorithms is on the same order of magnitude. In terms of area, LMS, while not nearly as large as the Vitis design (RSA2048), is larger than the VHDL-optimized RSA4096 module and similar to the RSA4096-Verilog one. Note that, even though it is not included in the RSA rows in Table 3, extra SHA256 footprint will still exist in an RSA verification scenario to calculate the digest of the image, which we expect to be similar to the additional LMS SHA256 logic reported in Table 3-footnote $^\#$.

It still remains feasible to further optimize an LMS verifier to fit into almost the smallest of recent-generation FPGAs. We expect that the footprint of verifier logic for other LMS/HSS and SPHINCS$^+$ parameters will be higher, but easily supported by most modern FPGAs.

In terms of total impact to the booting process if we assume the boot chain starts from a Xilinx verifier, it is clear that ~10 ms will be unnoticeable even in use-cases where booting up takes just a few seconds. In any case, booting from a HBS-signed Xilinx bitstream will not affect the total boot time more than a few milliseconds which is the case for classical signatures as well.

5   Conclusion

In conclusion, in this work we evaluated the impact of using Post-quantum hash-based signatures for secure boot and software signing. We proposed parameter sets at different security levels that would be useful for different software signing use-cases and introduced an architecture that would work for most vendors. We experimentally showed that the impact of switching to such signatures will be insignificant for the verifier compared to conventional RSA used today in various use-cases (i.e. hardware secure boot, FPGA). We also showed that the signer will be more impacted, but still at an acceptable level. Finally, we discussed practical issues and concerns of migrating to HBS signatures and their alternatives.

Acknowledgments. We would like to thank Scott Fluhrer for his LMS code, his optimizations and his valuable guidance and feedback. The authors would also like to thank Jason Moore and Jim Wesselkamper from Xilinx for their sample Xilinx design data points included in this work. The LMS FPGA logic measurements were based on code developed by Md Mahbub Alam, a Ph.D. Candidate at the University of Florida at the time. Thanks to Bruno Couillard and Jim Goodman from Crypto4A for the interesting discussions about HBS and their feedback. Finally, we would like to acknowledge Joost Rijneveld for his feedback and comments regarding SPHINCS+ parameters and the SPHINCS+ implementation and Dimitrios Sikeridis for his help with the experiments.

References

1. Ando, M., Guttman, J.D., Papaleo, A.R., Scire, J.: Hash-based TPM signatures for the quantum world. In: Manulis, M., Sadeghi, A.-R., Schneider, S. (eds.) ACNS 2016. LNCS, vol. 9696, pp. 77–94. Springer, Cham (2016). https://doi.org/10.1007/978-3-319-39555-5_5
2. Aumasson, J.P., et al.: SPHINCS+ - Submission to the 2nd round of the NIST post-quantum project. https://sphincs.org/data/sphincs+-round2-specification.pdf (2019). Specification document (part of the submission package)
3. Basu, K., Soni, D., Nabeel, M., Karri, R.: Nist post-quantum cryptography- a hardware evaluation study. Cryptology ePrint Archive, Report 2019/047 (2019). https://eprint.iacr.org/2019/047
4. Bernstein, D.J., et al.: SPHINCS: practical stateless hash-based signatures. In: Advances in Cryptology - EUROCRYPT 2015–34th Annual International Conference on the Theory and Applications of Cryptographic Techniques, pp. 368–397 (2015). https://doi.org/10.1007/978-3-662-46800-5_15
5. Boneh, D., Gueron, S.: Surnaming schemes, fast verification, and applications to SGX technology. In: Handschuh, H. (ed.) CT-RSA 2017. LNCS, vol. 10159, pp. 149–164. Springer, Cham (2017). https://doi.org/10.1007/978-3-319-52153-4_9

6. Buchmann, J., Dahmen, E., Hülsing, A.: XMSS - a practical forward secure signature scheme based on minimal security assumptions. In: Yang, B.-Y. (ed.) PQCrypto 2011. LNCS, vol. 7071, pp. 117–129. Springer, Heidelberg (2011). https://doi.org/10.1007/978-3-642-25405-5_8
7. Buchmann, J.A., Butin, D., Göpfert, F., Petzoldt, A.: Post-quantum cryptography: state of the art. In: Ryan, P.Y.A., Naccache, D., Quisquater, J.-J. (eds.) The New Codebreakers. LNCS, vol. 9100, pp. 88–108. Springer, Heidelberg (2016). https://doi.org/10.1007/978-3-662-49301-4_6
8. Cisco: Cisco Secure Boot and Trust Anchor Module differentiation solution overview (2017). https://www.cisco.com/c/en/us/products/collateral/security/cloud-access-security/secure-boot-trust.html
9. ETSI: ETSI TC Cyber Working Group for Quantum-Safe Cryptography. https://portal.etsi.org/TBSiteMap/CYBER/CYBERQSCToR.aspx (2017). Accessed 25 July 2019
10. Fluhrer, S.: LMS hash based signature open-source implementation (2019). https://github.com/cisco/hash-sigs
11. Fluhrer, S., Dang, Q.: Additional Parameter Sets for LMS Hash-based Signatures. Internet-Draft draft-fluhrer-lms-more-parm-sets-00, Internet Engineering Task Force, September 2019. https://datatracker.ietf.org/doc/html/draft-fluhrer-lms-more-parm-sets-00, work in Progress
12. Fluhrer, S., McGrew, D., Kampanakis, P., Smyslov, V.: Postquantum Preshared Keys for IKEv2. Internet-Draft draft-ietf-ipsecme-qr-ikev2-08, Internet Engineering Task Force, March 2019. https://datatracker.ietf.org/doc/html/draft-ietf-ipsecme-qr-ikev2-08, work in Progress
13. Ghosh, S., Misoczki, R., Sastry, M.R.: Lightweight post-quantum-secure digital signature approach for IoT motes. Cryptology ePrint Archive, Report 2019/122 (2019). https://eprint.iacr.org/2019/122
14. Stateful Hash-Based Signatures - Public Comments on Misuse Resistance (2019). https://csrc.nist.gov/CSRC/media/Projects/Stateful-Hash-Based-Signatures/documents/stateful-HBS-misuse-resistance-public-comments-April2019.pdf
15. Hoffman, P.E.: The Transition from Classical to Post-Quantum Cryptography. Internet-Draft draft-hoffman-c2pq-05, Internet Engineering Task Force, May 2019. https://datatracker.ietf.org/doc/html/draft-hoffman-c2pq-05, work in Progress
16. Huelsing, A., Butin, D., Gazdag, S.L., Rijneveld, J., Mohaisen, A.: XMSS: eXtended Merkle Signature Scheme. RFC 8391, May 2018. https://doi.org/10.17487/RFC8391, https://rfc-editor.org/rfc/rfc8391.txt
17. Hülsing, A., Busold, C., Buchmann, J.: Forward secure signatures on smart cards. In: Knudsen, L.R., Wu, H. (eds.) SAC 2012. LNCS, vol. 7707, pp. 66–80. Springer, Heidelberg (2013). https://doi.org/10.1007/978-3-642-35999-6_5
18. Hülsing, A., Rijneveld, J., Samardjiska, S., Schwabe, P.: From 5-pass MQ-based identification to MQ-based signatures. IACR Cryptology ePrint Archive, vol. 2016, p. 708 (2016)
19. Hülsing, A., Rijneveld, J., Schwabe, P.: Armed sphincs - computing a 41 kb signature in 16 kb of ram. Cryptology ePrint Archive, Report 2015/1042 (2015). https://eprint.iacr.org/2015/1042
20. Kampanakis, P.: Slim SPHINCS$^+$open-source implementation (2019). https://github.com/csosto-pk/slim_sphincsplus/tree/master/ref
21. Kannwischer, M.J., Rijneveld, J., Schwabe, P., Stoffelen, K.: pqm4: testing and Benchmarking NIST PQC on ARM Cortex-M4. Cryptology ePrint Archive, Report 2019/844 (2019). https://eprint.iacr.org/2019/844

22. Kölbl, S., Lauridsen, M.M., Mendel, F., Rechberger, C.: Haraka v2-efficient short-input hashing for post-quantum applications. IACR Trans. Symmetric Cryptol. 1–29 (2016)

23. Kumar, V.B.Y., Gupta, N., Chattopadhyay, A., Kaspert, M., Krauß, C., Nieder-hagen, R.: Post-quantum secure boot. In: Proceedings of the 23rd Conference on Design, Automation and Test in Europe, DATE 2020, EDA Consortium, San Jose, CA, USA, pp. 1582–1585 (2020)

24. Langley, A.: Email thread: proposed addition of hash-based signature algorithms for certificates to the LAMPS charter (2018). https://mailarchive.ietf.org/arch/msg/spasm/PgzLjPcg-jfywQFQs9gMLFcgRd8

25. McGrew, D., Curcio, M., Fluhrer, S.: Leighton-Micali Hash-Based Signatures. RFC 8554, April 2019. https://doi.org/10.17487/RFC8554, https://rfc-editor.org/rfc/rfc8554.txt

26. Microsoft: Windows Secure Boot Key Creation and Management Guidance (2017). https://docs.microsoft.com/en-us/windows-hardware/manufacture/desktop/windows-secure-boot-key-creation-and-management-guidance

27. Mosca, M.: Cybersecurity in an era with quantum computers: will we be ready? IEEE Secur. Privacy **16**(5), 38–41 (2018)

28. Ounsworth, M., Pala, M.: Composite Keys and Signatures For Use in Internet PKI. Internet-Draft draft-ounsworth-pq-composite-sigs-01, Internet Engineering Task Force, July 2019, https://datatracker.ietf.org/doc/html/draft-ounsworth-pq-composite-sigs-01, work in Progress

29. Panos Kampanakis, S.F.: LMS vs XMSS: a comparison of the Stateful Hash-Based Signature Proposed Standards. Cryptology ePrint Archive, Report 2017/349 (2017). http://eprint.iacr.org/2017/349

30. Proos, J., Zalka, C.: Shor's discrete logarithm quantum algorithm for elliptic curves. Quantum Info. Comput. **3**(4), 317–344 (2003), http://dl.acm.org/citation.cfm?id=2011528.2011531

31. Rohde, S., Eisenbarth, T., Dahmen, E., Buchmann, J., Paar, C.: Fast hash-based signatures on constrained devices. In: Grimaud, G., Standaert, F.-X. (eds.) CARDIS 2008. LNCS, vol. 5189, pp. 104–117. Springer, Heidelberg (2008). https://doi.org/10.1007/978-3-540-85893-5_8

32. Roma, C., Tai, C.E.A., Hasan, M.A.: Energy consumption of round 2 submissions for NIST PQC standards. In: Second PQC Standardization Conference, August 2019

33. Shor, P.W.: Polynomial-time algorithms for prime factorization and discrete logarithms on a quantum computer. SIAM J. Comput. **26**(5), 1484–1509 (1997)

34. Soni, D., Basu, K., Nabeel, M., Karri, R.: A hardware evaluation study of NIST post-quantum cryptographic signature schemes. In: Second PQC Standardization Conference, August 2019

35. Steblia, D., Fluhrer, S., Gueron, S.: Design issues for hybrid key exchange in TLS 1.3. Internet-Draft draft-stebila-tls-hybrid-design-01, Internet Engineering Task Force, July 2019. https://datatracker.ietf.org/doc/html/draft-stebila-tls-hybrid-design-01, work in Progress

36. SPHINCS+ team: SPHINCS+ open-source implementation (2019). https://github.com/sphincs/sphincsplus

37. Tjhai, C., Tomlinson, M., Fluhrer, S., Geest, D.V., Garcia-Morchon, O., Smyslov, V.: Framework to Integrate Post-quantum Key Exchanges into Internet Key Exchange Protocol Version 2 (IKEv2). Internet-Draft draft-tjhai-ipsecme-hybrid-qske-ikev2-04, Internet Engineering Task Force, July 2019. https://datatracker.ietf.org/doc/html/draft-tjhai-ipsecme-qske-ikev2-04, work in Progress. grbartle@cisco.com

38. Xilinx: Vitis Security Library (2019). https://github.com/Xilinx/Vitis_Libraries/blob/8ee9037aeb2bdf44096c256ec6779973387e0c0f/security/docs/guide_L1/internals/rsa.rst

39. Yoo, Y., Azarderakhsh, R., Jalali, A., Jao, D., Soukharev, V.: A Post-Quantum Digital Signature Scheme Based on Supersingular Isogenies. Cryptology ePrint Archive, Report 2017/186 (2017). http://eprint.iacr.org/2017/186

Exploring the Coverage of Existing Hardware Vulnerabilities in Community Standards

Paul A. Wortman[1]([⊠])[iD], Fatemeh Tehranipoor[2][iD], and John A. Chandy[1][iD]

[1] University of Connecticut, Storrs, CT, USA
{paul.wortman,john.chandy}@uconn.edu
[2] Santa Clara University, Santa Clara, CA, USA
ftehranipoor@scu.edu

Abstract. Hardware security vulnerabilities have taken on greater importance over the last decade as academic and industry research has brought the issue to the forefront. The scope and breadth of these vulnerabilities have made them difficult to classify as has been done for software and network systems with the well-known Common Vulnerabilities and Exposures (CVE) database maintained by the MITRE Corporation. As further hardware security research continues, there is a requirement to standardize the language and references of academics, industry, and government alike. Without this common lexicon it becomes exceedingly difficult and potentially confusing when exchanging ideas, concepts, and methodologies across various sectors. Building and maintaining a glossary of terms, concepts, and concerns allows for a focus towards further research and development in the field of hardware security. In this paper, we review the nascent efforts by academia and industry in categorizing and documenting the existing hardware security landscape. The contributions of our work is an examination of the existing community efforts in the classification of hardware weakness with a specific focus on the CWE database. While current efforts are helping to contour the hardware landscape, similar to the work already performed for software and networks, the field is still evolving, and more work is required.

Keywords: Hardware security · Security vulnerabilities · Security standards · Security metrics

1   Introduction and Motivations

Hardware security is still a fledgling field of cybersecurity. The majority of cybersecurity activity currently exists in the realms of software and networking, with active academic research efforts and significant standardization and information sharing mechanisms in industry. The exchange of this Cyber Threat Intelligence (CTI) has become so prolific that the OASIS Cyber Threat Intelligence Technical Committee [8] has produced a Structured Threat Information Expression

© Springer Nature Switzerland AG 2021
Y. Park et al. (Eds.): SVCC 2020, CCIS 1383, pp. 87–97, 2021.
https://doi.org/10.1007/978-3-030-72725-3_6

(STIX) [6] language for the serialized formatted exchange of CTI as well as a separate and independent Trusted Automation Exchange of Intelligence Information (TAXII) [7] protocol which acts as an application layer for the communication of CTI in a simple and scalable manner. Unlike software and network systems, however, the scope of hardware security is far more loosely defined. Hardware components/definitions can include the physical chips and boards present in electronics, embedded/IoT devices and networks [19], or even the less defined boundary of Cyber Physical Systems [10,13,15,16,22]. One of the largest issues facing the safe and secure implementation and development of hardware components is the "pass the buck" mentality that can occur with industry and academics alike when the requirements for security begin to cross boundaries into the software and networking spaces. Fortunately, most of the hardware community is actively working to improve the documentation of hardware weaknesses, vulnerabilities, and mitigations [11,12,14,18,21].

While there has been recent significant growth in hardware security research, there has been relatively minimal documented and standardized work in hardware, embedded systems, and integrated circuit security. In December 2019, a Trusted and Assured MicroElectronics (TAME) report was released as a review of hardware security efforts over the previous 18 months. With the release of the TAME report, new light and focus has been directed to the efforts of the hardware security community to bridge the gap between existing software/network weakness/vulnerability databases and the lack thereof for hardware. In February 2020, MITRE released version 4.0 of their Common Weaknesses Enumeration (CWE) standard [4], which came with the inclusion of a "Hardware Design" view to categorize known hardware weaknesses into 12 distinct groups. The purpose of this effort was the same as made in the software weaknesses and vulnerabilities space with inclusion of the CWE and Common Vulnerabilities and Exposures (CVE) databases. While this release does provide a solid starting point for attempting to classify hardware security weaknesses, the attack surface space has a large body of literature on a variety of topics (e.g. memory, hardware Trojans, VHDL, UART/JTAG, timing attacks). Unfortunately, this athenaeum of literature is not uniform in its distribution across hardware security fields, leading to gaps in knowledge/research in certain areas. The computer security landscape is always quickly changing and that is reflected in the frequent updates to the CWE. MITRE has released subsequent updates to the CWE in June 2020 (version 4.1), August 2020 (version 4.2), and December 2020 (version 4.3). The hardware security taxonomy represented by the new CWE is still developing and as a result may be inaccurate, repetitive, or not inclusive of the entire scope of hardware security research. These efforts are relatively new and therefore not as mature as the software and network counterparts.

In this paper, we examine and review various community efforts to document and standardize the hardware security field. These efforts range from providing taxonomies of known weaknesses and vulnerabilities to prescribing best practices to identify, mitigate, and prevent these issues within larger product design. Due to the extensive nature of these efforts, the focus of this paper is to present these works and better educate the hardware security community of these endeavors. Lastly, we briefly discuss our observation of this space, what issues our community faces moving forward, and recommendation for further improvements.

2   Survey of Hardware Security Categorizations

As mentioned before, there is a lack of standardization and documentation for hardware weaknesses and vulnerabilities. Many different areas of hardware-based security have a plethora of sub-classifications (e.g. PUFs, side-channel attacks, directed hardware attacks; probing, hardware Trojans, etc.). These classifications have grown over time, have incorporated changes, made adoptions, and alterations of the taxonomies based on application or scope. There is a difficulty when attempting to delineate between all the hardware-based security implementations because they can be classified as belonging to multiple groupings. This challenge of the field can lead to similar sub-categorization or unique naming schemes to describe the same security issues or concerns.

Additionally it is difficult to assign metrics of measurement to the risk associated with weaknesses and their implemented vulnerabilities. Furthermore, confusion can arise due to the large number of non-standard taxonomies and other cataloging of known attack surfaces. While each of the taxonomies may be valid in their own right, the separate groups can use varying terminology or differentiation between specific realms, subcategories, or even use of terms (e.g. weakness versus vulnerability). Groups tend to decide on their own arbitrary/proprietary metrics (e.g. Rostami et al. [17] chose their own metrics to evaluate defenses). The software and network community started developing standard terminology and definitions as far back as 1999. The standardization of terms and concepts allowed individuals to focus efforts on knowledge sharing and mitigation of these issues.

Finally, despite best efforts, there is a lack of clarity on the difference between a weakness and a vulnerability. The security community (from academia to industry), unfortunately, tends to interchangeably use these terms, which can lead to confusion and miscommunication. We adopt the definition given by the MITRE CWE: a vulnerability is the occurrence of a weakness (or multiple weaknesses) within a product [3]. For the purpose of this paper, we will assume a homogeneous usage unless clearly stated otherwise. In spite of these challenges, there are a number of recent community efforts to improve hardware weaknesses and vulnerabilities knowledge through the standardization and documentation of the existing field. The following discussion summarizes these existing community efforts in documenting hardware security.

2.1   Trusted and Assured MicroElectronics Forum

The Trusted and Assured MicroElectronics Forum (TAME) was created as the first US forum on trusted and assured microelectronics. As a result of the aggregation of three committees working over 18 months, TAME issued a report focused specifically on Hardware Assurance and Weakness Collaboration and Sharing (HAWCS), Design for Security, and Microelectronics Security and Trust Grand Challenges [20]. This TAME report interprets "hardware vulnerabilities/weaknesses" as those existing in the hardware or firmware of a system and extends a functional definition that the vulnerability or weakness can be potentially mitigated but not removed by software changes. The report identifies three essential ways in which hardware and software weaknesses/vulnerabilities differ. First, hardware vulnerabilities are not easily patchable. Second, if the hardware-based issue can be mitigated, it is often a partial mitigation, thereby leaving some variation of the attack surface to persist. Lastly, due to the persistence of vulnerabilities, measuring an attacker's effort is a central metric. Furthermore, the TAME group presents a trinary structure for summarizing security metrics based off of: Error Metrics (Impact), Trust Metrics (Reliability), and Subversion Resistance (Effort). The report inevitably concludes that there is a level of acceptance that hardware has various attack surfaces which will most likely never be entirely secured. This immense scope is a central theme that appears within the hardware security field.

In addition, the TAME report found that while a notable ecosystem of reporting and assessment structure exists for the software and networking security fields, there is a distinct lack of coverage for hardware. The deficiency of automated detection and identification systems is of particular concerns since these could not only improve detection of low-level issues (e.g. hardware Trojans) but also help provide inexpensive diagnosis of information leakage and counterfeits. The existence of some knowledge structures for hardware security concerns does cultivate a platform from which the standardization can begin, however, there was not currently an all-encompassing characterization that clearly linked hardware-based issues to their underlying mechanisms. The TAME report does not inventory the full range of hardware security vulnerabilities, but it does present a table of hardware security taxonomies that refer to other databases or research papers that provide detailed examples of each topic.

2.2 Common Attack Pattern Enumeration and Classification (CAPEC)

The Common Attack Pattern Enumeration and Classification (CAPEC) [1] is a MITRE resource intended as a community asset for the identification and understanding of attacks. Of this publicly accessibly catalog of common attack patterns, there are two "domains of attack" [1] that are applicable to hardware security: Hardware and Physical Security. These two taxonomies are represented below:

1. Hardware: Attack patterns that focus on exploitation of physical hardware
2. Physical Security: Attack patterns that focus on physical security

The "Hardware" domain contains attack patterns that focus on the exploitation of physical hardware. These attacks can fall into several broad categories that depend upon the sophistication of the attacker and the type of systems targeted. Hardware-based attacks include those against chips, circuit boards, device ports, etc. and can include attacks relating to the adding or removing of jumpers as well as the application of sensors for the reading or writing to the board. The hardware domain also includes replacement, destruction, modification, and exploitation of hardware components to achieve desired negative technical impact as within scope of the category. The "Physical Security" domain relates attack patterns that focus on physical security; techniques centralized around the exploitation of weaknesses in physical security of a system to achieve a desired technical impact. Topics associated with physical security include excavation, reverse engineering, hardware integrity attack, physical theft, obstruction, and the bypassing of physical security. While this domain is separate from the Hardware-domain, it appears that its intent is as a catch-all for attack patterns that do not fit within the Hardware domain. For this domain the focus is on techniques defined by exploitation of weaknesses in the physical security of a system to achieve desired negative technical impact.

2.3 SAE G-32 Cyber Physical Systems Security Committee

Another example of a community effort is the recent formation of the SAE G-32 Cyber Physical Systems Security Committee [5]. The group was established by SAE International to address critical needs for government, industry, and academia through collaboration to address the security of Cyber Physical Systems (CPS). Within the scope of this on-going work are technologies that combine cyber and physical spaces and that can respond, in real time, to their environments. These systems are taken to include electronic parts, assemblies, systems, and system elements that can operate as a single, self-contained device or as part of an interconnected network sharing and/or providing operations. These considerations attempt to coalesce knowledge and practices in the areas of software, hardware, system design, risk evaluation, and establishment of product assurances. While this work is central in presenting a common standardization of language and documentation, the committee is still working towards the development and release of this material. As such the G-32 standard is still not mature enough to be applicable at this time.

2.4 Trust-Hub

Trust-Hub [9] is a resource sponsored by the National Science Foundation (NSF) and hosted by the University of Florida for the purpose of exchanging knowledge and ideas to help develop/evaluate technologies in hardware security and trust domains. The Hardware Platform material of this group relates to efforts in developing a collection of data from application specific integrated circuit (ASIC) chips and insertion of hardware Trojans into FPGAs. The Trust-Hub Vulnerability Database contains a "Physical Attack" taxonomy that categorizes physical attacks upon hardware vulnerabilities as based on active or passive methodology, which both are further sub-categorized as either "Non-Invasive" or "Invasive & Semi-Invasive" attacks. These are further grouped based on the scope of attack or methodology implemented. The advantage of Trust-Hub is that it is an incredibly detailed taxonomy of "Physical Vulnerabilities". However, the scope of this information is limited to low-level chips and gates. The categorization of physical attacks is particularity relevant to integrated circuits but lacks the purview required for the larger range of hardware-based weaknesses and vulnerabilities.

2.5   CVE and CWE

Two of the more influential and widely used resources for networks and software security are the Common Vulnerabilities and Exposures (CVE) list and the later Common Weaknesses Enumeration (CWE) database; both produced by the MITRE Corporation.

The Common Vulnerabilities and Exposures (CVE) dictionary was created in 1999 to provide definitions of publicly disclosed cybersecurity vulnerabilities and exposures [2]. The goal of the CVE database is to allow for easier exchange/sharing of data across separate vulnerability tools, databases, and services. By 2005, MITRE's CVE team had developed primary classification and categorization of vulnerabilities, faults, attacks, and other common software weaknesses. However these categorizations were not refined appropriately for use within the CVE. In 2006 the CWE database was created to better address these needs for the security community.

The Common Weakness Enumeration (CWE) [4] is a list of common software and hardware weakness types compiled as a community-developed database. The "weaknesses" are flaws, faults, bugs, vulnerabilities, or other errors in hardware/software implementation, code, design or architecture. If these weaknesses are left un-addressed it could result in hardware, systems, or networks being vulnerable to attack. The purpose of the CWE list is to act as a common language (e.g. associated classification taxonomy) that can be used to identify and describe the documented weaknesses. By maintaining this database the CWE can be used to educate hardware and software engineers, architects, designers, and programmers to help eliminate the most common mistakes and stop vulnerabilities at the source. The 4.0 release of the CWE (Feb 29th, 2020) was the first to include hardware weaknesses and subsequent releases (4.1 (June 25th, 2020), 4.2 (August 20th, 2020), and 4.3 (December 10th, 2020)) have expanded the hardware weakness categorizations. Of all the reviewed community standardization and documentation efforts with respect to hardware security, the work by MITRE on the CWE is the most mature as well as actively being updated. Recently a Hardware CWE Special Interests Group (HW CWE SIG) was formed to further develop the CWE database, with their first meeting having been on October 30th, 2020. The purpose of the group was for researchers and representatives of active groups operating in hardware design, manufacturing, and security to be able to interact, share opinions and expertise, and leverage community knowledge to improve growth and adoption of the CWE as a standard for defining hardware security weaknesses.

Figure 1 illustrates the coverage of the various community efforts in standardizing documentation of the hardware security field. As can be seen, different groups have varied coverage depending on their specialization/focus. TAME and Trust-Hub are both focused on low-level hardware, though Trust-Hub also has a greater emphasis on supply chain security. G-32 is focused in the broader area of CPS security. CWE has the broadest coverage of hardware weaknesses, but the database is still a small subset of all known weaknesses. Though there is a separation of hardware weaknesses and hardware vulnerabilities, there is some overlap due to vulnerability being the exploitation of a given weakness or group of weaknesses. Due to the maturity and active nature of the CWE database, the CWE has done the best job in covering the entire scope of hardware weaknesses and vulnerabilities. As such, we will delve deeper into a summary of the CWE hardware efforts and review the categorization of these weaknesses further in the following section.

3   CWE 4.x Hardware Categories

The key addition in the 4.x standards release is the addition of the Hardware Design View. This view's purpose is to be an organization of weaknesses and concepts that are frequently encountered or used within hardware design. The categories presented in the CWE documentation are solely intended to simplify navigation, browsing, and mapping of characteristically similar base and class weaknesses. One should take note that the categories themselves are not technically weaknesses. Furthermore, the CWE documentation makes a note that it is possible for the same weakness to exist within multiple different categories. The MITRE CWE breaks up the common hardware view weaknesses into twelve separate categories. What follows is an examination of each of the twelve categories with a category definition, along with observations and assumptions made about each categorization.

Manufacturing and Life Cycle Management Concerns. This category groups weaknesses whose root-cause for defects arise from the semiconductor-manufacturing process or during the life cycle and supply chain. Examples of manufacturing weaknesses include defects in semiconductor logic with security implications and unprotected confidential information on devices. Life cycle management issues include improper scrubbing of data from decommissioned devices, products released in non-release configurations, device unlock credential sharing, and minimal protection against reverse engineering.

Security Flow Issues. This category relates weaknesses due to improper design of full-system security flows, including but not limited to secure boot, secure update, and hardware-device attestation. Examples of these weaknesses encompass improper design of security flows of the full-system and can include

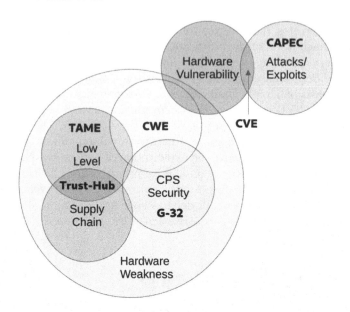

Fig. 1. Venn diagram of hardware security coverage

secure booting and updating, proof of a hardware device's security, and unrestricted access due to unexpected boot processes or early activation of hardware components.

Integration Issues. Weaknesses in this category arise due to multiple hardware Intellectual Property (IP) cores from third parties, or from the prior generation of products into a common System-on-Chip (SoC) or other hardware platform. This category of weaknesses includes incorrectly connecting IP blocks into a system or using old insecure or incompatible versions of third-party IP blocks. A simple example could be a company that wants to create some new product but tries to save costs by reusing existing IP blocks.

Privilege Separation and Access Control Issues. This category groups weaknesses related to features and mechanisms providing hardware-based isolation and access control (e.g. identity, policy, locking control) of sensitive shared hardware resources such as registers and fuses. Weaknesses within this space include lack of proper access control lists, lack of separation for trusted hardware components (e.g. TPM), no use of unique identifiers or properties to ensure the sources of high-level access/action, and inclusion/use of undocumented capabilities or features.

General Circuit and Logic Design Concerns. This category relates weaknesses due to hardware-circuit design and logic (e.g. CMOS transistors, finite state machines, and registers) as well as issues related to hardware description languages such as System Verilog and VHDL. This set of weaknesses include issues such as incorrect register defaults, race conditions, improper handling of single event upsets, hardware Trojans, malicious circuit paths, and other concerns relating to critical infrastructure paths.

Core and Compute Issues. There are a range of weaknesses typically associated with CPUs, Graphics, Vision, AI, FPGA and microcontrollers. Though this category is limited in its scope, it can be one of the more critical concerns. Examples include incorrect configuration of CPU hardware, lack of separation of access control (Meltdown), unexpected behavior due to particular sequences of instructions. In this scope the security/safety of communication standards is paramount, especially with regards to embedded system functionality.

Memory and Storage Issues. These include weaknesses associated with memory (e.g. DRAM, SRAM) and storage technologies (e.g. NAND Flash, OTP, EEPROM and eMMC). Vulnerability attacks that are relevant in this space include cold boot attacks, TSOP/direct chip read, chip decapping, ROWHAMMER, aging SRAM/DRAM, and others. Although there exist similar concerns within software and network spaces, these weaknesses are specific to hardware-based and physical-centric shortcomings.

Peripherals, On-Chip Fabric, and Interface/IO Problems. This category groups together weaknesses related to hardware security problems that apply to peripheral devices IO interfaces, on-chip interconnects, network-on-chip (NoC), and buses. Issues in scope relate to the design of hardware interconnect and/or protocols such as PCIe, USB, SMBUS general-purpose IO pins, and user-input peripherals such as mouse and keyboard. With the expansion of embedded systems into the larger consumer market, there is constant concern of how these systems can be protected against failure due to exploitable weaknesses and mitigations against them. These concerns grow with the number of interfaces and cyber-physical systems determined by an array of interactive systems (e.g. user input, bus communication, network-on-chip (NoC), hardware peripherals).

Security Primitives and Cryptography Issues. This category includes weaknesses related to hardware implementations of cryptographic protocols and other hardware-security primitives such as physical unclonable functions (PUFs) and random number generators (RNGs). Concerns could include overcoming/replicating PUFs (within tolerable error) and/or other techniques for altering the effectiveness of randomness within PUFs or RNGs. Examples of attacks include incorrect cryptographic hardware implementations, insufficient randomness in RNGs, controlling the hardware's environmental properties to limit the response space of PUFs, accessing the database of known values for the challenge-response of PUFs, controlling the random seed for RNGs, or other methods to control/limit effectiveness of circuit elements.

Power, Clock, and Reset Concerns. These relate to system power, voltage, current, temperature, clocks, system state saving/restoring, and resets at the platform and SoC level. Attacks under this category include clock glitching, under powering of circuits, as well as additional circuit manipulation. Weaknesses within this category include missing known values upon device/system reset, improper locking behavior when power state transitions occur, and missing protections/mitigations against voltage/clock glitches.

Debug and Test Problems. These are weaknesses that relate to hardware debug and test interfaces such as JTAG and scan chain. These include references to JTAG vulnerabilities, testpad PCB problems, debug interfaces left from manufacturing and design. The most well-known attack vector within this category is the exploitation of leftover debug interfaces, allowing for access to internal systems.

Cross-Cutting Problems. This category groups together weaknesses that can arise in multiple areas of hardware design or can apply to a wide cross-section of components. As the name implies, this category is intended to act as a "catch-all" for weaknesses that do not fit in the other categories nicely or span a number of categories. Examples include incorrect documentation, improper physical access control, violation of functional/behavior specs, etc.

4   Conclusion

A great deal of effort is currently being made in the field of hardware weaknesses and vulnerabilities. The scope of these research efforts has changed over time, though the work is becoming better focused as well. The security community has begun to formalize standard documentation and language around hardware security weaknesses and vulnerabilities. Specifically there is a distinct need to establish a glossary of hardware-specific terminology, while characterizing key differences that might cause confusion between similar language in software and networking spaces. The Common Weakness Enumeration (CWE) establishes an effective base to continue growing a characterization of hardware security concerns, however continued effort is necessary to fully encompass the current field of hardware security research. In particular, the CWE hardware categories need to be mapped against the latest hardware security research to identify potential gaps in its overall weakness coverage.

References

1. CAPEC view: Domains of attack. http://capec.mitre.org/data/definitions/3000.html
2. Common Vulnerabilities and Exposures. https://cve.mitre.org/index.html
3. CWE glossary. https://cwe.mitre.org/documents/glossary/index.html#Weakness

4. CWE view: Hardware design. https://cwe.mitre.org/data/definitions/1194.html
5. Cyber physical systems security committee G-32 established by SAE international. https://saemobilus.sae.org/cybersecurity/news/2019/03/cyber-physical-systems-security-committee-g-32-established-by-sae
6. Introduction to STIX. https://oasis-open.github.io/cti-documentation/stix/intro
7. Introduction to TAXII. https://oasis-open.github.io/cti-documentation/taxii/intro.html
8. OASIS cyber threat intelligence (CTI) TC. https://www.oasis-open.org/committees/tc_home.php?wg_abbrev=cti
9. Trust-hub - the vulnerability database. https://trust-hub.org/vulnerability-db/physical-vulnerabilities
10. Altawy, R., Youssef, A.M.: Security, privacy, and safety aspects of civilian drones: a survey. ACM Trans. Cyber-Phys. Syst. **1**(2), 1–25 (2016)
11. Bettayeb, M., Nasir, Q., Talib, M.A.: Firmware update attacks and security for IoT devices: survey. In: Proceedings of the ArabWIC 6th Annual International Conference Research Track, pp. 1–6 (2019)
12. Botero, U.J., et al.: Hardware trust and assurance through reverse engineering: a survey and outlook from image analysis and machine learning perspectives. arXiv preprint arXiv:2002.04210 (2020)
13. Camara, C., Peris-Lopez, P., Tapiador, J.E.: Security and privacy issues in implantable medical devices: a comprehensive survey. J. Biomed. Inform. **55**, 272–289 (2015)
14. Coppolino, L., D'Antonio, S., Mazzeo, G., Romano, L.: A comprehensive survey of hardware-assisted security: from the edge to the cloud. Internet Things **6**, 100055 (2019)
15. Giraldo, J., Sarkar, E., Cardenas, A.A., Maniatakos, M., Kantarcioglu, M.: Security and privacy in cyber-physical systems: a survey of surveys. IEEE Des. Test **34**(4), 7–17 (2017)
16. Humayed, A., Lin, J., Li, F., Luo, B.: Cyber-physical systems security–a survey. IEEE Internet Things J. **4**(6), 1802–1831 (2017)
17. Rostami, M., Koushanfar, F., Karri, R.: A primer on hardware security: models, methods, and metrics. In: Proceedings of the IEEE, vol. 102, no. 8, pp. 1283–1295 (2014)
18. Szefer, J.: Survey of microarchitectural side and covert channels, attacks, and defenses. J. Hardware Syst. Secur. **3**(3), 219–234 (2019)
19. Tehranipoor, F., Karimian, N., Wortman, P.A., Haque, A., Fahrny, J., Chandy, J.A.: Exploring methods of authentication for the Internet of Things. In: Internet of Things, pp. 71–90. Chapman and Hall/CRC (2017)
20. Tehranipoor, M., et al.: TAME: trusted and assured microelectronics forum working groups report. https://www.erai.com/CustomUploads/ca/wp/TAME_Report.pdf, December 2019
21. Tschofenig, H., Baccelli, E.: Cyberphysical security for the masses: a survey of the internet protocol suite for internet of things security. IEEE Secur. Privacy **17**(5), 47–57 (2019)
22. Urbina, D.I., et al.: Survey and new directions for physics-based attack detection in control systems. National Institute of Standards and Technology, US Department of Commerce (2016)

MurQRI: Encrypted Multi-layer QR Codes for Electronic Identity Management

Bonha Koo[ID], Taegeun Moon[ID], and Hyoungshick Kim[✉][ID]

Department of Computer Science and Engineering, Sungkyunkwan University,
Suwon, South Korea
bonhak@andrew.cmu.edu, {taegeun,hyoung}@skku.edu

Abstract. Quick Response (QR) codes are widely used due to their
versatility and low deployment cost. However, the existing QR code
standard is ineffective for security-critical applications (e.g., electronic
identity management) as the stored information can be easily exposed
to unauthorized parties. Moreover, it does not provide sufficient storage
capacity to employ robust encryption schemes for complex access control and authentication. In this paper, we present a novel approach of
employing encrypted multi-layer QR codes, MurQRI (pronounced "Mer-
cury"), for secure user authentication and fine-grained access control
in various domains (e.g., airport and hospital). MurQRI is designed to
store up to 45 kilobytes of data and protect the stored information via
biometric authentication and encryption. To support fine-grained access
control, we employ attribute-based encryption. We also introduce real-
world applications where MurQRI can be used effectively and discuss possible methods to enhance security.

Keywords: QR code · Multi-layer QR · Access control · User
identification · User authentication

1 Introduction

A Quick Response (QR) code is a two-dimensional barcode that can encode various types of information. Because the QR code can be used to transfer large
data between devices through their display (sender) and camera (receiver), it has
been widely used in numerous applications—mobile purchases, print advertise-
ments, and information delivery—to represent an individual's data or authorization ticket. However, the use of QR codes also brings security issues [8,18]. As
anyone can easily read the barcode, it can leak confidential information to unauthorized entities. Moreover, QR codes can be generated for malicious purposes
(e.g., forgery, impersonation) from one's public or easily accessible data. For
example, Jaroszewski [16] presented a forgery attack with a maliciously modified QR code. The demonstration involved a crafted QR boarding pass used
to access airline lounges and fast-tracks. The attack was successful by simply

© Springer Nature Switzerland AG 2021
Y. Park et al. (Eds.): SVCC 2020, CCIS 1383, pp. 98–108, 2021.
https://doi.org/10.1007/978-3-030-72725-3_7

generating a QR code altering the traveler's name and flight information. This example shows that data embedded in a QR code should be carefully considered for security-critical applications such as electronic identity management.

Several approaches have been proposed to protect QR codes. As explained in Sect. 6, previous attempts extend from simple secret embedding methods to key encryption [12, 13, 26, 28]. However, existing methods cause inconvenience by requiring large storage space or revealing documented data as plain-text. Further problems of existing methods are high dependency on the server and the absence of fine access control. Ultimately, previous studies integrate conventional QR codes, which are limited to containing trivial data when generated in practical sizes [2]. Overall, there has not been a holistic approach to solving these limitations to establish a reliable electronic identity management scheme.

To overcome such limitations, we propose MurQRI, a novel QR code representation scheme to safely store personal data for electronic identification jointly providing fine access-control. Unfortunately, the existing QR code standard cannot directly be used for this purpose because there is no standard protection method for the QR code. It is limited to holding maximum data of 2,953 bytes (in binary mode), which is not sufficient to store an individual's photo or biometric data (see Sect. 2.1) [15]. As a solution, MurQRI expands its data capacity by taking the form of a multi-layer QR and protecting each layer's content with ciphertext-policy attribute-based encryption (CP-ABE). Moreover, MurQRI can be further extended with secret hiding techniques to meet the requirements of environments where more complex access control is demanded among multiple parties conveying various privileges to access others' data.

The rest of this paper is organized as follows. Section 2 explains multi-layer QR codes and attribute-based encryption used in MurQRI. Section 3 and 4 introduce the proposed MurQRI system and describe real-world applications. Section 5 evaluates the effectiveness of biometric input and secret hiding techniques. Section 6 discusses related work. Finally, Sect. 7 concludes the paper and suggests future work.

2   Background

2.1   Multi-layer QR Code

A Quick Response (QR) code [15] is a two-dimensional barcode that consists of black and white square modules arranged on a grid. The QR code supports 40 versions which differ in size ranging from 21×21 (version 1) to 144×144 (version 40), and 4 different error correction levels: L (7%), M (15%), Q (25%), and H (30%). The amount of data each holds accords to the input mode (e.g., numeric, binary) and error correction level. The QR code can contain diverse forms of data, including simple texts, URLs, and contacts. Due to its attractive features such as error correction and high-speed scanning, QR codes are widely used in multiple fields today.

Multi-layer QR is a relatively new topic introduced to support larger data by expanding the conventional QR code of two dimensions to three. Whereas

Fig. 1. Example of multi-layer QR code

the standard QR code can store up to 2,953 bytes (in binary mode) [15], multi-layer QR can store much more data because of its extended dimension. Figure 1 shows an example of a 3-layer QR code. Pioneering studies of multi-layer QR [6,11,22,25] suggested utilizing different color channels of the barcode and scanner. Specifically, Dean et al. [11] divided data into three equal-length strings to be embedded into three separate QR codes, allowing the use of a smaller QR version with the same data. Each string was then encoded in the QR format with white modules assigned to red, green, and blue color spaces, respectively. When decoding, layers were separated after color correction, then combined to reconstruct the original string. This scheme observed that any three linearly independent colors are effective in constructing a multi-layer QR code.

However, discoloration of a printed QR code using the RGB channel is yet a problem. To address this issue, Bulan et al. [6] designed an algorithm solving cross-channel color-interference between print-colorant and camera channels. The method they proposed outperformed the preceding method of thresholding for each RGB channel. To develop more practical ways in decoding the multi-layer QR, Noppakaew et al. [25] proposed an algorithm to compute a collection of suitable colors needed to construct n-layered QR codes. They generated a partition of positive numbers, namely 255, with the length of $\lceil l/3 \rceil$ to construct an l-layered QR code. With the maximum l being 15 in this particular study, the multi-layer QR code can store up to 45 kilobytes, which is about 15 times greater than that of the standard QR code.

2.2 Attribute-Based Encryption

Shamir [28] introduced an identity-based cryptosystem as an extended version of the traditional public key cryptography. Unlike the conventional version, which requires the message to be encrypted with the receiver's public key, identity-based encryption (IBE) can utilize an arbitrary public string (e.g., email address) as the public key. Later, fully functional IBE schemes were devised in [4,27], which expands "identities" to "descriptive attributes." Ciphertext-policy attribute-based encryption (CP-ABE) takes a further step and links attributes that describe each user to their private key, and embeds the attribute policy within the ciphertext [3,14]. Therefore, users can decrypt the ciphertext only if their attributes satisfy the access policy.

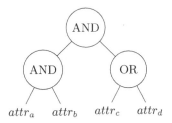

Fig. 2. Access policy tree using AND/OR gates

In CP-ABE, there is a trusted key generator. The trusted party takes charge of setting up the access tree ($\mathbb{A}$) and policy, manages the private master-key, and generates private keys for different parties. Each node in the access tree acts as a threshold gate, and leaf nodes describe attributes (see Fig. 2). In addition, although the key generator can be a server for initialization, it is not required for the server to be constantly available after initialization.

The followings are simplified explanations of four algorithms in CP-ABE:

1. Setup (λ): The Setup algorithm takes the initial security parameter λ as input. The outputs are public parameters p and the master-key K_M. p is open to everyone (similar to public key), while K_M should be kept as a secret by the trusted key generator. All entities in one system use the same p for authentication.
2. KeyGen (p, K_M, γ): The KeyGen algorithm takes p, K_M, and a set of attributes γ as the input. It outputs a secret key K_S for the user with corresponding features.
3. Encrypt (p, M, $\mathbb{A}$): The Encrypt algorithm takes p, message to encrypt M, and the access structure $\mathbb{A}$ as input. It outputs a ciphertext C.
4. Decrypt (p, K_S, C): The Decrypt algorithm takes p, secret key of a user K_S, and the ciphertext C. It outputs the original message M.

The algorithm reveals M if and only if K_S satisfies γ encrypted in C.

3 Proposed Scheme

MurQRI aims to provide an adaptable identification method secure against privacy violation, data misuse, and other security breaches. Figure 3 illustrates the structure of `MurQRI`. `MurQRI` adopts a multi-layer QR code scheme (see Sect. 2.1) to store larger data organized in categories. In addition, `MurQRI` employs attribute-based encryption (see Sect. 2.2) to provide stricter authentication and complex access-control. Authorized individuals can hold private attribute keys according to their authority or permission to access the data encoded in users' tag.

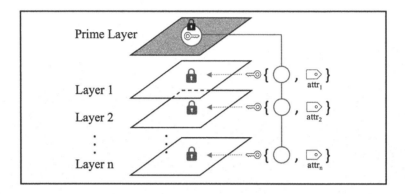

Fig. 3. Overview of `MurQRI`

Figure 4 illustrates encryption and decryption algorithms for a 3-layer `MurQRI`. QR_p, QR_1, and QR_2 are stacked to form the multi-layer QR according to an algorithm devised in Sect. 2.1. The proposed scheme contains two types of layers with distinct functions: *prime* and *non-prime*. The top-most layer is referred to as *prime layer*. Its sole purpose is to verify the ID holder's authenticity. Therefore, the only data within this layer is an encrypted version of the implicit key (K_i), which can be inferred from the name that this is only used internally. Nevertheless, we discuss encoding additional data in the prime layer in Sect. 5.2. Encryption and authentication methods for the prime layer differ upon implementation, described later in this section. *Non-prime layers*, also referred to as "bottom" layers, hold information originally contained in traditional identification documents (see Sect. 4). Bottom layers are encrypted with two keys, K_i and a layer-specific K_{attr}.

Upon issuance of `MurQRI`, there are multiple ways to encrypt the prime layer. For example, the owner can set a simple passcode (e.g., 4-digit code) or use her biometric data as *Password*. Under this setting, the prime layer encodes K_i, encrypted with a selected *Password*, into a QR code QR_p. In Sect. 5.1, we discuss how to employ biometric data as an authentication mechanism for `MurQRI`.

The bottom layers deploy ciphertext-policy attribute-based encryption (CP-ABE) for fine-grained access control. To set up non-prime layers, let T and K_{attr} be the access policy tree and private key, respectively. Following the algorithm `Setup` and `KeyGen` in Sect. 2.2, the trusted key generator sets T and K_{attr}. Then,

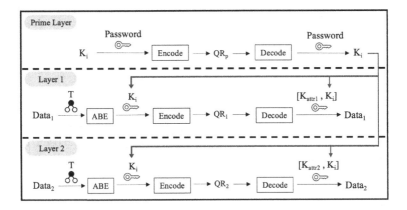

Fig. 4. Example of a 3-layer `MurQRI`

the ciphertext of plain data is generated according to `Encrypt`. Again, ciphertext for each layer (layer n) is encrypted with K_i, which parties other than the key generator can only obtain by correctly decrypting the prime layer, and then encoded into a QR code QR_n.

This method serves the purpose of both proving the authenticity of the user and providing selective restriction. For example, it is impracticable for a malicious attacker to access data in bottom layers of a stolen tag encrypted with the owner's biometric data, because her biometric input will not match that in the target user's ID. Furthermore, characteristics of CP-ABE convey that users cannot collect private keys and combine them to act as a private key with desired privileges [19]. Along with the infeasibility of a collusion attack, revocation and delegation of a private key are convenient in this algorithm. Therefore, `MurQRI` implementing CP-ABE can be useful in a large universe with many users and authority levels.

4   Real-World Applications

To demonstrate the practicality of `MurQRI`, we provide two specific real-world use cases.

4.1   `MurQRI` for Electronic Identification in Airports

Because of its convenience, electronic identification is widely used in airports for ePassports and electronic boarding passes [1,29]. Unlike the conventional isolated system, `MurQRI` can serve both functions of an ePassport and a boarding pass to meet real-world efficiency utilizing its security features. The following is a list of information that `MurQRI` could carry in such an environment:

- Default Data: Name, Contact
- Flight Data: Valid flight number, Time, Gate, Seating
- Passport Data: Valid passport number, VISA status
- Biometric Data: Face, Iris, Fingerprint recognition data
- Billing Information

While there are many places this ID could be read, confidential information should not be revealed to those without appropriate permission. For example, the prime layer can be encrypted with a biometric measure (chosen by standard); then, the bottom layers can only be deciphered directly from the owner's correct biometric input. In addition, layer 1 can contain passport information, including confidential data such as her VISA status. Among multiple authorities who can access this ID, airline staff and airport security members should be able to access layer 1, while customer service representatives or cargo handlers should not access or modify this particular information.

4.2 MurQRI for Patient Data in Hospitals

Utilizing barcode technology in healthcare is not a new concept. Indeed, advantages in the industry have been proven across multiple years [17,24]. People are making efforts to put in more data in the barcode, which led to implementing QR codes in line. The main purpose of this is to prevent human-made medical errors and support faster workflow. Additionally, compared to the previous airport scenario, data transmission in a hospital can be more critical.

Consider an example where patient P visits physician H_1 for a health screening, only to find the results be severe cancer. Medical information that could be included in P's ID is as follows:

- Diagnosis and Test Results
- Medication Management: Prescription, Progress logs
- Chemotherapy Instruction: Radiation dose

Regarding medical confidentiality, Physician-Patient privileges are needed to protect P's physical and mental states between P and H_1 [7]. Another physician H_2 cannot access this data even though H_2 has the access level of 'physician.' Additionally, access privileges can be delegated among doctors and hospitals if P chooses to transfer hospitals. MurQRI can be useful in this situation as CP-ABE supports easy delegation and revocation of attribute keys. Furthermore, unauthorized staff members are strictly prohibited from modifying drugs or radiation doses of P. By incorporating MurQRI in the hospital industry, critical accidents and unintentional data breaches can be prevented.

5 Discussion

In this section, we discuss the effectiveness of biometric data as a key for encrypting K_i and a method of further subdividing a single layer.

5.1 Utilizing Biometric Authentications

The goal of implementing biometric data as a key is to prove the ID owner's authenticity. Face, fingerprint, or iris data can be stored along with biometric engines. For example, templates for each biometric data in [23] are 194 or 322, 800 to 8,000, and 2,348 bytes respectively. Consider the algorithm of Fig. 4 with *Password* as the owner's facial recognition data. Once the reader verifies that a user's face matches the encrypted data, K_i is retrieved. Therefore, bottom layers can be assessed as valid and also be decrypted with appropriate private attribute keys. Real-time comparison of input against the biometric key prevents replay and impersonation attacks. Modifying the prime layer or replacing the QR code is not feasible because attribute policies are defined upon the distributor's issuance. However, as an individual can only generate one key from each biometric feature, security breaches where the biometric data is compromised can be a problem. To prevent this attack, we can embed biometric data with a distributor-generated token, which alters when MurQRI is issued. Although generating a fixed key for biometric measures and stability of scanning depends on the environment and selected engine, biometric recognition can further enhance security by linking the owner to the verified document.

5.2 Utilizing Secret Hiding

As MurQRI is an electronic identity management scheme, a conventional ID's basic identification functions cannot be ignored. In many cases, revealing the owner's name is not a controversial issue; ID holders do not find it a security breach. Indeed, adding an unencrypted layer for basic identification factors can serve such a function. Even so, there may be cases in which only specific data within layers should be revealed to the general public. Therefore, we suggest the utilization of secret hiding to disclose data selectively. This scheme can enhance the functionality of an ID and conserve the property of data-categorization.

Secret hiding is a scheme that exploits error correction codewords to conceal secret messages within a cover QR code [20]. QR codewords of a secret message is extracted and embedded into a QR code containing a cover message. Encryption methods or embedding positions differ according to implementation details. Hence, any ordinary decoder can read the cover message, while authorities with prior knowledge of the corresponding decryption method can successfully read the secret message [5,9,10].

Returning to the airport scenario in Sect. 4.1, each layer can embed different public information according to how sensitive the data is. Indeed, the prime layer can select Default Data as the cover message, while ciphertext resulting from encrypting K_i can be the secret. In addition, the layer that includes flight information can select valid flight number, gate, departure time, and seating as public data, while flight validation or reservation codes can be concealed. A recent and most-promising study constructed an algorithm that allows a conventional QR code to hide 10,208 bits of secret message [21]. Adding multiple layers in this scheme provides sufficient space for data in the scenarios mentioned above.

6   Related Work

Previous attempts to secure data within a QR code extend from simple secret embedding methods to key encryption, including employing facial recognition keys. Trujillo et al. [13] introduced an ID authentication system that takes advantage of a (2,2) threshold secret sharing scheme [28]. Two QR code shares, belonging to the distributor and user each, are simultaneously presented and stacked to reveal the secret distinguishable by the human visual system. Yet, this method requires extra storage space to save paired barcodes in order to successfully evaluate authenticity. Similarly, Qryptal [26] suggested IDs including a QR code signed by PKI organization keys and private multi-step pipeline compression. Although this guarantees the authenticity of the document, it still reveals all data to the public in plain-text. The QR code only acts as a tool for authentication while no data is concealed. In contrast, Denso Wave developed Face SQRC [12], which is based on encoding facial recognition data in employee IDs. Although facial recognition data effectively prevents impersonation attacks, the tag can only hold trivial information due to limited data capacity. Overall, existing methods do not address problems of limited encoding space and lack of access control, especially when generated in suitable sizes.

7   Conclusion and Further Work

In this paper, we proposed MurQRI, an encryption-based multi-layer QR code scheme for secure electronic identity management. MurQRI provides enhanced security of electronic identification by using encryption and fine-grained access control while providing larger data capacity. The QR code consists of a single prime layer and multiple non-prime layers. The prime layer stores an implicit key, encrypted with a user's password or biometric factor (e.g., fingerprint). Non-prime layers store confidential data encrypted with the implicit key. For the encryption of non-prime layers, we suggest using CP-ABE for fine-grained access control—when a user holds the valid password and private attribute key, the content at non-prime layers can successfully be decrypted. In addition, we suggest a supplementary scheme of secret hiding in QR to enhance the performance of MurQRI by providing an option to select public and private data discreetly.

Overall, the proposed scheme allows safer distribution of the ID in public and complex access control. Adopting biometric information as an encryption key assures the integrity and authenticity of the owner. However, any symmetric and asymmetric encryption protocol can be used as well. This flexible scheme could be useful in various applications, such as airports, hospitals, or environments that involve multiple users and different authority properties. For future work, we plan to implement a fully working system of the proposed QR scheme. Given that implementing CP-ABE augments the ciphertext to a substantial size, we also plan to conduct feasibility and usability studies utilizing different cryptographic primitives to find the optimal data size and multi-layering techniques for storing personal data and biometrics.

Acknowledgement. This research was supported by the ICT R&D program (No.2017-0-00545) and the National Research Foundation of Korea (NRF) grant funded by the Korea government (MSIT) (No. 2019R1C1C1007118).

References

1. The electronic passport in 2020 and beyond. https://www.thalesgroup.com/en/markets/digital-identity-and-security/government/passport/electronic-passport-trends
2. QR code basics: Getting started with QR codes, June 2020. https://www.qr-code-generator.com/qr-code-marketing/qr-codes-basics/
3. Bethencourt, J., Sahai, A., Waters, B.: Ciphertext-policy attribute-based encryption. In: 2007 IEEE Symposium on Security and Privacy (SP 2007), pp. 321–334 (2007). https://doi.org/10.1109/SP.2007.11
4. Boneh, D., Franklin, M.: Identity-based encryption from the Weil pairing. In: Kilian, J. (ed.) CRYPTO 2001. LNCS, vol. 2139, pp. 213–229. Springer, Heidelberg (2001). https://doi.org/10.1007/3-540-44647-8_13
5. Bui, T.V., Vu, N.K., Nguyen, T.T.P., Echizen, I., Nguyen, T.D.: Robust message hiding for QR code. In: 2014 Tenth International Conference on Intelligent Information Hiding and Multimedia Signal Processing, pp. 520–523 (2014). https://doi.org/10.1109/IIH-MSP.2014.135
6. Bulan, O., Blasinski, H., Sharma, G.: Color QR codes: increased capacity via per-channel data encoding and interference cancellation. In: Color Imaging Conference (2011)
7. California State Legislature: (1965). https://leginfo.legislature.ca.gov/faces/codes_displayText.xhtml?lawCode=EVID&division=8.&title=&part=&chapter=4.&article=6, division 8. Priviliges Chapter 4. Particular Priviliges Article 6. Physician-Patient Privilege
8. Chambers, B.: How COVID-19 Has Accelerated QR Code Adoption in the UK and EU. Mobileiron.com, October 2020. https://www.mobileiron.com/en/blog/how-covid-19-has-accelerated-qr-code-adoption-uk-eu
9. Chiang, Y.J., Lin, P.Y., Wang, R.Z., Chen, Y.H.: Blind QR code steganographic approach based upon error correction capability. KSII Trans. Internet Inf. Syst. **7**, 2527–2543 (2013). https://doi.org/10.3837/tiis.2013.10.012
10. Chow, Y.-W., Susilo, W., Baek, J.: Covert QR codes: how to hide in the crowd. In: Liu, J.K., Samarati, P. (eds.) ISPEC 2017. LNCS, vol. 10701, pp. 678–693. Springer, Cham (2017). https://doi.org/10.1007/978-3-319-72359-4_42
11. Dean, T., Dunn, C.: Quick layered response (QLR) codes (2012)
12. DENSO WAVE: Face authentication SQRC. https://www.denso-wave.com/en/system/qr/product/facesqrc.html
13. Espejel-Trujillo, A., Castillo Camacho, I., Nakano-Miyatake, M., Perez-Meana, H.: Identity document authentication based on VSS and QR codes. Procedia Technol. **3**, 241–250 (2012). https://doi.org/10.1016/j.protcy.2012.03.026
14. Goyal, V., Jain, A., Pandey, O., Sahai, A.: Bounded ciphertext policy attribute based encryption. In: Aceto, L., Damgård, I., Goldberg, L.A., Halldórsson, M.M., Ingólfsdóttir, A., Walukiewicz, I. (eds.) ICALP 2008. LNCS, vol. 5126, pp. 579–591. Springer, Heidelberg (2008). https://doi.org/10.1007/978-3-540-70583-3_47
15. ISO/IEC 18004:2015(E): Information technology – automatic identification and data capture techniques – QR code bar code symbology specification. Standard, International Organization for Standardization (2015)

16. Jaroszewski, P.: How to get good seats in the security theater? Hacking boarding passes for fun and profit, May 2016. https://www.defcon.org

17. Khammarnia, M., Kassani, A., Eslahi, M.: The efficacy of patients' wristband bar-code on prevention of medical errors. Appl. Clin. Inform. **6**, 716–727 (2015). https://doi.org/10.4338/ACI-2015-06-R-0077

18. Krombholz, K., Frühwirt, P., Kieseberg, P., Kapsalis, I., Huber, M., Weippl, E.: QR code security: a survey of attacks and challenges for usable security. In: Tryfonas, T., Askoxylakis, I. (eds.) HAS 2014. LNCS, vol. 8533, pp. 79–90. Springer, Cham (2014). https://doi.org/10.1007/978-3-319-07620-1_8

19. Lai, J., Deng, R.H., Li, Y.: Fully secure cipertext-policy hiding CP-ABE. In: Bao, F., Weng, J. (eds.) ISPEC 2011. LNCS, vol. 6672, pp. 24–39. Springer, Heidelberg (2011). https://doi.org/10.1007/978-3-642-21031-0_3

20. Lin, P., Chen, Y., Lu, E.J., Chen, P.: Secret hiding mechanism using QR barcode. In: 2013 International Conference on Signal-Image Technology Internet-Based Systems, pp. 22–25 (2013). https://doi.org/10.1109/SITIS.2013.15

21. Lin, P.-Y., Chen, Y.-H.: High payload secret hiding technology for QR codes. EURASIP J. Image Video Process. **2017**(1), 1–8 (2017). https://doi.org/10.1186/s13640-016-0155-0

22. Meruga, J., et al.: Multi-layered covert QR codes for increased capacity and security **37**, 17–27 (2015). https://doi.org/10.1080/1206212X.2015.1061254

23. Neurotechnology: Megamatcher SDK, November 2020. https://www.neurotechnology.com/megamatcher-algorithm-tests.html#tests_finger_face_iris

24. Niceware International LLC: Patient Safety with Bar Code and RFID Labeling Identification. White paper, December 2006

25. Noppakaew, P., Khomkuth, S., Sriwilas, S.: Construction of multi-layered QR codes utilizing partitions of positive integers. J. Math. Comput. Sci. **18**, 306–313 (2018). https://doi.org/10.22436/jmcs.018.03.06

26. Qryptal: The simpler approach to secure and verify documents. https://www.qryptal.com/landingpages/signed-qr-code/

27. Sahai, A., Waters, B.: Fuzzy identity-based encryption. In: Cramer, R. (ed.) EUROCRYPT 2005. LNCS, vol. 3494, pp. 457–473. Springer, Heidelberg (2005). https://doi.org/10.1007/11426639_27

28. Shamir, A.: How to share a secret. Commun. ACM **22**(11), 612–613 (1979). https://doi.org/10.1145/359168.359176

29. SITA: Air Transport IT Insights 2019. SITA. https://www.sita.aero/resources/type/surveys-reports/air-transport-it-insights-2019

An Attack on Quantum Circuits Based on the Error Rates of NISQ Systems and a Countermeasure

Nikita Acharya, Vedika Saravanan, and Samah Mohamed Saeed[(✉)]

City College of New York, City University of New York, New York, USA
{nachary000,vsarava000}@citymail.cuny.edu, ssaeed@ccny.cuny.edu

Abstract. Noisy Intermediate Scale Quantum (NISQ) computers are subject to different sources of noise. To enhance the reliability of quantum computers, noise-aware quantum compilers are used to generate the quantum circuit. A quantum compiler maps the quantum circuit to a physical circuit that can be executed on the quantum hardware. A malicious compiler can launch several attacks to increase the error rates in the circuit, and thus, corrupt the circuit output. To detect these attacks, we utilize circuit test points, which provide the meta-information of the circuit errors, and thus, detect any unexpected changes in the circuit error rates.

1 Introduction

Quantum computing is a rapidly growing field in computing. Applications of quantum computing are based on well-known quantum algorithms including but not limited to the Harrow-Hassidim-Lloyd (HHL) algorithm for linear systems of equations [6], the Grover Search [4], the Variational-Quantum-Eigensolver (VQE) [12], the Quantum Fourier Transform (QFT) [10], and the Quantum Approximate Optimization Algorithm (QAOA) [17]. Potential applications are cryptography [14], searching in big database [4], chemical simulations [8], and solving optimization problems [17]. Many companies like Google, Intel, and IBM have developed quantum computers with a limited number of noisy quantum bits (qubits). These machines do not have enough number of qubits to support error correction. We referred to these computers as Noisy Intermediate Scale Quantum (NISQ) computers.

The input to the quantum computer is a quantum circuit. Each circuit consists of gates, which modify the state of the qubits. In NISQ systems, noisy physical qubits are allocated to create a physical quantum circuit. To enhance the reliability of the circuit output, noise-aware quantum compilers are used to generate the physical quantum circuit. A quantum compiler decomposes complex quantum operations into elementary gates [10]. Then, it allocates physical qubits and schedules their operations based on the device fidelity information and its coupling constraint [5,7,13,15,19,21]. It also optimizes the quantum circuit using several optimization approaches (e.g. rule-based optimization [9]). Finally,

© Springer Nature Switzerland AG 2021
Y. Park et al. (Eds.): SVCC 2020, CCIS 1383, pp. 109–114, 2021.
https://doi.org/10.1007/978-3-030-72725-3_8

the optimized physical quantum circuit is executed on the quantum computer. This process can reduce the impact of errors on the circuit output. In order to select qubits and schedule the circuit operations, a compiler utilizes the back-end physical properties including the measurement and the gate error rates, the qubit coherence time, and the coupling constraint of the quantum device.

The compiler generates quantum circuits with the objective of minimizing their error rates while satisfying the coherence requirement of the qubits. A malicious compiler, on the other hand, can inject more errors into the circuit. We exploit such vulnerability to launch an attack on quantum circuits and propose a countermeasure to thwart this attack.

2   Attack

The output of the quantum circuit is sensitive to variable errors, which depend on the allocated physical qubits and the scheduled operations [16]. The variability in the hardware error rates can be exploited by a compromised compiler, which can select qubits with low fidelity, and thus, impact the circuit output. Malicious qubit allocations can also result in very noisy operations or additional gates in the form of swap operations. Each swap operation consists of three two-qubit (Controlled Not) gates. The user is unaware of any malicious changes made to the quantum compiler since the resulting circuit to be executed on the quantum computer is still functionally equivalent to the original quantum algorithm. This attack can also impact the reputation of the quantum hardware company.

To illustrate the impact of the attack, we consider a quantum circuit that consists of a single Toffoli gate with three control lines as shown in Fig. 1(a). The expected output of the Toffoli circuit when all the control lines are set to one is 1111. Two possible qubit allocations of the Toffoli quantum circuit, which satisfy the coupling constraint of IBM Q16 Melbourne quantum computer are shown in Fig. 1(b). The qubit allocation of the quantum circuit, which minimizes the circuit error rates, is highlighted in green color (q_0, q_1, q_2 and q_{14}). On the other hand, the qubit allocation under the attack is highlighted in red color. The attacker chooses q_4, q_8, q_9 and q_{10} qubits with low gate and qubit fidelity to increase the circuit error rates. Figure 1(c) shows the output distribution of the quantum circuit in the absence and the presence of the attack. The results show that the expected output can only be extracted from the attack-free circuit with a probability of 70%.

3   Countermeasure

We proposed a software-based approach to provide error rates of the quantum circuit at runtime [2]. A user can rely on these error rates to decide whether to accept the circuit output. We utilize different test points to generate a set of test circuits including classical, superposition [20], and un-compute tests [2]. The test circuits are executed on a NISQ computer in addition to the entire physical quantum circuit to provide meta-information of the runtime error rates

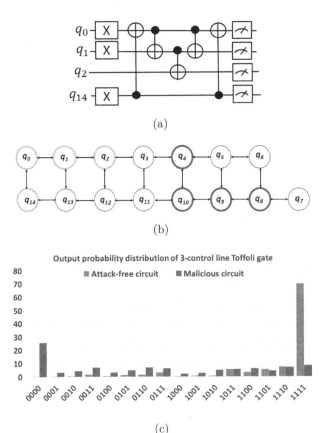

Fig. 1. (a) Toffoli circuit satisfying IBM Q16 Melbourne coupling constraint. (b) The coupling graph of IBM Q16 Melbourne architecture with two possible physical qubit allocations for the Toffoli circuit in the absence (highlighted in green) and the presence (highlighted in red) of the attack. (c) The resulting output distribution of the Toffoli circuit generated using the two qubit allocations. (Color figure online)

at different points of the circuit. In classical assertion, the qubits are inspected to check whether they are in a classical state 0 or 1. The test point outcome is validated by measuring the circuit qubits that are in a classical state. For superposition tests, ancillary qubits are utilized which are entangled with the test qubits and measured to provide information about the superposition state of the qubits. To generate uncompute test circuits, the quantum circuit is divided into partitions. For each subset of the partitions, we uncompute all the gates within these partitions by applying their inverse operations in a reverse order such that the qubits state is returned back to the initial state. All the qubits are then measured, which evaluate to zero in the absence of noise. The output of the test circuits can be used to learn the quantum circuit error rates.

To detect any suspicious changes in the circuit behavior due to false error rates, we verify the backend error rates using a minimum number of test circuits by comparing error rates of two diverse physical implementations of the same quantum circuit. A simple reliability model, referred to as Estimated Success Probability (ESP), is used to allocate another set of qubits and operations with lower success rate to construct the physical quantum circuit. ESP is computed by multiplying the success probability of every gate and measurement operation in the quantum circuit [11].

We generate and execute the same test circuits under the two qubit allocations and compare the corresponding test circuit outputs. We count the number of the test circuit pairs, which behave as expected (ET), and use it to compute the Percentage of Effective Tests (PET) as $\frac{ET}{N} \times 100$, where N is the total number of test pairs. A high PET (greater than 50%) indicates that the circuit behaves as expected.

4   Validation

We validated our approach using different quantum circuit executed on IBM Q16 Melbourne quantum computer. We use Bernstein–Vazirani(BV) [3] quantum algorithm with different numbers of qubits, Grover Search algorithm (Grover) [4], and other reversible circuits including Decoder, Adder, and Toffoli gates obtained from RevLib [18]. All the benchmark circuits are compiled using the Qiskit SDK compiler [1]. We use the highest level of optimization given by Qiskit compiler which maps the logical quantum circuit to a physical quantum circuit that satisfies the hardware constraints with high ESP. This mapping is referred to as the *Original Mapping*. Next, we generate another physical qubit allocation that has the lowest ESP. We refer to this allocation as the *Compromised Mapping*. We generate classical, superposition and uncompute test circuits for both of these mappings. The Original Mapping and the Compromised Mapping circuits in addition to their test circuits are executed in the quantum computer for 8192 runs and the output distributions are extracted based on which the PET is computed.

Figure 2 shows the percentage of the expected output of the two mappings for each circuit executed on IBM Q16 Melbourne quantum computer in addition to the corresponding PET. The green bars are the percentage of the expected output of the Original Mapping circuits while the red bars are the percentage of the expected output of the Compromised Mapping circuits. We notice that all the Compromised Mapping circuits fail to provide the expected output as the most dominant output in the output distribution, which indicates that by manipulating the error rates an attacker can change the circuit output. Thus, we rely on the PET with respect to the Original Mapping circuits. The PET in blue color is always greater than 50%, which indicates that the Original Mapping circuits utilize the actual error rates of the hardware, and therefore, behave as expected.

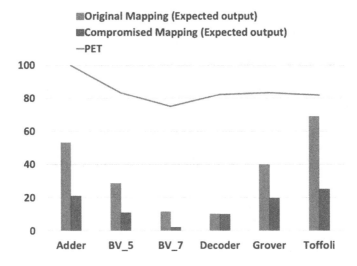

Fig. 2. The expected output percentage of the original and compromised mapping circuits and their corresponding PET.

5   Conclusion

In this paper, we explore a possible attack on quantum circuits executed on NISQ computers based on the variation in the qubit error rates and propose a countermeasure to detect this attack. We leverage different types of tests including superposition, classical, and uncompute tests to study the error rates of the circuit. We identify the test points of the quantum circuit under different qubit allocations. The test circuits are executed on the quantum computer. We show that PET can detect unexpected changes in the circuit error rates. Our approach will help to set up a path to monitor the quantum circuit behavior.

References

1. Abraham, H., et al.: Qiskit: an open-source framework for quantum computing (2019). https://doi.org/10.5281/zenodo.2562110
2. Acharya, N., Saeed, S.M.: A lightweight approach to detect malicious/unexpected changes in the error rates of NISQ computers. In: Proceedings of 2020 IEEE/ACM International Conference On Computer Aided Design (ICCAD), pp. 1–9 (2020)
3. Du, J., et al.: Implementation of a quantum algorithm to solve the Bernstein-Vazirani parity problem without entanglement on an ensemble quantum computer. Phys. Rev. A **64**(4) (2001). https://doi.org/10.1103/physreva.64.042306
4. Grover, L.K.: A fast quantum mechanical algorithm for database search. In: Proceedings of the Twenty-Eighth Annual ACM Symposium on Theory of Computing. STOC 1996, pp. 212–219. Association for Computing Machinery, New York (1996). https://doi.org/10.1145/237814.237866
5. Guerreschi, G.G., Park, J.: Two-step approach to scheduling quantum circuits. Quantum Sci. Technol. **3**(4), 045003 (2018)

6. Harrow, A.W., Hassidim, A., Lloyd, S.: Quantum algorithm for linear systems of equations. Phys. Rev. Lett. **103**, 150502 (2009). https://doi.org/10.1103/PhysRevLett.103.150502
7. Li, G., Ding, Y., Xie, Y.: Tackling the qubit mapping problem for NISQ-era quantum devices. In: Proceedings of the Twenty-Fourth International Conference on Architectural Support for Programming Languages and Operating Systems, pp. 1001–1014. ACM (2019)
8. McCaskey, A.J., et al.: Quantum chemistry as a benchmark for near-term quantum computers. npj Quantum Inf. **5**(1), 99 (2019)
9. Miller, D.M., Maslov, D., Dueck, G.W.: A transformation based algorithm for reversible logic synthesis. In: Proceedings of Design Automation Conference, pp. 318–323 (2003)
10. Nielsen, M., Chuang, I.: Quantum Computation and Quantum Information. Cambridge University Press, Cambridge (2000)
11. Nishio, S., Pan, Y., Satoh, T., Amano, H., Meter, R.V.: Extracting success from IBM's 20-qubit machines using error-aware compilation. CoRR abs/1903.10963 (2019). http://arxiv.org/abs/1903.10963
12. Peruzzo, A., et al.: A variational eigenvalue solver on a photonic quantum processor. Nat. Commun. **5**(1), 4213 (2014). https://doi.org/10.1038/ncomms5213
13. Rasconi, R., Oddi, A.: An innovative genetic algorithm for the quantum circuit compilation problem. In: Proceedings of the AAAI Conference on Artificial Intelligence, vol. 33, pp. 7707–7714, July 2019. https://doi.org/10.1609/aaai.v33i01.33017707
14. Shor, P.W.: Algorithms for quantum computation: discrete logarithms and factoring. In: Proceedings of the Annual Symposium on Foundations of Computer Science, pp. 124–134 (1994)
15. Siraichi, M.Y., dos Santos, V.F., Collange, S., Pereira, F.M.Q.: Qubit allocation. In: Proceedings of International Symposium on Code Generation and Optimization, pp. 113–125. ACM (2018)
16. Tannu, S.S., Qureshi, M.K.: Not all qubits are created equal: a case for variability-aware policies for NISQ-era quantum computers. In: Proceedings of International Conference on Architectural Support for Programming Languages and Operating Systems, pp. 987–999. ACM (2019)
17. Wang, Z., Hadfield, S., Jiang, Z., Rieffel, E.G.: Quantum approximate optimization algorithm for MaxCut: a fermionic view. Phys. Rev. A **97**, 022304 (2018). https://doi.org/10.1103/PhysRevA.97.022304
18. Wille, R., Grosse, D., Teuber, L., Dueck, G.W., Drechsler, R.: RevLib: an online resource for reversible functions and reversible circuits. In: Proceedings of International Symposium on Multiple Valued Logic, pp. 220–225 (2008)
19. Wille, R., Burgholzer, L., Zulehner, A.: Mapping quantum circuits to IBM QX architectures using the minimal number of SWAP and H operations. In: Proceedings of Design Automation Conference, p. 142–1 (2019)
20. Zhou, H., Byrd, G.T.: Quantum circuits for dynamic runtime assertions in quantum computation. IEEE Comput. Archit. Lett. **18**(2), 111–114 (2019). https://doi.org/10.1109/lca.2019.2935049
21. Zulehner, A., Wille, R.: Make it reversible: efficient embedding of non-reversible functions. In: Proceedings of Design Automation and Test in Europe, pp. 458–463 (2017)

Blockchain and Security

SpartanGold: A Blockchain for Education, Experimentation, and Rapid Prototyping

Thomas H. Austin$^{(\boxtimes)}$ (ID)

San José State University, San Jose, CA 95192, USA
thomas.austin@sjsu.edu

Abstract. Since the introduction of Bitcoin and the blockchain, the cryptocurrency space has seen rapid innovation in both academic research and in cutting edge designs from industry. Student interest has likewise increased rapidly.

All of these areas would benefit from the ability to rapidly prototype ideas without becoming bogged down in complex code bases: academic researchers need a way to highlight key concepts of their designs; industry engineers could vet their early designs and identify potential challenges; and students would be able to play with key concepts of the blockchain in a simple, easy to understand codebase.

This paper introduces SpartanGold, a blockchain implementation written in JavaScript patterned after Bitcoin. Several features of Bitcoin's design are simplified or eliminated, though those features may be added in easily. SpartanGold supports a single-threaded mode where miners communicate via JavaScript events, and a multi-process mode where miners and clients send messages over TCP/IP. While the former mode simplifies testing and can provide cleaner demonstrations, the latter mode provides a more realistic experience. We show the utility of SpartanGold by implementing different designs of mining pools and by showing how Bitcoin's UTXO model could be added to SpartanGold.

Keywords: Blockchain · Cryptocurrency · Education

1 Introduction

Since the introduction of Bitcoin [21], interest in cryptocurrencies and the blockchain has exploded. As the Bitcoin ecosystem has evolved, new challenges have emerged like selfish mining [7] and mining pools [29]. Problems with Bitcoin's proof-of-work model have become evident, and alternate consensus mechanisms [15–18] have been proposed or used in practice. Finally, alternate protocols have tried to extend the promise of what Bitcoin's design hinted at, such as Ethereum's quasi-Turing complete virtual machine [38].

Despite the excitement surrounding these mechanisms, they are often not well understood. In part, the code bases for many of the leading cryptocurrencies are written in high-performing programming languages such as C++, Rust,

© Springer Nature Switzerland AG 2021
Y. Park et al. (Eds.): SVCC 2020, CCIS 1383, pp. 117–133, 2021.
https://doi.org/10.1007/978-3-030-72725-3_9

or Go; while these languages seem like good choices for the real-world implementations, they introduce a barrier to understanding the design for programmers not already familiar with these languages.

Within industry, many blockchain startups promote their ideas through the use of whitepapers and public presentations. While they can be useful, many key issues of the design are often left unclear. Furthermore, subtle challenges can be left undiscovered until companies have already committed substantial engineering effort to a project.

This paper introduces *SpartanGold*[1], a simplified blockchain-based cryptocurrency designed for experimentation and rapid prototyping. Its design is patterned after Bitcoin, but with many features either simplified or removed. The codebase is written in JavaScript, a language widely used in a variety of domains and a language already of interest to developers of blockchain-based distributed apps (Dapps).

With SpartanGold, students can experiment with different features of blockchain designs and study those features in isolation. For industry, SpartanGold serves as a tool to prototype different concepts and to promote new ideas.

2 Popular Cryptocurrency Code Bases

Before we delve into the design of SpartanGold, we first informally survey the other cryptocurrency codebases out there. While all of these projects involve a mixture of programming languages, usually the core of the codebase is written in a single language. By far, the two most commonly used languages seem to be C++ and Go, though there are occasional projects or project components written in Rust.

Bitcoin's reference implementation [2] is written in C++. As a result, cryptocurrencies that initially forked off of Bitcoin like Primecoin [27] and Peercoin [24] are also predominantly C++ code bases. Other early cryptocurrencies such as Litecoin [19] and Dogecoin [5] also seemed to follow suit and have code bases in C++.

Since those early currencies, there has been a noticeable rise in the use of the Go programming language, though many newer projects still use C++. Algorand [10], Thundercore [23, 37], and 0Chain [1] all use Go, whereas Monero [20], Ripple's XRP [36] and EOS [6] rely on C++ instead. (We should note that a significant chunk of the EOS codebase appears to be written in WebAssembly.) Dfinity [4, 14] instead seems to rely on Rust.

Some projects involve a mix of multiple codebases written in different programming languages. For Cosmos, its Tendermint Core [31] is a Go codebase, though a Rust implementation [34] is available. However, certain of its components, such as the ABCI server [32], are written in Rust. Similarly, Filecoin [8] uses Go for Project Lotus [28], but instead uses Rust for its Filecoin Proving

---

[1] https://www.spartangold.net/.

Subsystem [9]. Ethereum [11] and related projects are written in Go. However, the Solidity compiler [30] for Ethereum is written in C++.

A smattering of other programming languages are used for other projects, with a noticeable bent towards statically typed functional programming languages for projects growing out of academia. For example, Cardano [3] is primarily written in Haskell, whereas Tezos [12,35] prefers OCaml.

3   Choice of JavaScript

The survey in Sect. 2 shows a clear preference for languages that offer high performance (C++/Go), strong security guarantees (Haskell/OCaml), or both (Rust). While these languages make strong choices for production implementations, they introduce significant barriers for starting new projects.

Complaints about C++ are very common, especially its slow build times and lack of memory safety. In fact, complaints about C++ were part of the motivation for the designers of both the Go programming language and for Rust.

An obvious question arises: why JavaScript, and not Go or Rust? This section reviews the advantages of JavaScript, and why it serves as an ideal choice for an experimental code base.

Familiarity to Students. Java and Python are the two most common languages in introductory courses [13], which is an argument for using these languages instead. However, while JavaScript is not as well known by students, its design makes it relatively easy for Java or Python programmers to learn. Like these other languages, JavaScript supports object-oriented programming. SpartanGold uses classes, available since ECMAScript 2015, rather than prototypes in order to minimize the learning curve for students new to the language. Particularly for Java programmers, the coding style and naming conventions in JavaScript are very familiar.

Ubiquitous Nature of JavaScript. Perhaps more than any other language, JavaScript shows up everywhere. Though it began as a language for client-side programming, it is often used with Node.js as a server-side language. Of particular interest to developers in the blockchain space, JavaScript is one of the core components used in the development of Ethereum decentralized applications (Dapps). Due to its prevalence, many developers are already very familiar with this language.

Run-to-Completion Model. In JavaScript, the current task always runs to completion. While this complicates some aspects of SpartanGold's design such as mining, it avoids many subtle problems that can arise with concurrency bugs.

Extensive Library Support. Due to its prevalence, JavaScript offers a large number of libraries and frameworks. For some of the more advanced blockchain protocols, this wealth of tools is a strong advantage.

4   SpartanGold Design

The name SpartanGold is intended to highlight both its minimalist nature as well as its focus on cryptocurrencies. SpartanGold is patterned after Bitcoin's design, but several features are simplified or removed. The goal of the project is to strip down the design to its essence, and thereby avoid distracting developers with less central concepts. In this section, we review which features of Bitcoin we kept and which we discarded. In addition, we highlight some key parts of SpartanGold's architecture.

Like Bitcoin, SpartanGold uses a proof-of-work mechanism to achieve Nakamoto consensus, where miners earn transaction fees paid by clients and newly-minted coins (the coinbase amount) in exchange for their work. Unlike Bitcoin, the proof-of-work is fixed at creation and not adjusted over time. Transactions are stored in a JavaScript Map rather than in a Merkle tree, and there is no limit on the total size of blocks.

Two design features in particular change the nature of SpartanGold:

1. It uses an account-based model, similar to Ethereum's design, rather than an unspent-transaction output (UTXO) model.
2. There is no support for a scripting language built in to the blockchain.

The UTXO model is interesting, and the first incarnation of SpartanGold did in fact use a UTXO model to follow Bitcoin more closely. However, students struggled to understand this feature, and it unnecessarily complicated the design of some projects extending SpartanGold. Therefore, the project was refactored to change to an account-based model instead.

In the account-based model, every user is associated with some amount of coins (or "gold", in SpartanGold's parlance). This design makes it somewhat easier to identify the chain of transactions belonging to a user, unless they make multiple accounts. Additional information can then be associated with the accounts. For instance, in Ethereum each account uses a nonce value to order the transactions of a given client.

Fortunately, SpartanGold can be extended to use a UTXO model if desired. Section 5.2 describes how that is done.

Bitcoin offers a scripting language of limited power to provide for a variety of transaction forms. This design gives Bitcoin surprising flexibility. However, we felt that its introduction would overcomplicate SpartanGold's design. Instead, SpartanGold only allows for the transfer of funds from one user to (one or more) other users.

4.1   Classes

As mentioned previously, SpartanGold is organized in classes. The key classes are:

– **Transaction**, storing information about a specific transaction.

- **Block**, storing a collection of transactions. This class is also responsible for tracking balances and validating transactions.
- **Client**, responsible for managing the client's keys, for posting transactions, and for storing blocks.
- **Miner**, extending **Client**. Miners are responsible for collecting transactions into blocks and for finding valid proof-of-work values.
- **Blockchain**, storing configuration settings and constants for the blockchain. It also includes several utility methods.

These different pieces are reviewed below.

Transactions. Transactions in SpartanGold are sent across the network in JavaScript Object Notation format (JSON). The fields are:

- **from**: indicating the account of the sender, derived from the sender's public key.
- **nonce**: specifying a sequential nonce, specific to the sender's account.
- **sig**: The senders signature for the transaction.
- **pubKey**: The public key, matching the sender's account.
- **fee**: A transaction fee, specifying the amount of gold given to the miner that finds a proof for the block.
- **outputs**: An array of account/amount pairs, indicating how much gold should be given to each account.
- **data**: A free-form JSON object (optional).

The **data** field is worth special mention. By design, it can include whatever the user desires. However, when the sender signs the transaction, this field is included, so any attempt to modify its contents can be detected. With this field, it is possible to add any information needed for different blockchain designs.

Block. As with transactions, blocks are sent across the network in JSON format. However, blocks include additional information about balances that are *not* included when serialized.

The **addTransaction** method accepts a transaction. It verifies that the transaction is properly formed and signed, that it is not a replayed transaction (checking the nonce value), and that the sender has sufficient funds. If so, the transaction is added to the block. The block then updates the balances for the sender and for all receivers.

The **rerun** method is used whenever a block is received from another miner. It accepts the previous block in the blockchain as its argument and initializes all balances to match that of the previous block. All of the transactions in the current block are then re-added, verifying that there are sufficient funds and that there are no other problems. If any transaction fails, this method returns **false** to indicate that the block is invalid.

Client. The client is responsible for tracking a user's keys, for posting transactions, and for storing blocks.

The `receiveBlock` method accepts a block from a miner. It verifies the block is valid and stores it. However, if the client is missing blocks preceding this block in the blockchain, it requests the previous block from the network. This mechanism allows a client to gather the blocks that it is missing if it starts after the blockchain is already running.

If the received block is further in the chain than the client's current best block, the client switches to treat this block as the most current block in the blockchain. (This design is similar to Bitcoin, but slightly simplified. Instead of taking the longest chain, Bitcoin miners select the chain with the most computational work. In most cases, the longest chain also involves the most computational work, but due to Bitcoin's variable proof-of-work target, that is not necessarily so.)

The `postTransaction` method takes an array of outputs (client account/gold amount pairs) and a transaction fee, and creates a transaction with this information. It then signs the transaction with the client's private key and broadcasts it to the network.

Miner. A miner is a client that also collects transactions into blocks and searches for a valid proof-of-work.

This class features a `startNewSearch` method, which creates a new block and begins searching for a valid proof of work. This method is therefore the ideal place to add any additional information that might be needed for a block.

The `findProof` method increments the `proof` field of a block until the hash value of that block is lower than the proof-of-work target. At that point, the miner broadcasts the block to the network. Once that block has been validated, every miner accepts the block and begins a new search for the subsequent block.

Due to JavaScript's run-to-completion design, setting up the `findProof` method takes some care or else no other code could run until it found a valid proof. To address this issue, every miner has a `miningRounds` property. This property dictates how long a miner will search for a proof before pausing to allow other events to be processed.

Changing the `miningRounds` property does not have much impact on the miner's behavior in multi-process mode. However, in single-threaded mode, this property directly correlates to mining power. For instance, if one miner has a `miningRounds` value of 500, and another miner has a value of 2000, the second miner will perform four times as many hashes whenever it is its turn to mine.

Blockchain. This class stores various configuration details for the blockchain, such as the proof-of-work target and the amount of coinbase rewards given to a miner for finding a block. It also includes various utility methods, including a `makeGenesis` method responsible for making the first block in the blockchain and initializing client balances.

4.2   Single-Threaded Mode

SpartanGold's clients and miners respond to various events, which serve as the core mechanism for simulating messages across the network. A `FakeNet` class is responsible for sending messages between clients and miners.

```
sendMessage(address, msg, o) {
  if (typeof o !== 'object')
    throw new Error(`Expecting an object, but
        got a ${typeof o}`);

  // Serializing/deserializing the object to
    prevent
  // cheating in single threaded mode.
  let o2 = JSON.parse(JSON.stringify(o));

  const client = this.clients.get(address);

  let delay = Math.floor(Math.random() * this.
    messageDelayMax);

  if (Math.random() > this.chanceMessageFails)
      {
    setTimeout(() => client.emit(msg, o2),
      delay);
  }
}
```

Fig. 1. sendMessage method from FakeNet class.

Figure 1 shows how the message passing works. The `sendMessage` primitive accepts an address to receive the message, a `msg` field that specifies the event to trigger, and the object representing the actual message to be passed. To avoid any accidental cheats, the object is stringified and then parsed. (This design helps to catch problems where a codebase would work in a single-threaded simulation, but not when communicating over the network.) After looking up the client by address, `client.emit` can then be used to send the message.

By default, messages are guaranteed delivery and always show up in order. However, it is possible to simulate less ideal network conditions by introducing random message delays or a probability of messages being dropped.

Figure 2 shows an example of a sample simulation. In this scenario, there are 2 miners, `minnie` and `mickey`, as well as three additional clients `alice`, `bob`, and `charlie`. Alice transfers 40 gold to Bob, and after 5 s the simulation terminates, displaying the balances for all accounts according to Minnie's perspective.

4.3 Multi-process Mode

While single-threaded mode allows us to set up simple, easy-to-run experiments, it lacks a touch of realism. Fortunately, it is easy to modify SpartanGold so that miners communicate over the network instead. By extending the `FakeNet` class and overriding the `sendMessage` method, different network protocols may be used instead.

The SpartanGold module comes built in with a `TcpMiner` that extends the `Miner` class with methods to register and connect with other miners over TCP/IP. Modifying the `FakeNet` class itself is straightforward; only the `sendMessage` method needs to be overridden, and the rest of its logic remains unchanged. With this change, SpartanGold miners can now be run in separate processes, and will send all messages to one another over the network. Figure 3 shows the text-based interface for this mode.

5 Use Cases

SpartanGold has been used to model various scenarios in an upper-division "blockchain and cryptocurrencies" computer science course at San José State University. In addition, it has been the basis of a few master's thesis projects. Pillai [25] used it as the basis for her model on *earmarked UTXOs*, and Pardeshi [22] implemented the TontineCoin model of Pollett et al. [26]. It has also been used for the design of a proof-of-stake protocol [33] patterned after Tendermint.

In this section, we review a few additional cases in more depth to show the utility of SpartanGold.

5.1 Mining Pools

Bitcoin miners have become increasingly specialized. While the early vision of Bitcoin was that everyone could mine using their desktop or laptop machines, the landscape changed as first GPU mining rigs and then ASIC miners came to dominate. These specialized machines are good for mining Bitcoin, and not much else. They also tend to consume a significant amount of electricity. As a result, miners have become a specialized group of investors very concerned about receiving a payout for their investment.

The irregular payout mechanism makes mining as an investment vaguely akin to buying a bunch of lottery tickets, albeit for a well-paying lottery. To achieve a

```
let fakeNet = new FakeNet();

// Clients
let alice = new Client({
  name: "Alice",
  net: fakeNet
});
let bob = new Client({
  name: "Bob",
  net: fakeNet
});
let charlie = new Client({
  name: "Charlie",
  net: fakeNet
});

// Miners
let minnie = new Miner({
  name: "Minnie",
  net: fakeNet});
let mickey = new Miner({
  name: "Mickey",
  net: fakeNet
});

// Creating genesis block
let genesis = Blockchain.makeGenesis({
  blockClass: Block,
  transactionClass: Transaction,
  clientBalanceMap: new Map([
    [alice,  233],
    [bob,  99],
    [charlie,  67],
    [minnie,  400],
    [mickey,  300],
  ]),
});

fakeNet.register(alice,bob,charlie,minnie,mickey);

// Miners start mining.
minnie.initialize();
mickey.initialize();

// Alice transfers some money to Bob.
alice.postTransaction([{
  amount: 40,
  address: bob.address
}]);

// Print out the final balances after 5 seconds.
setTimeout(() => {
  minnie.showAllBalances();
  process.exit(0);
}, 5000);
```

Fig. 2. Sample simulation setup using single-threaded mode

```
Balances:
   hDDXlpBFlnKViXVhbpJbf+tua7F8yMPIYtjJ+8KbWbk=:  501
   6NMB4xXkGniLmeGBemXUZ7QOEDeo3uXP15fuGpcUq0A=:  402


Funds: 501
Address: hDDXlpBFlnKViXVhbpJbf+tua7F8yMPIYtjJ+8KbWbk=
Pending transactions:

What would you like to do?
*(c)onnect to miner?
*(t)ransfer funds?
*(r)esend pending transactions?
*show (b)alances?
*show blocks for (d)ebugging and exit?
*(s)ave your state?
*e(x)it without saving?

Your choice:
```

Fig. 3. Multi-process mode interface

more regular payout, miners have formed *mining pools*, combining their hashing power and dividing the rewards with one another according to the work that they contributed.

An *operator* manages the pool, assigning blocks to the other miners and tracking the rewards that should be paid to each miner in the pool. In order to prove how much computational effort they are contributing, miners send *shares* to the operator. A share is a block with a hash value that does not meet the required proof-of-work target, but which does meet a second target value specified by the mining pool.

Several different forms of mining pools exist, with pay-per-share (PPS), proportional (PROP), and pay-per-last-N-shares (PPLNS) being the most common designs. Rosenfeld [29] provides an excellent overview of mining pools, their designs, and the attacks that they are vulnerable to. In the remainder of this section, we show how SpartanGold can be used to highlight the difference between the different styles of mining pools.

Both operators and pool miners handle some of the responsibilities of a standalone miner. The operator handles the collection of transactions into a block, but does not search for a valid proof-of-work. The pool miners do not collect transactions or attempt to create blocks, but instead focus on finding valid proofs. In our implementation, both `PoolMiner` and `PoolOperator` extend the `Miner` class. The `PoolMiner` behavior does not change with the different mining pool designs; we omit its implementation, instead focusing on the `PoolOperator` class.

The operator includes a `poolNet` field, which is a `FakeNet` instance connecting it to the miners in the pool that it manages. When starting a new search, the operator creates a block, adds transactions to it, and then sends it to its miners, as the code below shows:

```
startNewSearch () {
    let block = Blockchain.makeBlock(
        this.address,
        this.lastBlock);

    // Add queued-up transactions to block.
    this.transactions.forEach((tx) => {
        block.addTransaction(tx, this);
    });
    this.transactions.clear();

    // Sending the block to the pool miners
    this.poolNet.broadcast(NEW_POOL_BLOCK, block);
}
```

Whenever the operator receives a share from a miner in the pool, it verifies that the share is valid. If so, it calls the **rewardMiner** method. If the share is also valid as a block proof, the operator announces the block to the rest of the SpartanGold network, and calls the **payRewards** method.

The code below shows this behavior of operators when receiving shares:

```
receiveShare (msg) {
    let { block, minerAddress } = msg;
    block = Blockchain.deserializeBlock(block);

    if (!this.hasValidShare(block)) {
        this.log(`Invalid share.`);
        return;
    }

    this.rewardMiner(minerAddress);

    if (block.hasValidProof()) {
        this.log(`Mining pool proof: ${block.proof}`);
        this.currentBlock = block;
        this.announceProof();
        this.payRewards();
    }
}
```

The behavior of calling these methods varies based on the design of the mining pool. We review the code for each of the three mining pool styles discussed previously.

For a PPS miner, the operator immediately pays a reward to a miner as soon as that miner reports a share. Once a valid proof for a block is found, the operator takes the entire reward for itself. Figure 4 shows the implementation of the reward methods.

With a PPS mining pool, the operator bears significant financial risk, potentially going broke if the miners in the pool find many shares but never report a

```
rewardMiner(minerAddress) {
  this.postTransaction([{
    address: minerAddress,
    amount: SHARE_REWARD
  }], 0);
}

payRewards() {
  // Do nothing.
}
```

Fig. 4. Reward method implementations for a PPS mining pool operator

valid block proof. As a result, the fees for this style of mining pool tend to be higher than other styles.

A PROP mining pool follows a different strategy, paying miners nothing initially when they find a share, instead just recording that a share was discovered. Once a proof for a block is discovered, the operator writes a transaction paying all miners who contributed to the block based on the number of shares they discovered. Figure 5 shows the methods implementing this reward structure.

While PROP mining pools eliminate the operator's risk, looking at the code highlights a potentially significant issue. As the number of shares increases, the reward paid to each miner drops. At some point, it becomes in the financial best interest of miners in the mining pool to switch to a different mining pool that is paying better rewards. This mining strategy is referred to as a *pool hopping attack*.

To address this weakness, PPLNS mining pools only reward the most recent N shares. For instance, if $N = 10$ and 10 shares have already been discovered, the oldest of these shares is discarded when the 11th share comes in. This design eliminates the incentive for pool hopping, while still avoiding any financial risk for the operator. Because of its benefits, PPLNS pools have come to dominate over time. Figure 6 shows the reward methods for this style of mining pool.

5.2 Unspent Transaction Output Model

As mentioned previously, SpartanGold does not follow Bitcoin's UTXO model, opting instead for the simpler account-based approach. However, by extending SpartanGold it is possible to introduce this design into the protocol.

Although the full implementation is too complex to include in this paper, the modified `Client.postTransaction` method is illuminating. Figure 7 shows that method.

The first ten lines of this method are no different than the standard `postTransaction` method. On lines 11–13, we begin to see a difference. Unlike with an account-based model, the UTXO model assumes that a client has multiple addresses, each associated with its own key. On line 16–23, the client collects

```
rewardMiner(minerAddress) {
  this.pendingShares.push(minerAddress);
}

payRewards() {
  let outputs = [];
  let shareReward = Math.floor(TOTAL_SHARE_REWARDS / this.
      pendingShares.length);

  this.pendingShares.forEach((address) => {
    outputs.push({
      address: address,
      amount: shareReward
    });
  });

  this.postTransaction(outputs, 0);

  // Clean out pending shares after payment.
  this.pendingShares = [];
}
```

Fig. 5. Reward method implementations for a PROP mining pool operator

```
rewardMiner(minerAddress) {
  let output = { address: minerAddress,
                 amount: SHARE_REWARD };
  this.pendingShares.push(output);

  // Removing old shares.
  while (this.pendingShares.length > N) {
    this.pendingShares.shift();
  }
}

payRewards() {
  this.postTransaction(this.pendingShares, 0);

  // Once paid, we clean out the pending shares.
  this.pendingShares = [];
}
```

Fig. 6. Reward method implementations for a PPLNS mining pool operator

sufficient UTXOs to meet the required payment, starting with the oldest UTXOs first since they are more likely to have already been accepted and confirmed by the network.

```
1   postTransaction: function(outputs, fee=Blockchain.
        DEFAULT_TX_FEE) {
2
3       // We calculate the total value of gold needed.
4       let totalPayments = outputs.reduce(((acc, {amount}) => acc +
            amount, 0) + fee;
5
6       // Make sure the client has enough gold.
7       if (totalPayments > this.availableGold) {
8         throw new Error(`Requested ${totalPayments}, but account
              only has ${this.balance}.`);
9       }
10
11      let addresses = [];
12      let pubKeys = []
13      let privKeys = [];
14
15      // Collecting UTXOs to gather sufficient payment.
16      let total = 0;
17      while (total < totalPayments) {
18        let utxo = this.wallet.shift();
19        total += this.lastConfirmedBlock.balanceOf(utxo.address);
20        addresses.push(utxo.address);
21        pubKeys.push(utxo.keyPair.public);
22        privKeys.push(utxo.keyPair.private);
23      }
24
25      // Calculating change, if any.
26      let change = total − totalPayments;
27      if (change > 0) {
28        let addr = this.createAddress();
29        outputs.push({ address: addr, amount: change });
30      }
31
32      // Making the new transaction.
33      let tx = Blockchain.makeTransaction({
34        from: addresses,
35        nonce: 0, // Nonces are not needed for the UTXO model
36        pubKey: pubKeys,
37        outputs: outputs,
38        fee: fee,
39      });
40
41      for (let i=0; i<privKeys.length; i++) {
42        let privKey = privKeys[i];
43        tx.sign(privKey);
44      }
45
46      this.net.broadcast(Blockchain.POST_TRANSACTION, tx);
47
48      return tx;
49  }
```

Fig. 7. The postTransaction method for the UTXO model.

When a transaction output is spent, all of the funds must be allocated. Within Bitcoin, any funds not going to a specified address are implicitly reserved as transaction fees paid to the miner; our implementation still leaves these fees explicit, but requires that all funds are allocated to some address.

As a result, if the total of the available UTXOs exceeds the amount of funds, the additional gold must be allocated to a new address. Lines 26–30 handle this requirement. A new address is created, which also generates a new public key/private key pair. This address is then added to the list of outputs, receiving the excess amount of gold.

Lines 33–39 create a new transaction. Since the UTXO model includes a replay defense by its design, we set the nonce value to '0'. The other parameters are similar to the standard transaction form, except that the `from` and `pubKey` fields are arrays rather than single values.

Lines 41–44 sign the transaction with every private key associated with a UTXO used as an input for this transaction. The method then broadcasts the transaction to the network.

By highlighting this feature of Bitcoin in isolation, it becomes a bit easier to appreciate the intricacies of its design.

6   Conclusion and Future Work

In this paper, we have reviewed the design of SpartanGold and shown how its design served to make it a good tool for educational use and for prototyping different designs. To demonstrate its utility, we have shown how SpartanGold can be used to illustrate differences in mining pool strategies and how it may help to explain the UTXO model used by Bitcoin.

Development in SpartanGold continues. In future work, we intend to build out additional implementations of blockchain protocol designs and attacks. Ultimately, the end goal is to provide a rich set of simulations to foster better understanding of the blockchain space.

References

1. 0chain/gosdk. https://github.com/0chain/gosdk. Accessed November 2020
2. Bitcoin core integration/staging tree. https://github.com/bitcoin/bitcoin. Accessed November 2020
3. https://github.com/input-output-hk/cardano-node. Accessed November 2020
4. Dfinity's rust agent repository. https://github.com/dfinity/agent-rs. Accessed November 2020
5. Dogecoin core. https://github.com/dogecoin/dogecoin. Accessed November 2020
6. Eosio - the most powerful infrastructure for decentralized applications. https://github.com/EOSIO/eos. Accessed November 2020
7. Eyal, I., Sirer, E.G.: Majority is not enough: bitcoin mining is vulnerable. Commun. ACM **61**(7), 95–102 (2018)
8. Filecoin: A decentralized storage network. Technical report, Protocol Labs, August 2017

9. Filecoin proving subsystem. https://github.com/filecoin-project/rust-fil-proofs. Accessed November 2020
10. Go-algorand. https://github.com/algorand/go-algorand. Accessed November 2020
11. Go ethereum. https://github.com/ethereum/go-ethereum. Accessed November 2020
12. Goodman, L.: Tezos - a self-amending crypto-ledger. Technical report, Tezos Foundation (2014)
13. Guo, P.: Python is now the most popular introductory language at top U.S. universities. Communications OPF the ACM: BLOC@CACM (2014). https://cacm.acm.org/blogs/blog-cacm/176450-python-is-now-the-most-popular-introductory-teaching-language-at-top-u-s-universities/fulltext
14. Hanke, T., Movahedi, M., Williams, D.: DFINITY technology overview series, consensus system. CoRR abs/1805.04548 (2018). http://arxiv.org/abs/1805.04548
15. King, S.: Primecoin: cryptocurrency with prime number proof-of-work (2013). http://primecoin.org/static/primecoin-paper.pdf
16. King, S., Nadal, S.: Ppcoin: peer-to-peer crypto-currency with proof-of-stake (2012). http://primecoin.org/static/primecoin-paper.pdf
17. Kwon, J.: Tendermint: consensus without mining (2014). https://tendermint.com/static/docs/tendermint.pdf
18. Larimer, D.: Delegated proof-of-stake (DPoS) (2014)
19. Litecoin core integration/staging tree. https://github.com/litecoin-project/litecoin. Accessed November 2020
20. Monero. https://github.com/monero-project/monero. Accessed November 2020
21. Nakamoto, S.: Bitcoin: a peer-to-peer electronic cash system (2009). http://www.bitcoin.org/bitcoin.pdf
22. Pardeshi, P.: Implementing TontineCoin. Master's thesis, San José State University (2020)
23. Pass, R., Shi, E.: Thunderella: blockchains with optimistic instant confirmation. In: Nielsen, J.B., Rijmen, V. (eds.) EUROCRYPT 2018. LNCS, vol. 10821, pp. 3–33. Springer, Cham (2018). https://doi.org/10.1007/978-3-319-78375-8_1
24. Peercoin official development repo. https://github.com/peercoin/peercoin. Accessed November 2020
25. Pillai, J.: Earmarked UTXOs For escrow services and two-factor authentication on the blockchain. Master's thesis, San José State University (2019)
26. Pollett, C., Austin, T.H., Potika, K., Rietz, J.: Tontinecoin: murder-based proof-of-stake. In: 2020 IEEE International Conference on Decentralized Applications and Infrastructures (DAPPS), pp. 82–87 (2020). https://doi.org/10.1109/DAPPS49028.2020.00009
27. Primecoin integration/staging tree. https://github.com/primecoin/primecoin. Accessed November 2020
28. Project lotus. https://github.com/filecoin-project/lotus. Accessed November 2020
29. Rosenfeld, M.: Analysis of bitcoin pooled mining reward systems. Computing Research Repository (CoRR) abs/1112.4980 (2011). http://arxiv.org/abs/1112.4980
30. The solidity contract-oriented programming language. https://github.com/ethereum/solidity. Accessed November 2020
31. Tendermint core. https://github.com/tendermint/tendermint. Accessed November 2020
32. Tendermint rust ABCI. https://github.com/tendermint/rust-abci. Accessed November 2020

33. tendermint-sg: a variant of spartangold patterned after Tendermint's proof-of-stake. https://github.com/taustin/tendermint-sg. Accessed November 2020
34. tendermint.rs. https://github.com/informalsystems/tendermint-rs. Accessed November 2020
35. Tezos gitlab page. https://gitlab.com/tezos/tezos. Accessed November 2020
36. XRP ledger. https://github.com/ripple/rippled. Accessed November 2020
37. Thundercore local chain. https://github.com/thundercore/thundercore-localchain. Accessed November 2020
38. Wood, G.: Ethereum: a secure decentralised generalised transaction ledger (2014). https://gavwood.com/paper.pdf

BIOT: A Blockchain-Based IoT Platform for Distributed Energy Resource Management

Mostafa Yalpanian[1] , Naser Mirzaei[1] , Alireza Parvizimosaed[2(✉)] ,
Farid Farmani[3] , Mehdi Parvizimosaed[4] , and Behdad Bahrami[4]

[1] Boof Corporation, Tehran, Iran
{myalpanian,nasermirzaei89}@boof.tech
[2] University of Ottawa, Ottawa, ON, Canada
aparv007@uottawa.ca
[3] Fareng Group Ltd., Toronto, ON, Canada
ffarmani@farenggroup.com
[4] Edgecom Energy Corporation, Toronto, ON, Canada
{mehdi,bbahrami}@edgecomenergy.ca
https://www.edgecomenergy.ca

Abstract. Smart grids are IoT-enabled grids at which communication devices can be used to interconnect, monitor and manage distributed energy resources (DERs). The emerging efficient and clean energy DERs such as Lithium-ion batteries and Photovoltaic have been widely used in IoT-enabled smart grids that makes their secure operation challenging. In this paper, a blockchain-based IoT platform, namely BIoT, is proposed to maintain security of energy supply network including DERs against IoT platform's security issues, e.g., single point of failure, malicious code and data leak. BIoT verifies resource management requests in a consensus process, provides certificate-based authentication as well as attribute-based access control, and ensures data integrity. BIoT's performance has been evaluated on Ontario Energy Board (OEB) Cybersecurity framework and a performance benchmark.

Keywords: Internet of Things (IoT) · Blockchain · Cybersecurity · Distributed energy resource · Smart grid

1 Introduction

Centralized device controllers have been conventionally used to control a large group of controllable devices. However, due to their reliability issues, the

Funded by IRAP under the project "Blockchain IoT Security Solution for Distributed Energy System Network".

© Springer Nature Switzerland AG 2021
Y. Park et al. (Eds.): SVCC 2020, CCIS 1383, pp. 134–147, 2021.
https://doi.org/10.1007/978-3-030-72725-3_10

inclination towards Internet of Things (IoT) has been increasing rapidly. Predictions indicate that there will be 24 billion machine-to-machine (M-To-M) connections by 2025 while around 114 million autonomous intelligent and embedded systems have already been installed in Canada. Smart grid, smart facilities, and energy management systems are examples to real applications of IoT[24].

Smart grid is the next generation of electrical networks that interconnects distributed energy resources (DERs) and controls energy demand and load in an intelligent manner. Sustainability and resilience of smart grids directly rely on operation of DERs that are managed and monitored through sensors and actuators in an IoT network. IoT can provide device monitoring (e.g., smart metering), failure prediction, autonomous maintenance, remote device controlling, IT security, generation optimization and load balancing services in several applications such as residential and industrial buildings, hospitals, greenhouses, factories, etc. [14]. For instance, facilities equipped with energy storage systems in Ontario often charge batteries in off-peak times, and release battery energy in peak times resulting in energy cost savings. These charging and discharging signals can be provided by an IoT platform. However, 97% of customers who are interested in migrating to IoT are concerned about security [14]. Security of IoT is investigated in different levels ranging from physical and data link to the application. These security issues can be organized in sensing, network, middleware, gateway and application layers [5]. Hence, secure communication solely never guarantees the security of an IoT system. Microsoft survey shows that network-level security (e.g., authentication, access control, single point of failure), data integrity and encryption, remote hardware and firmware updation, and device management are generic IoT concerns [14].

The paper proposes an IoT platform, called BIoT, enriched by permissioned (private) blockchain, edge computing and off-chain cloud to address IoT security issues. The major purpose is to autonomously monitor, maintain and control DERs in facilities. BIoT satisfies data immutability and integrity, provides a certificate-based authentication mechanism and an attribute-based access control, and resolves single point of failure, malicious code injection and data leak threats. BIoT interconnects DERs in a secure manner that addresses a set of security issues and provides immune logs that enhance the accuracy of threat detection tools. We have evaluated security and performance of BIoT through Ontario Energy Board (OEB) cybersecurity framework and a benchmark.

The rest of this paper is structured as follows. Section 2 presents our research baseline, including a background regarding blockchain systems. Our proposed IoT platform is presented in Sect. 3. Model evaluation is presented in Sect. 4. Section 5 discusses related work. Finally, conclusion and highlights of future work is provided in Sect. 6.

2   Research Baseline

Blockchain is a distributed ledger technology (DLT) that stores a chain of blocks with cryptographic hash in multiple peers. This immutable technology keeps data unchanged and indelible. Using smart contracts, blockchain is able to process transactions on peers independently and run a consensus mechanism to integrate results and update ledgers. Blockchains are either permissioned or non-permissioned. The former requires a user approval whereas the latter is open for participants. Permissioned blockchain fits into private smart facilities or microgrids since only authorized users can interact with DERs remotely and privacy of customers is significantly important and data must remain confidential. In addition, consensus process in permissioned type takes less energy than non-permissioned one [1,18,23]. Corda [21], Quorum [20], Enterprise Ethereum [3], Openchain [16], MultiChain [2], XuperChain [26], HydraChain [7], Hyperledger Ursa, Fabric, Sawtooth, Iroha and Indy [13] are examples of permissioned blockchain projects that have been developed by blockchain pioneer companies recently.

3 BIoT Distributed Platform

BIoT is an IoT platform based on Hyperledger Fabric blockchain that distributes processes among peer-to-peer(P2P) interconnected nodes (i.e., peers) which enables secure control of DERs remotely. Figure 1 shows high level architecture of the platform. A set of gateways and servers provide access points to a BIoT network. Gateways are installed in facilities and communicate with sensors and actuators through local Wi-Fi networks. A gateway frequently receives data from sensors and sends requests to actuators while a server is hosted on cloud and serves user requests.

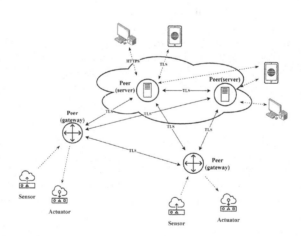

Fig. 1. Architecture of BIoT

BIoT encodes DER management policies and verification rules in smart contracts that are deployed on and executed by peers. A consensus mechanism collects votes of peers about an incoming transaction and verifies the safety of transactions, e.g., it investigates the state of charge (SOC) of batteries and rejects charging request in case the battery is full. Duplicate smart contracts protect BIoT against malicious code injection in the sense that an invalid smart contract raises votes dissimilar to the majority of votes, and then they are rejected through consensus. Furthermore, the consensus mechanism reduces the risk of attacks since penetration to at least half of servers and gateways is required to manipulate votes and update ledgers.

The platform records critical information such as status of DERs in distributed ledgers by cryptography. Encrypted data is capsuled in a block which is attached to a chain of blocks by a hash value. Therefore, if a pre-recorded block is manipulated, the remaining chain is disconnected and consequently invalidates the chain. This mechanism partially guarantees data integrity of BIoT at the network level.

Peers of a network store at least one ledger per smart contract and keep ledgers synchronous with other peers. Despite locating at various places, peers store a copy of ledgers. BIoT uses duplication to provide decentralized applications in addition to tackling the single point of failure security concern. In other words, applications are able to simultaneously send requests to multiple peers. In case a peer is unavailable, the remaining peers process data using the same smart contracts and up-to-date ledgers.

BIoT conserves the privacy of customers by dedicating a private virtual network to facilities. In fact, facilities' data crosses over individual gateways and dedicated server-side containers. Figure 2 represents a sample network of two facilities. Facilities X and Y manage their own gateways separately and share two cloud servers.

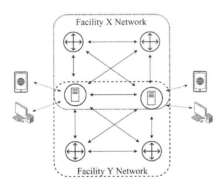

Fig. 2. BIoT networks of two facilities

The platform has been developed in multiple layers as Fig. 3 shows. Layers are described as follows.

- **Application:** It provides decentralized applications such as a command-line interface (CLI), mobile, and web applications that use X.509 certificates to authenticate users, and sign, encrypt, and decrypt messages. The mobile application and CLI transmit data through TLS protocol whereas web applications use HTTPS.

- **Service:** It contains subsidiary services that facilitate communication with the core of BIoT. A software development kit (SDK) is a library of reusable functions that are used to interface with BIoT blockchain and certificate authority (CA). Similarly, a set of application programming interfaces (APIs) allow web applications to access and interact with CA and BIoT. A trusted CA service registers identities and issues X.509 certificates that validate identities and make communications secure by using public and private keys. Furthermore, the service can expire, revoke, and re-issue certificates. A wallet service securely keeps identities of a user and streamlines identity management. A user may register in the BIoT platform multiple times. For instance, he/she may own multiple facilities and requires an identity per facility. Users store identities in their own wallets and further they can choose an identity for signing up to the platform. Moreover, the service supports basic operations such as identity addition and deletion, and keeps track of private keys to sign transactions.
- **Blockchain:** It is the core of BIoT that verifies data, manages users and devices, protects users privacy and records critical information in on-chain. User and device management policies have been encoded in smart contracts. They carry out addition, deletion, edition and grouping actions for users, gateways and devices. Herein, devices are DERs, sensors and actuators. New devices and gateways are inactive until they acquire administrators approval. Sensors and actuators can dynamically connect or disconnect gateways and DERs. BIoT composes a role and attribute-based access control for setting privileges of roles by using attributes. Roles and their attributes are defined at run-time. Attributes grant roles permission to smart contract functions. Identities are assigned to a role and permissions such as charging and discharging a battery, approving a new sensor, or activating a gateway are granted to identities based on attributes. All P2P communication channels among gateways and servers are encrypted using TLS protocol.

  DERs are sensitive to operational commands such as speeding up/down motors or charging/discharging batteries. Commands shall be verified regarding safety rules and current status of DERs to ensure the target DER remains in safe and healthy status, nonetheless advanced DERs refuse irregular commands. BIoT programs hazard protection rules in smart contracts, and evaluates operational commands during a Byzantine Fault Tolerance (BFT) consensus process. In case of hazard, BIoT refuses the command, raises an event and alarms operators.

  Network management specifies settings of BIoT network using a set of configuration scripts. These settings characterize peers, facilities, smart contracts, ledgers, communication protocols, etc. A network is configured during deployment, however, BIoT is able to connect or disconnect peers at run-time.
- **Middleware:** This intermediate layer converts messages between blockchain and devices. Drivers control actuators using MQTT protocol. Middleware

services are able to read ledger independently and process devices' data stream at the edge of network.

– **Hardware:** It contains DERs, sensors and actuators that provide data or perform an action.

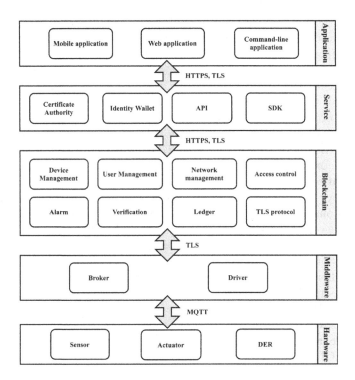

Fig. 3. BIoT layered architecture

4   Evaluation

BIoT is configured for lithium battery management of a facility. The network contains a Raspberry Pi (ARM Quad core Cortex-A72 CPU with 4G RAM) gateway, which runs the facility's peer, and two cloud servers (Intel 2 GHz CPU with 4 GB RAM), which run the energy management company's peers. At least one peer of the company and facility shall validate a request before updating ledgers. We evaluate the performance, reliability, and performance of BIoT, and will consider scalability in the future.

4.1   Cybersecurity

The Ontario Energy Board (OEB) ensures the energy sector is sustainable, by regulating Ontario's electricity and natural gas sectors. Such regulations include, setting valid and rational rates, approving leave to construct applications, and licensing all participants in the electricity sector, as well as natural gas marketers who sell to low volume consumers.

A recent article from the OEB represents a framework consisting of an Inherent Risk Profile Tool and a related Self-Assessment Questionnaire [15]. This framework illustrates a process and recommends tools and means to boost improvement in organizations that are subject to OEB regulatory oversight.

The cybersecurity controls in this framework are mainly based on the U.S. National Institute of Standards and Technology (NIST) Framework for Improving Critical Infrastructure Cybersecurity, which has been widely adopted and endorsed as a fundamental cybersecurity resource by regulators and industry associations around the world, including Canada. The check list in this framework is based on RS.AN-3 illustrative example. The categories and subcategories are mapped to standards and frameworks such as CCS CSC, COBIT 5, NIST SP 800-53, GAAP, ISA 62443, ISO/IEC 27001, PIPEDA. The privacy controls reflect Fair Information Principles (which are the foundation of Canadian personal information protection laws) and Generally Accepted Privacy Principles (established by the American Institute of Certified Public Accountants and Chartered Professional Accountants Canada).

This framework contains an Inherent Risk Profile Tool specifically tailored to the inherent cybersecurity risks in Ontario's LDC (Local Distribution Company) community. Depending on size, maturity and capability, each company may apply different risk profiles which will require a varying degree of security controls to be applied for security measurement. These risk profiles are defined as three types: High (HR), Medium (MR) and Low (LR) (baseline).

The goal is to make the organization's service and product more secure. Using OEB cybersecurity framework, we can check many controls on our organization and product. OEB framework has five main categories including Identify, Protect, Detect, Respond and Recover. Each category is decomposed into subcategories.

The framework addresses 109 subcategories. By analyzing them we detected 49 subcategories that are most applicable to BIoT. Our preliminary self-assessment has been summarized in Table 1. Although BIoT is under development and will be launched in the close future, early assessment represents the security status of BIoT. Eight of seventeen protection items have been satisfied and six items are in progress while three unsatisfied items rely on the operational environment. The results show that blockchain has totally satisfied PR-DS-5, PR-IP.4, PR-MA.2, PR-PT.4 and partially satisfied PR.AC-1, PR-AC-3, PR-AC-4, PR-DS-1, PR.DS-2. Data encryption, ledger and peer duplication, detailed logs, and strong access control are the most effective features of blockchain. Furthermore, blockchain contributes to threat detection. It can help IoT platforms in satisfying item DE.CM-4 by preventing malicious code injection. Moreover, It can strengthen threat monitoring by providing detailed logs, preventing unauthorized access, and rejecting invalid data. BIoT will consider detection, response, and recovery features in the future.

Table 1. Security self-assessmen with OEB framework.

Function	Category	Subcategory	HR	MR	LR	Self Assessment	Reason	Next Improvement
ID: Identify	ID-AM: Asset Management	ID.AM-1: Physical devices and systems within the organization are inventoried.	X	X	X	Yes with CCW	A list of servers, gateways, sensors, actuators, cables and other physical devices have been prepared.	-
		ID.AM-2: Software platforms and applications within the organization are inventoried.	X	X	X	Yes with CCW	A list of services, applications, APIs, containers, scripts, configurations, executable files, libraries and other software related components have been documented.	-
		ID.AM-3: Organizational communication and data flows are mapped.	X	X	X	Work In Progress	Architecture and data flow have been drawn. Installation and deployment have been automated by scripts. Requirements have been documented.	Business processes shall be clarified by activity diagrams.
		ID.AM-P1: Identify the personal information or customer proprietary information, its authority for the collection, use and disclosure of such information, and the sensitivity of such information.	X	X	X	Yes with CCW	BIOT manages users' information (i.e., username, password, facility name and certificates). Sensitivity of information is in highest level.	-
	ID.BE: Business Environment	ID.BE-5: Resilience requirements to support delivery of critical services are established.	X	X		Work In Progress	BIoT duplicates data in distributed ledgers. If a server/gateway fails, there are always backup processors and ledgers.	Make a mechanism for recovering BIoT if all servers/gateways stop working.
	ID.GV: Governance	ID.GV-P1: A policy is established for collection, use and disclosure of customer personal and proprietary information.	X	X	X	Yes with CCW	BIoT policy is to circulates data of a customer in the facility private network. Certificates and blockchain solution ensure that valid users have access to data.	-
		ID.GV-4: Governance and risk management processes address cybersecurity risks	X	X	X	No	-	A continuous risk management process is required.
	ID.RA: Risk Assessment	ID.RA-1: Asset vulnerabilities are identified and documented.	X	X		Work In Progress	Vulnerability of APIs were evaluated through a web vulnerability assessment benchmark. Some application and protocol(HTTP, TLS) based resource exhausting attacks have been simulated and weaknesses of the platform have been identified.	Vulnerability of other assets (e.g., services, ledgers and etc) should be assessed.
		ID.RA-2: Threat and vulnerability information is received from information sharing forums and sources.	X	X		No	-	-
PR: Protect	PR.AC: Access Control	PR.AC-1: Identities and credentials are managed for authorized devices and users.	X	X	X	Yes with CCW	BIoT provides access control and certificate management. Users can revoke and order new certificates.	-
		PR.AC-3: Remote access is managed.	X	X	X	Work In Progress	Direct access to gateways is through OpenVPN while indirect access is through TLS.	Add two factor authentication.

(continued)

Table 1. (*continued*)

Category	Subcategory				Status	Description	Notes
PR.AT:Awareness and Training	PR.AC-4: Access permissions are managed, incorporating the principles of least privilege and separation of duties.	X	X		Yes	BIoT control management is configured to minify accesses to the assets and entities.	-
	PR.AT-1: All users are informed and trained.	X	X	X	No	-	Users will be trained in security awareness course.
PR.DS: Data Security	PR.DS-1: Data-at-rest is protected.	X	X	X	Yes	Only permitted users has access to data due to access control policies. All data is encrypted before storing in ledger.	-
	PR.DS-2: Data-in-transit is protected.	X	X	X	Yes	BIoT uses TLS for all communications.	-
	PR.DS-5: Protections against data leaks are implemented.	X	X		Work In Progress	BIoT encrypts messages, stores encrypted data in ledger and restricts unauthorized users to read, write or edit data.	A Pretty Good Privacy (PGP) encryption strengths data protection.
	PR.DS-6: Integrity checking mechanisms are used to verify software, firmware, and information integrity.	X			Work In Progress	A test benchmark autonomously runs critical transactions and ensures correctness of smart contracts and peers. Network installation is verified manually.	Still we need to document manual verification.
	PR.DS-7: The development and testing environment(s) are separate from the production environment.	X			Work In Progress	We are still in development phase. Servers and gateways have been configured for development environment.	An operational environment should be prepared.
PR.IP: Information Protection Processes and Procedures	PR.IP-1: A baseline configuration of information technology/industrial control systems is created and maintained.	X			Yes	Gitlab CI/CD has been configured to perform some test cases before merging codes with the repository.	-
	PR.IP-2: A System Development Life Cycle to manage systems is implemented.	X			Yes	BIoT has been developed based on agile and test driven methodology. Codes are reviewed and tested by a separate employee, and an automatic test evaluates changes. In addition, GitLab CI/CD tests codes before storing in a repository.	-
	PR.IP-4: Backups of information are conducted, maintained, and tested periodically.	X	X	X	Work In Progress	BIoT spreads a copy of ledger to each peer.	A periodic backup of off-chain PostgreSQL database is required.
	PR.IP-7: Protection processes are continuously improved.	X	X		No	-	-
	PR.IP-12: A vulnerability management plan is developed and implemented.	X	X		Work In Progress	Vulnerabilities are scanned every 6 months. Still, there exist an API vulnerability detection and some DDOS attack simulators.	Some other scripts and tools shall be prepared to check vulnerability of other assets.
PR.MA: Maintenance	PR.MA-2: Remote maintenance of organizational assets is approved, logged, and performed in a manner that prevents unauthorized access.	X			Yes	Ledger and peers logs all transactions in detail.	-

(*continued*)

Table 1. (*continued*)

Function	Category	Subcategory				Status	Implementation in BIoT	Remarks
DE: Detect	PR.PT: Protective Technology	PR.PT-1: Audit/log records are determined, documented, implemented, and reviewed in accordance with policy.	X			No		Needs to implement a security information event monitoring (SIEM).
		PR.PT-4: Communications and control networks are protected.	X	X	X	Yes	A private network is created per facility and TLS protocol makes communications secure.	-
	DE.CM: Security Continuous Monitoring	DE.CM-4: Malicious code is detected.	X	X		Yes	BIoT ignores peers that executes invalid smart contract (e.g., malicious codes).	-
		DE.CM-7: Monitoring for unauthorized personnel, connections, devices, and software is performed.	X			Work In Progress	BIoT prevents unauthorized connections since all users and devices must be approved and must get certificate from CA. Blockchain also verifies that valid devices send data.	A traffic analyzer tool shall collect and analyse logs and monitor traffic.
		Status of 4 medium risk subcategories (i.e., DE.AE-1, DE.AE-5, DE.CM-1,DE.CM-8, DE.DP-1) and 6 high risk subcategories (i.g., DE.AE-2, DE.AE-3, DE.AE-4, DE.CM-5, DE.CM-6 are No.						
RS: Respond	RS.RP: Response Planning	RS.RP-1: Response plan is executed during or after an event.	X	X	X	No		-
	RS.CO: Communications	RS.CO-2: Events are reported consistent with established criteria.	X	X	X	Work In Progress	BIoT verifies data and requests and notify operators if verification fails(e.g., if a gateway sends data by another gateway's sensor identifier.	Define rules in Security Operation Center (SoC) to autonomously report incidents.
	RS.AN: Analysis	RS.AN-1: Notifications from detection systems are investigated.	X	X		Work In Progress	Events are already recorded in ledger and alarms users.	Needs to define rules in SoC and also needs a threat hunting for investigation.
		RS.AN-3: Forensics are performed.	X			No		-
	RS.MI: Mitigation	RS.MI-2: Incidents are mitigated.	X	X	X	No		-
	RS.IM: Improvements	RS.IM-1: Response plans incorporate lessons learned.	X	X		Work In Progress		-
		RS.IM-2: Response strategies are updated.	X	X		No		-
RC: Recover	RC.RP: Recovery Planning	RC.RP-1: Recovery plan is executed during or after an event.	X	X		No		-
	RC.IM: Improvements	RC.IM-1: Recovery plans incorporate lessons learned.	X	X		No		-
		RC.IM-2: Recovery strategies are updated.	X	X		No		-
	RC.CO: Communications	RC.CO-2: Reputation after an event is repaired.	X			No		-

4.2   Performance

Several benchmarks have been implemented for testing performance and reliability of BIoT. A performance benchmark sent 1000 read (i.e., ListFacilities), write (i.e., RegisterGateway), and edit (i.e., ActivateGateway) transactions at a rate of 10 transactions per second (TPS) to simulate a performance stress test over the facility network. As Table 2 represents, throughput and average latency of the reading transactions were 10 TPS and 0.27 s, respectively, writing transactions were processed with 7.9 TPS throughput and 14.95 s latency while edit transactions were processed at rate of 7.4 TPS with average 10.26 s latency. All read and write transactions were successful whereas 984 of 1000 edit transactions failed. The failure reason was that transactions are buffered due to network latency, and will update the same variable, concurrently. Even though the high rate edition is an abnormal behavior that might damage DERs, actuators, or gateways, concurrency is an upfront issue of BIoT. Latency of reading requests is less than one second even in high transaction rates. In contrast, latency of writing requests correlates with the rate of transactions.

Table 2. Stress test result.

Request	Succ	Fail	Send Rate (TPS)	Max Latency (s)	Min Latency (s)	Avg Latency (s)	Throughput (TPS)
ListFacilities	1000	0	10.0	0.55	0.18	0.27	10.0
RegisterGateway	1000	0	10.0	35.36	0.64	14.95	7.9
ActivateGateway	16	984	10.0	33.93	0.62	10.26	7.4

The higher transaction rate, the more cumulative blocks, and more latency. Latency of transactions and number of failures are reduced dramatically in lower rates, as shown on Table 3. Average latency of writing and editing requests are reduced to 2.69 and 0.88 s respectively, with only 52 editing transactions failures. In addition, Table 3 represents reliability of BIoT in a two-hour time span in which servers and services of BIoT were working continuously for two hours. This preliminary result shows BIoT is reliable, although an accurate evaluation shall involve all transactions in a real operational environment.

Table 3. Reliability evaluation result.

Request	Succ	Fail	Send Rate (TPS)	Max Latency (s)	Min Latency (s)	Avg Latency (s)	Throughput (TPS)
ListFacilities	1000	0	1.0	20.47	0.41	0.77	1.0
RegisterGateway	1000	0	0.2	31.48	0.45	2.69	0.2
ActivateGateway	948	52	0.2	31.22	0.44	0.88	0.2

Another feature of BIoT is its significantly low resource usage. The Raspberry Pi used 35% CPU and 500MB RAM on average, and servers used less than 15% CPU and 400MB RAM despite the number of transactions. The given snapshot, Fig. 4, shows the status of resource allocations.

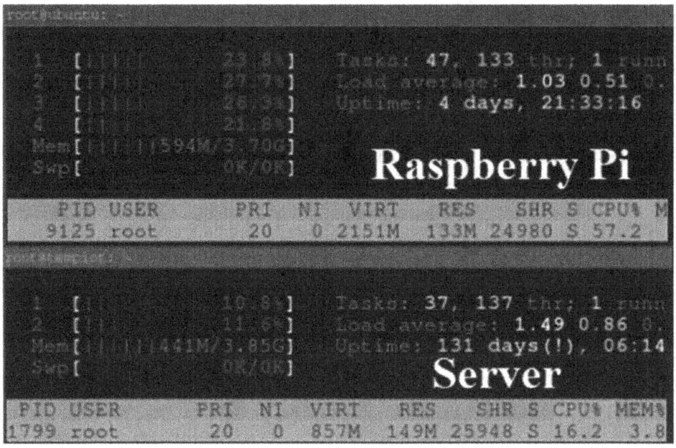

Fig. 4. Resource usage snapshot

5   Related Works

A systematic literature review surveys 244 IoT and blockchain research works to discover key challenges and benefits of Blockchain in IoT applications as well as generic IoT and blockchain security attacks and threats [25]. Although the survey concludes that composition faces issues such as high computation and storage, extra communication in P2P networks, high energy consumption, and latency problems, BIoT has overcome the issues because only essential data is recorded in on-chain while the remaining is stored in off-chain. Kshetri claims that blockchain can address IoT challenges such as cost and capacity constraints, unavailability of services, susceptibility to manipulation, single point of failure, and vulnerability to distributed denial of service (DDOS) attacks and data theft and remote hijacking [9]. Khan and Salah argue that blockchain resolves some IoT security problems such as lack of device ownership tracking, weak data authentication and integrity, inefficient and insecure authentication, authorization and privacy protection mechanisms, and use of heavy and complex communication protocols [8]. Likewise, blockchain might prevent data loss, spoofing attack and unauthorized access. Permissioned blockchains can secure IoT devices that deal with private data. In addition, data and validity of IoT devices might be verified, data provenance might be achieved using blockchain. Ledger replication also ensures fault tolerance [5, 22]. Blockchain has been investigated as an emerging technology that can solve smart grids security issues. Guan et al. [4] used Rainbowchain blockchain to keep smart meters data confidential and preserve the privacy of customers. Huang et al. proposed consortium blockchains for scheduling electric vehicle charging, and protecting data [6]. Li et al. [11] improved security of nontransparent energy trading market by using consortium blockchain technology.

Some researchers have proposed smart grid management solutions using IoT and blockchain technologies. Pop et al. [19] made a P2P smart metering network among consumers and system operators for collecting energy consumption and production. A self-enforcing smart contract has also been designed to encode energy balancing rules. Although the solution deals with DER monitoring, it does not contribute to DER controlling. Similarly, Li et al. [12] overviewed how distributed ledgers and smart contracts address cybersecurity challenges of smart grids and transactive energy markets. They offered a vision for taking advantage of blockchain and IoT technologies in energy markets. Kumar et al. [10] considered application of blockchain, IoT, and artificial intelligence in smart grid. All these research works are true examples of blockchain capabilities to solve many challenges that are present in traditional systems.

6   Conclusions and Future Work

A blockchain-based IoT (BIoT) platform was organized in four layers for DER management systems. Security of the platform was assessed via Ontario Energy Board's cybersecurity framework. Early evaluation indicated that blockchain protects IoT platforms and can enhance security in terms of detection and response. The performance and reliability of BIoT was also evaluated on three benchmarks. The average latency of transactions was less than 3 seconds in normal mode while the rate of transactions influenced latency. The application processed read and write transactions without failure whereas editing transactions faced concurrency problems regarding the rate of transactions. BIoT will be further developed in the future to integrate a security information event monitoring (SIEM) into BIoT to overcome detection, response, and recovery weaknesses. In addition, BIoT will be enriched with a compliance checker that models and monitors privacy regulations through smart contracts [17].

References

1. Christidis, K., Devetsikiotis, M.: Blockchains and smart contracts for the internet of things. IEEE Access **4**, 2292–2303 (2016)
2. Coin Sciences Ltd.: MultiChain: an enterprise blockchain (2020). https://www.multichain.com
3. Enterprise Ethereum Alliance: Enterprise Ethereum (2020). https://entethalliance.org
4. Guan, Z., et al.: Privacy-preserving and efficient aggregation based on blockchain for power grid communications in smart communities. IEEE Commun. Mag. **56**(7), 82–88 (2018)
5. Hassija, V., Chamola, V., Saxena, V., Jain, D., Goyal, P., Sikdar, B.: A survey on IoT security: application areas, security threats, and solution architectures. IEEE Access **7**, 82721–82743 (2019)
6. Huang, X., Zhang, Y., Li, D., Han, L.: An optimal scheduling algorithm for hybrid EV charging scenario using consortium blockchains. Futur. Gener. Comput. Syst. **91**, 555–562 (2019)
7. HydraChain: HydraChain (2020). https://github.com/HydraChain/hydrachain

8. Khan, M.A., Salah, K.: IoT security: review, blockchain solutions, and open challenges. Futur. Gener. Comput. Syst. **82**, 395–411 (2018)

9. Kshetri, N.: Can blockchain strengthen the internet of things? IT Prof. **19**(4), 68–72 (2017)

10. Kumar, N.M., et al.: Distributed energy resources and the application of AI, IoT, and blockchain in smart grids. Energies **13**(21), 5739 (2020)

11. Li, Z., Kang, J., Yu, R., Ye, D., Deng, Q., Zhang, Y.: Consortium blockchain for secure energy trading in industrial internet of things. IEEE Trans. Industr. Inf. **14**(8), 3690–3700 (2017)

12. Li, Z., Shahidehpour, M., Liu, X.: Cyber-secure decentralized energy management for IoT-enabled active distribution networks. J. Mod. Power Syst. Clean Energy **6**(5), 900–917 (2018)

13. Linux Foundation: Hyperledger Project (2020). https://www.hyperledger.org/

14. Microsoft: Report: IoT signals (2020). https://azure.microsoft.com/en-ca/resources/iot-signals/

15. Ontario Energy Board: Ontario cyber security framework. https://www.oeb.ca/sites/default/files/Ontario-Cyber-Security-Framework-20171206.pdf. Accessed 21 Nov 2020

16. Openchain Project: Openchain (2020). https://www.openchainproject.org

17. Parvizimosaed, A.: Towards the specification and verification of legal contracts. In: 2020 IEEE 28th International Requirements Engineering Conference (RE), pp. 445–450. IEEE (2020)

18. Peters, G.W., Panayi, E.: Understanding modern banking ledgers through blockchain technologies: future of transaction processing and smart contracts on the internet of money. In: Tasca, P., Aste, T., Pelizzon, L., Perony, N. (eds.) Banking Beyond Banks and Money. NEW, pp. 239–278. Springer, Cham (2016). https://doi.org/10.1007/978-3-319-42448-4_13

19. Pop, C., Cioara, T., Antal, M., Anghel, I., Salomie, I., Bertoncini, M.: Blockchain based decentralized management of demand response programs in smart energy grids. Sensors **18**(1), 162 (2018)

20. Quorum: Quorum: a complete open source blockchain platform for business (2020). https://consensys.net/quorum

21. R3: Corda: an open-source blockchain platform for business (2020). https://www.corda.net

22. Sengupta, J., Ruj, S., Bit, S.D.: A comprehensive survey on attacks, security issues and blockchain solutions for IoT and IIoT. J. Netw. Comput. Appl. **149**, 102481 (2020)

23. Szabo, N.: Formalizing and securing relationships on public networks. First Monday **2**(9) (1997)

24. Valerio, P.: GSMA forecasts slight, short-term IoT market disruption (2020). https://iot.eetimes.com/gsma-forecasts-slight-short-term-iot-market-disruption/

25. Wang, X., et al.: Survey on blockchain for internet of things. Comput. Commun. **136**, 10–29 (2019)

26. XuperChain Lab: XuperChain (2020). https://github.com/xuperchain/xuperchain

A Privacy Preserving E-Voting System Based on Blockchain

Wenjun Fan[1], Shubham Kumar[2], Vrushali Jadhav[2], Sang-Yoon Chang[1],
and Younghee Park[2(✉)]

[1] Computer Science Department, University of Colorado Colorado Springs,
Colorado Springs, CO 80918, USA
{wfan,schang2}@uccs.edu
[2] Computer Engineering Department, San Jose State University,
San Jose, CA 95192, USA
{shubham.kumar,vrushali.jadhav,younghee.park}@sjsu.edu

Abstract. An electronic voting system can enable greater democracy
by allowing virtual and remote voting and facilitating greater participation. However, the e-voting systems have experienced allegations due to
corruption and unfair practices including voter impersonation, fraud, or
duplicate votes. This has caused a decline in transparency and faith in
the electoral process, resulting in reduced participation of citizens in the
democratic process. To address these challenges, this paper proposes a
blockchain-based e-voting system to ensure the fairness of the electoral
process and restore people's faith while protecting the users' privacy.
First, we utilize face recognition technology to authenticate voters after
extracting feature sets from images while users actively make actions.
Second, we design a smart contract to secure voter information during
the election. Our approach involves analyzing the limitations of the existing electoral voting system and applies the blockchain-based solution to
the vulnerable aspects of the existing system. We implement our approach by using Ethereum, smart contract, and OpenCV Haar Cascade
detection classifiers, and our evaluation based on the prototype shows
that our approach is effective and efficient.

Keywords: E-voting · Blockchain · Privacy preserving · Smart
contract · Ethereum

1 Introduction

Blockchain technology has been introduced by the cryptocurrencies such as Bitcoin, while its capabilities have been extended to diverse industry and government applications [19]. Blockchain has revolutionized the whole of industry and
academic research and even drive economic change on a global scale because
of its attractive properties including decentralization, immutability, trustworthi-
ness, anonymity, persistency, and audibility. Such security-related characteristics

---

S. Kumar—The author contributed equally to the first author.

© Springer Nature Switzerland AG 2021
Y. Park et al. (Eds.): SVCC 2020, CCIS 1383, pp. 148–159, 2021.
https://doi.org/10.1007/978-3-030-72725-3_11

make blockchain technology, a.k.a. distributed ledger technology (DLT), advantageous in the development of not only cryptocurrencies but also other decentralized applications (dApps) [3], including distributed PKI [11,13], distributed banking [4], health care [17], supply chain [21], and IoT [10].

The security features in blockchain technology also enable us to improve an online voting system, such as using the blockchain database to ensure the integrity of the electronic voting (e-voting) results [7]. Elections are the fundamental foundation of democracy and can be used to select significant policies or rules and decide the leader of an organization or a country. E-voting can provide automation and efficiency in the election process and facilitate greater participation in voting. However, e-voting has several security problems and challenges, including privacy breaches, manipulated voting results, and unintended user voting. It is important to ensure that the voting process is secure and immutable.

In this paper, we design and build a new decentralized application for an e-voting system based on blockchain technology. To prevent vote tampering, we take advantage of blockchain as a key technology because of its immutability and decentralization properties. Using the blockchain framework for processing all critical transactions not only ensures its correctness but also makes the transaction data available to the public. That reduces the chance of fraud, as anyone can verify the transaction information. Apart from securing every involved transaction, it is also essential to verify the authenticity of the voter in order to defend against the integrity threats of duplicate voting, voter information tampering, and illegal voting. Therefore, the proposed system has multiple contributions which can be summarized as follows.

- First, we design a reliable e-voting system by preserving all the transactions in blockchain taking advantage of the blockchain ledger's immutability.
- Second, the proposed system provides integrity and privacy protection by hashing the ballot information.
- Third, we implement our system and evaluate our approach. The experimental results show that our system is effective and efficient.

The rest of this paper is organized as follows: Sect. 2 states the general research problem for e-voting system and the general background of the blockchain technology; Sect. 3 proposes our privacy-preserving e-voting system using blockchain; Sect. 4 presents our implementation using Ethereum and smart contract and the experimental results built on the prototype; Sect. 5 reviews some related work to our paper; Sect. 6 makes a conclusion to this paper.

2 Background

2.1 Problem of E-Voting Systems

E-voting [8] has become increasingly popular in the past few years because of its great potential to efficiently deal with a great number of voters with time and cost-saving. The existing e-voting systems aim to not only improve the accessibility of voting but also maintain a secure system resistant to tampering. A number of countries such as Australia, Brazil, Estonia, Netherlands, and Norway have adopted e-voting for national elections. However, such attempts to implement e-voting protocols and systems showed that several security problems were still not solved [6,16].

A case in point is the well-known Helios [1], which is the first web-based, open-audit e-voting system. However, it is unsuitable for government elections where vote purchasing and intimidation becomes an issue; voter privacy is an essential component of government elections. Also, Helios is not suitable for larger applications due to risks of denial of service (DoS) attacks and data tampering, since the conventional deployments of the voting system rely on a centralized database service, which suffers a single point of failure essentially [12].

Therefore, the e-voting systems have experienced allegations because of corruption and unfair practices such as voter impersonation, fraud, and duplicate votes, owing to its design and implementation drawbacks like centralized database service, nontransparent auditing, and integrity protection lacking [5,18]. Those issues have caused a decline in faith in the electoral process, resulting in reduced participation in the democratic process. In this paper, we use blockchain technology to address those problems to enhance e-voting.

2.2 Blockchain Technology

Blockchain technology has been rapidly developing in recent times [19]. It is created specifically to make it possible to come to an agreement even in a nontrusted environment. Blockchain builds on distributed consensus protocol, peer-to-peer (P2P) networking, distributed storage, and the cryptographic primitives of hash function and public-key ciphers to provide an immutable and verifiable ledger of transactions. The blockchain technology enables secure distributed computing and operations since the ledger is processed by and shared with the participants contributing to the ledger, and the integrity of the transactions or records are secured through the cryptographic primitives.

Because the blockchain's successful application in digital currencies and financial transactions, e.g., Bitcoin and Ethereum, there has been a surge of dApps powered by blockchain. Blockchain is expected to be well suited with the addition of smart contracts [2] that use computerized transaction protocols to execute the terms of contracts agreed by users of a blockchain, to dApps domain including product manufacturing, supply chain management, vehicle provenance, distributed banking, e-voting, etc. Therefore, in this paper, we take advantage of the blockchain as well as the smart contract to propose a privacy preserved e-voting system.

3 Our Approach

In this section, we propose our system design and a follow-up description for each functional component in detail.

Fig. 1. An overview of our system design

3.1 System Overview

An overview of our system architecture is presented by Fig. 1. In general, our system combines machine learning, distributed ledger, and smart contract technologies together to empower the privacy-preserving e-voting system. Our system consists of three major components, i.e., *registration*, *e-voting smart contract*, and *verification*, which will be described in the next subsection. In this subsection, we present the high-level workflow through these three components for carrying out the voting process as follows.

A voter needs to register with the e-voting system first through the *registration* component. The voter's personal data, like name, birthday, address, and driver's license number (considered as privacy data) will be stored in a user data store. Later on, the stored user data is utilized to authenticate the voter to log in to the system to vote for the candidate. The *e-voting smart contract* component is in charge of processing the voting, whereby the voter's ballot will be counted into the corresponding candidate, and the voter will be set as an already voted user which means the same user will not able to vote for any candidate again. Thereafter, the *verification* component will verify the current ballot by checking the voting and the candidate matching. If the voting is verified, which means the vote casting succeeds, so the ballot will be written to the ledger and the voter will be notified that the voting is successful.

3.2 System Components in Detail

The three integrated components aforementioned realize the voting functionality of our system. In this subsection, we present every functional component in greater detail. Table 1 describes the variables used in the following content.

Registration. Our registration component leverages the machine learning approach to facilitate the registration and authentication process. The system generates a feature vector from the voter's image during the registration process and then evaluates the feature vector during the voter's login by measuring the level of similarity. Blockchain securely stores the voter's information that is encrypted using the voter's token given by the system, which allows voters to anonymously cast their votes without revealing any personal data. Blockchain also handles the cases of duplicate and fraud voting by tracking the voter ID during vote cast.

Table 1. Definition of variables

Variable	Definition
V	The set of voters
n	The number of total voters
V_i	The ith voter, $i \in \{1, 2, ..., n\}$
T_i	The token for $V_i \in V$
vID_i	The ith voter's ID returned by database

We describe the registration and authentication phases in greater details as follows:

Registering User Information. i) First, while creating an account, a user is asked to choose a username and set a password, and also to fill in a personal profile including name, birthday, identification number (e.g., driver license number), email address, phone number, etc. Also, the user must take a headshot photo, and the image will be used for facial recognition. With this, any user can only have one unique account, which avoids using multiple email addresses to create multiple accounts. ii) Second, an one-time password (OTP) is sent to the user's email address for verification, after which the user's facial feature vector of the voter's image is generated[1]. The system then creates a new account object (associating with the username and password) for the user as voter V_i, assuming $i \in \{1, 2, ..., n\} = V$, and generates a token T_i. The system then prompts the user to securely keep the token T_i, as this will be required by the user during future logins. iii) Third, the system stores the username and password in the backend database which returns a new voter ID, vID_i. The other vital information of the user such as name, phone number, and the facial feature vector is encrypted using the T_i generated in the second step. Such encrypted information is then stored in the blockchain along with the vID_i. This helps in preserving the identity of the user because all the identifiable information is encrypted and can only be decrypted using the user's T_i.

Authenticating Users for Voting. i) First, this process starts with prompting V_i to provide the username, password, and T_i to the voting platform. After successful verification of the account object V_i, the system then retrieves the vID_i for the

---

[1] Note that the system only stores the feature vector of the image instead of the raw image.

voter from the backend database. ii) Second, the system retrieves the encrypted user information for the vID_i retrieved in the previous step. Thereafter, the user is asked to do a biometric authentication using facial recognition through the platform for generating the facial feature vector data. iii) Third, the T_i provided by the user during login is used to decrypt the user information retrieved from the blockchain which also contains the V_i's facial feature vector data captured during the user's registration. This facial feature data retrieved from the blockchain is then evaluated against the current facial feature data for a match. If the facial recognition process is successful, the user can log in to the voting system.

E-Voting Smart Contract. The e-voting smart contract is used to deal with the voting by processing the voter's ballot as a blockchain transaction and returning transaction results back to the server. The vote cast by the user is added to the Blockchain by calling the deployed smart contract. To make the voter anonymous a new account is created on the Blockchain network and the coins are transferred from the user's account to a new account. The transfer of coins takes place after verification of Blockchain transaction. The candidate with the highest number of coins is the winner of the elections.

We describe the detailed voting process as follows: i) First, after successful login, the voter gets displayed a list of candidates participating in the election. ii) Second, the user votes for the desired candidate. In this step, the smart contract checks the V_i to see whether it has already voted or not. If the V_i already voted, the smart contract stops the voting process, if not, the smart contract continually goes to the next step. iii) Third, a new account is created on the blockchain, and coins are transferred from the voter's account to the new account to realize anonymity. iv) Fourth, if the vote succeeds according to the verification which will be described in Subsect. 3.2, the user is notified. v) Fifth, the vote count is then incremented for the candidate, for which the voter voted.

Verification. The verification component is responsible for checking the effectiveness of the votes. We describe the process as follows: i) First, the smart contract needs to verify the transaction between the voter and the new account, and also, from the new account to the candidate. Later, the transfer of coins will take place from the new account to the candidate's account, which is initially zero at the start of the election process. ii) Second, the voter is notified about the successful cast of a vote. At any time the number of voters (i.e. the users who cast their votes) should be equal to the total number of votes of all the candidates.

4 Evaluation

In this section, we first present the implementation and the experimental setup, e.g., Ethereum and the APIs used for development, and then analyze the experimental results.

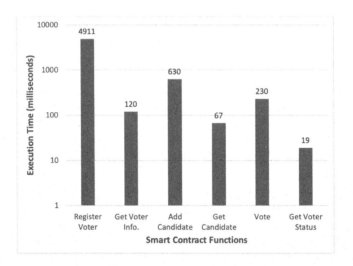

Fig. 2. Smart contract function execution time

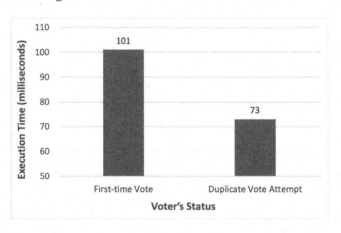

Fig. 3. Voting execution time analysis

4.1 Experiment Setup

We implement our system by using the following software and APIs.

Ganache (Truffle Suite) Version 2.4.0. This is a test environment that can be used to set up personal Ethereum Blockchain. It can be used to execute commands and run tests. It provides CLI and GUI support. We have used a GUI for our evaluation purposes.

Solidity Version 0.4.17. Our electoral smart contracts are developed using Solidity, and compiled using solidity compiler version 0.4.17.

Python Version 3.5. This version of Python is used to support and install different dependencies and Flask server. It is also used to create a virtual environment, activate it, and install different packages for running our machine learning facial recognition models.

Flask Server Version 1.1.1. A Flask based server uses OpenCV Haar Cascade detection classifiers to generate feature vectors from the user image. It uses cosine similarity to evaluate the match metrics for facial recognition.

Node.js Version 15.2.1. We use Node.js to create a back-end server that has multiple REST endpoints to serve requests for user registration, login, candidate profile setup, and election result storage.

MySQL Database Version 8.0.22. It stores the user's authentication credentials and can return voter's identification information back to the backend server.

4.2   Experimental Results

Built on our implementation, we conduct some experiments to evaluate our approach. The evaluation results are presented as follows.

Smart Contract Execution Time. This subsection presents the execution time of various smart contract functions based on our implementation. We evaluate the execution time for the functions including the actions like Register Voter, Get Voter Info., Add Candidate, Get Candidate, Vote, and Get Voter Status. Figure 2 presents the smart contract execution time in terms of different functions.

The execution time for Register Voter is significantly higher than the execution time of other functions as it involves the writing of the largest payload size to the smart contract. This payload has an encrypted facial feature vector and the voter's other information. Add Candidate action has the second-largest execution time as compared to the other functions, as it involves adding candidate information to the smart contract, but it does not have the facial feature vector stored in it.

The Vote function has a check, which verifies if the user has already voted or not. Figure 3 shows that the time taken for the First-time Vote function is higher than the time taken for the Duplicate Vote Attempt function, because in the case of the Duplicate Vote Attempt function, the smart contract blocks the duplicate voting attempt.

Smart Contract Gas Usage Analysis. We also present the gas usage and the ETH cost of various smart contract functions based on our implementation (see Table 2). We mainly focus on evaluating the gas usage of write operation intensive smart contract functions like Register Voter, Add Candidate, and Vote. Note that Get Voter Info., Get Candidate, and Get Voter Status are purely read functions that do not cost gas and ETH.

Table 2. Smart contract function analysis ($1 \text{ ETH} = 10^9 \text{ Gwei}$)

Smart contract functions	Gas used (Gwei)	ETH used
Register voter	1506948	0.001506948
Add candidate	131529	0.000131529
Vote	104939	0.000104939

The gas usage of the Register Voter function is significantly higher than the gas usage of other functions since it involves the writing of the largest amount of data through the heaviest payload size to the smart contract. This payload has an encrypted facial feature vector and the voter's other information.

Add Candidate function has the second-largest gas usage as compared to the other functions, as it also involves adding Candidate information to the smart contract, but it does not have the facial feature vector stored in it. The vote candidate function has the least gas usage among the smart contract write functions, as it has the smallest payload size among the other functions to write to the smart contract.

5   Related Work

In this section, we perform a literature review of the work in the context of e-voting systems. Helios [1] is a web-based and open-audit voting system. Helios is publicly accessible, and anyone can create and run an election. It greatly supports elections for small clubs, online communities, and student governments that need trustworthy elections without the significant overhead of coercion-freeness. However, the traditional Helios deployment relies on a centralized database service which makes it vulnerable to DoS attacks and data tampering. Our work uses blockchain to decentralize the database service which solves the single point of failure. In [14], the authors propose a novel voting credential management system (VCMS), which can preserve voting privacy against advanced attackers who do not only monitor the voting transactions and communications but are also capable of compromising an authority involved in the credential management and generation. VCMS uses multiple authorities to process the voter's registration and voting, and so one attacker cannot reveal the voter's privacy data if the attacker can only compromise one authority. Unless the attacker compromises multiple authorities and can correlate the compromised information, while that is very hard. Though our work simply uses a hash function to the ballot to preserve the voter's privacy information, we can also adopt the VCMS approach to perform the voting credential management to realize the privacy-preserving in e-voting.

Nowadays, with the rapid growth of blockchain technology's development, a number of blockchain-based e-voting systems have been proposed and implemented. To address the issue of voter data access, time-consuming in paper ballots, and voting fraud, the Blockchain-Enabled E-Voting (BEV) [9] system is proposed, which issues each voter a wallet and a single coin in that wallet which would act as a single opportunity to vote. BEV uses an encrypted key and tamper-proof personal IDs, whereby Blockchain generates cryptographically secure voting records to stop tamper with voter data while being open to public inspection. The work [12] improves the Helios e-voting system by replacing the centralized bulletin board with decentralized blockchain storage. Similarly, Zhou et al. [22] improve the traditional FOO e-voting system by replacing the trusted third party with a blockchain smart contract. Voatz [20] is a mobile-phone-based e-voting approach, which uses blockchain technology to ensure that votes are verified and immutably stored on multiple, geographically diverse verifying servers. However, Specter et al. [15] find that assuming optimistic use of the blockchain, the Voatz system has many vulnerabilities that allow different sorts of adversaries to alter, stop, or expose a user's ballot before the blockchain. Our work uses blockchain to store the vote/ballot information in a distributed manner as well, while we store the hash output of the information on the ledger to preserve the voter's ID to protect the voter's privacy.

6   Conclusion

We propose a privacy-preserving e-voting system to help users to register and cast their votes securely to their desired candidates. As the majority of people have email accounts, access to computers with external webcam or laptops with built-in cameras there is no additional cost associated with casting a vote using this platform. Users can log in to the web application after they have successfully verified their login credentials and identified themselves via facial recognition effectively. Users will get confirmation after their vote is successfully casted and they can also see the results of the election after the voting time frame is over. The existing applications in the literature do not have secure means to identify and authenticate the user, and due to this reason, there are more chances of malicious acts. The e-voting system that we have developed overcomes the problems of currently available systems.

Acknowledgment. This research was supported in part by Colorado State Bill 18-086.

References

1. Adida, B.: Helios: web-based open-audit voting. In: USENIX Security Symposium, vol. 17, pp. 335–348 (2008)
2. Buterin, V., et al.: A next-generation smart contract and decentralized application platform. White Pap. **3**(37) (2014)
3. Cai, W., Wang, Z., Ernst, J.B., Hong, Z., Feng, C., Leung, V.C.M.: Decentralized applications: the blockchain-empowered software system. IEEE Access **6**, 53019–53033 (2018)

4. Fan, W., Chang, S.Y., Emery, S., Zhou, X.: Blockchain-based distributed banking for permissioned and accountable financial transaction processing. In: 29th International Conference on Computer Communications and Networks (ICCCN), pp. 1–9 (2020)

5. Gibson, J.P., Krimmer, R., Teague, V., Pomares, J.: A review of e-voting: the past, present and future. Ann. Telecommun. **71**(7–8), 279–286 (2016)

6. Halderman, J.A., Teague, V.: The new South Wales iVote system: security failures and verification flaws in a live online election. In: Haenni, R., Koenig, R.E., Wikström, D. (eds.) VOTELID 2015. LNCS, vol. 9269, pp. 35–53. Springer, Cham (2015). https://doi.org/10.1007/978-3-319-22270-7_3

7. McKay, H.: First presidential vote cast using blockchain technology. https://www.foxnews.com/tech/first-presidential-vote-cast-using-blockchain-technology. Accessed 16 Oct 2016

8. Kohno, T., Stubblefield, A., Rubin, A.D., Wallach, D.S.: Analysis of an electronic voting system. In: 2004 Proceedings of IEEE Symposium on Security and Privacy, pp. 27–40. IEEE (2004)

9. Kshetri, N., Voas, J.: Blockchain-enabled e-voting. IEEE Softw. **35**(4), 95–99 (2018)

10. Li, Z., Kang, J., Yu, R., Ye, D., Deng, Q., Zhang, Y.: Consortium blockchain for secure energy trading in industrial internet of things. IEEE Trans. Industr. Inf. **14**(8), 3690–3700 (2018)

11. Matsumoto, S., Reischuk, R.M.: IKP: turning a pki around with decentralized automated incentives. In: 2017 IEEE Symposium on Security and Privacy (SP), pp. 410–426, May 2017

12. Perez, A.J., Ceesay, E.N.: Improving end-to-end verifiable voting systems with blockchain technologies. In: 2018 IEEE International Conference on Internet of Things (iThings) and IEEE Green Computing and Communications (GreenCom) and IEEE Cyber, Physical and Social Computing (CPSCom) and IEEE Smart Data (SmartData), pp. 1108–1115 (2018)

13. Sarker, A., Byun, S., Fan, W., Chang, S.Y.: Blockchain-based root of trust management in security credential management system for vehicular communications. In: ACM/SIGAPP Symposium On Applied Computing (SAC) (2021)

14. Sarker, A., Byun, S., Fan, W., Psarakis, M., Chang, S.: Voting credential management system for electronic voting privacy. In: 2020 IFIP Networking Conference (Networking), pp. 589–593 (2020)

15. Specter, M.A., Koppel, J., Weitzner, D.: The ballot is busted before the blockchain: A security analysis of voatz, the first internet voting application used in us federal elections. In: 29th {USENIX} Security Symposium ({USENIX} Security 2020), pp. 1535–1553 (2020)

16. Springall, D., et al.: Security analysis of the estonian internet voting system. In: Proceedings of the 2014 ACM SIGSAC Conference on Computer and Communications Security, CCS 2014, pp. 703–715. Association for Computing Machinery, New York (2014)

17. Sun, Y., Zhang, R., Wang, X., Gao, K., Liu, L.: A decentralizing attribute-based signature for healthcare blockchain. In: 27th International Conference on Computer Communication and Networks (ICCCN), pp. 1–9 (2018)

18. Taş, R., Tanrıöver, Ö.Ö.: A systematic review of challenges and opportunities of blockchain for e-voting. Symmetry **12**(8), 1328 (2020)

19. Underwood, S.: Blockchain beyond bitcoin. Commun. ACM **59**(11), 15–17 (2016)

20. Weiss, M., Halyard, M.: Voatz (2019)

21. Wu, H., et al.: Data management in supply chain using blockchain: challenges and a case study. In: 28th International Conference on Computer Communication and Networks (ICCCN), pp. 1–8, July 2019
22. Zhou, Y., Liu, Y., Jiang, C., Wang, S.: An improved foo voting scheme using blockchain. Int. J. Inf. Secur. **19**(3), 303–310 (2020)

BioBlockchain: Useful Proof-of-Work with Multiple Sequence Alignment

Yan Chen$^{(\boxtimes)}$ (ID), Thomas H. Austin (ID), and Philip Heller (ID)

San José State University, San Jose, CA 92009, USA
{yan.chen01,thomas.austin,philip.heller}@sjsu.edu

Abstract. Although Bitcoin is a successful electronic cash system, mining bitcoin wastes computation resources since the proof-of-work requires the miners to solve computational puzzles that have no intrinsic benefit to society. On the other hand, multiple sequence alignment is widely used in bioinformatics for analyzing similarities or differences among sequences, but it takes time and computational efforts. To reduce the waste of mining bitcoin, this paper proposes a modification to the Bitcoin protocol so that it requires the miners to find a multiple sequence alignment of protein sequences for proof-or-work.

Keywords: Blockchain · Bioinformatics · Multiple sequence alignment

1 Introduction

Bitcoin [1] is an electronic cash system that is purely peer-to-peer without a financial institution. To generate coins, clients need to go through a process of "mining", that is, solving a computational puzzle by incrementing a nonce until a required value is found ("proof-of-work"). These puzzles consume a huge amount of computational resources: the power consumed is equivalent to seven nuclear power plants [2]. However, these computational puzzles do not provide any benefit to society beyond their use in validating Bitcoin transactions.

One solution is to re-purpose the mining resources so the proof-of-work can be utilized for something useful. For example, Primecoin [3] uses proof-of-work to find prime numbers and form a primechain for mathematical research; Permacoin [4] uses proof-of-work for verifying distributed storage of archival data. The challenge of re-purposing is that the proof-of-work must have several essential properties to ensure the security of the Bitcoin network; these properties will be discussed in more detail in Sect. 4.

This project proposes a new proof-of-work system, called "BioBlockchain", that requires the miners to find multiple sequence alignments (MSA) for protein sequences to generate coins. MSA is an important bioinformatic tool that elucidates evolutionary relationships among similar DNA, RNA, or protein sequences [5]. Alignment is valuable in its own right, and is also the initial step of several other bioinformatic analyses, including computation of phylogenetic trees

© Springer Nature Switzerland AG 2021
Y. Park et al. (Eds.): SVCC 2020, CCIS 1383, pp. 160–166, 2021.
https://doi.org/10.1007/978-3-030-72725-3_12

and construction of profile Hidden Markov Models [6]. The time and memory complexity for computing the optimal MSA of n sequences with mean length L are both $O(L^n)$, so heuristic approaches are necessary. Thus BioBlockchain combines the computational difficulty required for a proof-of-work, with the societal benefit of providing a service to the bioinformatics community.

The rest of this paper is organized as follows: Sect. 2 gives background information about MSA in bioinformatics; Sect. 3 explains the mining process of BioBlockchain; Sect. 4 discusses the features needed for proof-of-work and how BioBlockchain achieves them; Sect. 5 demonstrates the architecture of this project, followed by a brief Conclusion.

2   Multiple Sequence Alignment in Bioinformatics

Multiple sequence alignment (MSA) is a method to align three or more related sequences by inserting gaps (usually represented as hyphens) into each input sequence so that all resulting sequences are the same length and the characters in each column are as consistent as possible. MSA is widely used in bioinformatics to analyze similarities or differences among sequences. Most of the applications involve aligning sequences of nucleotides (for DNA and RNA) or amino acids (for proteins), to compute phylogenetic trees to infer the evolutionary descent of related species, or to build profile Hidden Markov Models for computing if a new sequence matches a profile.

The proof-of-work in this project involves MSA for protein sequences. The sequences are provided in FASTA format, with each amino acid represented by a single character. Alignments are scored by scoring pairwise members of each column using the BLOSUM62 [7] matrix, which assigns high scores to pairs of amino acids with similar chemical properties such as charge or hydrophobicity, and low scores to pairs with dissimilar chemical properties.

2.1   Common Tool for MSA

Clustal Omega [8] is the most widely used tool for MSA. It is the latest version of a program that produces biologically meaningful alignments for DNA, RNA, or protein sequences. Research [8] showed that Clustal Omega can align a large scale of sequences faster and more accurately than earlier Clustal versions or other tools. Note that Clustal Omega, as well as all the tools for MSA, use heuristic approaches since the exact algorithm (dynamic programming) has an exponential complexity which is not tractable. Thus there is opportunity for improving the alignments computed by Clustal Omega.

2.2   Multiple Sequence Alignment Using Genetic Algorithms

Genetic algorithms [9,10] are a promising approach for improving Clustal's alignments. Genetic algorithms are a heuristic and nondeterministic approach that simulates natural selection over many generations within a population. Each individual in the population represents a candidate solution, encoded as a vector of values called the solution's "chromosome". In each generation (iteration), the fittest individuals (i.e. those representing the best solutions, as computed using BLOSUM62 [7]) are selected to produce offspring by exchanging solution traits (sections of their "chromosomes") with one another. To avoid local optima, implementations often have multiple independent populations which do not interact. The process ends when iteration no longer generates improvements. Genetic algorithms are highly parallelizable and therefore appropriate for blockchain proof-of-work.

This project uses a genetic algorithm named Multiple Sequence Genetic (MSG) [11] for computing MSA. MSG is a multiple population implementation. One population is initialized from a solution computed by Clustal Omega [8]. The other populations are initialized randomly. Miners use MSG to find a better alignment than the Clustal solution.

3   Mining Process

In this project, the number of sequences to align and the alignment score needed are configurable. For mining, the miner will first produce and hash a block of transactions. The sequences the miner needs to align will be based on the hash. Then the miner calculates the score of the MSA produced by Clustal Omega [8], which is used as a base score. The miner runs MSG [11] until finding an MSA with a score that improves the base score by a sufficient amount and announces the MSA found as the proof.

Similar to Bitcoin, the proof needs to be validated before adding the new block to the blockchain. To verify the proof, other miners need to first hash the proposed block to find the sequences being aligned, calculate the base score, and check if the proof announced indeed has a score that improves the base score by the desired amount. The new block will be added to the BioBlockchain only if the announced Multiple Sequence Alignment is verified. Figure 1 demonstrates the mining process.

4   Essential Properties of Proof-of-Work

The calculations involved in the proof-of-work must have the following features to ensure the system is efficient and secure.

4.1   Difficulty Adjustability

The difficulty should be adjustable to control the minting rate. The difficulty curve needs to be linear continuous. For Bitcoin, the hashed value required is adjusted every 2016 blocks so that new blocks are generated about every 10 min. Similarly, in Primecoin [3], the remainder of the Fermat primality test can be configured to adjust the difficulty. In this project, the difficulty will be adjusted by modifying the number of sequences to align and the alignment score needed.

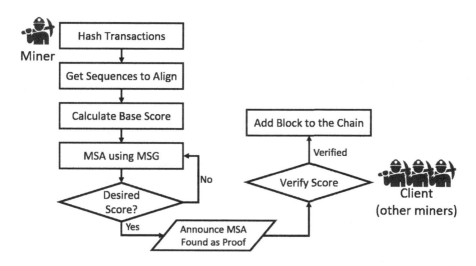

Fig. 1. Mining process

4.2   Efficient Verification

The process for finding the proof takes a long time but the verification of the proof should be fast. This is achieved by one-way functions, which means it is easy to calculate the output based on the input, but hard to find the input if given an output. For BioBlockchain, finding an MSA needs time and effort, but scoring the alignment is fast. So, the verification should be efficient since other miners only need to hash the proposed block once and calculate the scores to verify if the new alignment has the required score.

4.3   Precomputation Resistance

Miners should not be able to guess or precompute the proof before mining. This is also ensured by the one-way property of the hash function. In Bitcoin, the computational puzzles rely on the transactions, which makes it hard to guess because the miner didn't know the transaction before mining. Similarly, for BioBlockchain, the proof is the MSA of the sequences that are based on the hash of the transactions, so that it is feasible to precompute without knowing the actual transactions.

4.4   Non-reusability

The proof-of-work on one block should not be reusable for another block to prevent double-spending. In Bitcoin, a collision, which means different values have the same hash value, rarely happens. In BioBlockchain, the sequences to align are based on the hash of the transaction so it is not likely that the same sequences occur in different blocks. Moreover, since the algorithm used for MSA is nondeterministic, even the same sequences can have different alignments. But this needs further experiments.

5   BioBlockchain Architecture

BioBlockchain uses MSG [11] for finding MSA and scoring the result. To implement the MSA-based proof-of-work, SpartanGold (SG) [12], a simplified Bitcoin-like cryptocurrency written in JavaScript, is used as a foundation. Since MSG is written in Java, a class named `CallingJava` is implemented to call the classes and methods of MSG by executing shell commands with Node.js [13].

To modify the proof-of-work so that the miners find MSAs as proofs, the `Block` class and the `Miner` class in SG [12] are extended as the `BioBlock` class and the `BioMiner` class. The `BioBlock` class represents a block of transactions and has a method called `hasValidProof` that checks if the alignment (proof) is scored higher than the Clustal Omega [8] score by a required amount. The `findProof` method in the `BioMiner` class finds the alignment for a block. The scoring and aligning are both done by calling the corresponding method in MSG [11] through the `CallingJava` class, as shown in Fig. 2.

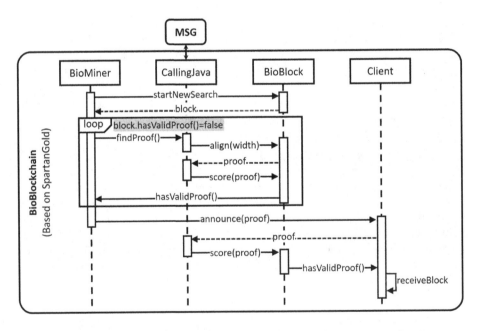

Fig. 2. Architecture and sequence diagram of finding a proof

When executing the `startNewSearch` method in the `BioMiner` class, a block is initialized. Then the miner uses the `findProof` method to find the alignment for the block. The alignment is based on the width and the MSG [11] will pre-compute a set of widths that are most likely to produce better alignments than Clustal Omega [8]. So `findProof` will go through the set of widths one by one to align the sequences until the `hasValidProof` method of the block returns true, that is, the score of the MSA meets the requirement. Once a proof is found, the miner will announce the alignment. A class called `Client` in SG [12], which is a superclass of the `BioMiner` class, will verify the block and store it in the BioBlockchain if the proof is validated.

6 Conclusion

To generate societal value from the computational resources used for mining, this project introduced a cryptocurrency with a proof-of-work that requires the miners to find a multiple sequence alignment for a list of protein sequences. MSA is essential in bioinformatics for analyzing the evolutionary relationships of different species. This paper showed that BioBlockchain has all properties needed for proof-of-work and thus the system is feasible.

Further work is needed to advance BioBlockchain from a successful proof-of-concept to a deployable resource. Future steps include examining how the number of sequences and the target score affect the mining rate, and improving architecture, particularly with respect to interactions between JavaScript and Java.

References

1. Nakamoto, S.: Bitcoin: a peer-to-peer electronic cash system. Technical report, Manubot (2019)
2. Redman, J.: The bitcoin network now consumes 7 nuclear plants worth of power. https://news.bitcoin.com/the-bitcoin-network-now-consumes-7-nuclear-plants-worth-of-power/
3. King, S.: Primecoin: Cryptocurrency with prime number proof-of-work (2013). http://primecoin.org/
4. Miller, A., Juels, A., Shi, E., Parno, B., Katz, J.: Permacoin: repurposing bitcoin work for data preservation. In: 2014 IEEE Symposium on Security and Privacy, pp. 475–490. IEEE (2014)
5. Altschul, S.F., et al.: Protein database searches using compositionally adjusted substitution matrices. FEBS J. **272**(20), 5101–5109 (2005)
6. Krogh, A., Brown, M., Mian, I.S., Sjölander, K., Haussler, D.: Hidden Markov models in computational biology: applications to protein modeling. J. Mol. Biol. **235**(5), 1501–1531 (1994)
7. Henikoff, S., Henikoff, J.G.: Amino acid substitution matrices from protein blocks. Proc. Natl. Acad. Sci. **89**(22), 10915–10919 (1992)
8. Sievers, F., Wilm, A., Dineen, D., et al.: Fast, scalable generation of high-quality protein multiple sequence alignments using clustal omega. Mol. Syst. Biol. **7**(1), 539 (2011)
9. Notredame, C., Higgins, D.G.: Saga: sequence alignment by genetic algorithm. Nucleic Acids Res. **24**(8), 1515–1524 (1996)

10. Zhang, C., Wong, A.K.: A genetic algorithm for multiple molecular sequence alignment. Bioinformatics **13**(6), 565–581 (1997)
11. Heller, P.: MSG: a gap-oriented genetic algorithm for multiple sequence alignment. Master's thesis, San José State University (2009)
12. Austin, T.: A simplified blockchain-based cryptocurrency for experimentation. http://www.spartangold.net/
13. Node.js v15.6.0 documentation. https://nodejs.org/api/child_process.html

Machine Learning for Security

Reconstructing Classification to Enhance Machine-Learning Based Network Intrusion Detection by Embracing Ambiguity

Chungsik Song[2], Wenjun Fan[1], Sang-Yoon Chang[1],
and Younghee Park[2(✉)]

[1] Computer Science Department, University of Colorado Colorado Springs,
Colorado Springs, CO 80918, USA
{wfan,schang2}@uccs.edu
[2] Computer Engineering Department, San Jose State University, San Jose,
CA 95192, USA
{chungsik,younghee.park}@sjsu.edu

Abstract. Network intrusion detection systems (IDS) has efficiently identified the profiles of normal network activities, extracted intrusion patterns, and constructed generalized models to evaluate (un)known attacks using a wide range of machine learning approaches. In spite of the effectiveness of machine learning-based IDS, it has been still challenging to reduce high false alarms due to data misclassification. In this paper, by using multiple decision mechanisms, we propose a new classification method to identify misclassified data and then to classify them into three different classes, called a malicious, benign, and ambiguous dataset. In other words, the ambiguous dataset contains a majority of the misclassified dataset and is thus the most informative for improving the model and anomaly detection because of the lack of confidence for the data classification in the model. We evaluate our approach with the recent real-world network traffic data, Kyoto2006+ datasets, and show that the ambiguous dataset contains 77.2% of the previously misclassified data. Re-evaluating the ambiguous dataset effectively reduces the false prediction rate with minimal overhead and improves accuracy by 15%.

Keywords: Network intrusion detection · Machine learning · Ensemble classifiers

1 Introduction

The interest to apply advanced machine learning techniques for the intrusion detection system has been steadily growing since the late 1990s [1–4]. Machine

This work is supported by NSF Award #1723663.

© Springer Nature Switzerland AG 2021
Y. Park et al. (Eds.): SVCC 2020, CCIS 1383, pp. 169–187, 2021.
https://doi.org/10.1007/978-3-030-72725-3_13

learning methods discover hidden, valid patterns and relationships among the attributes in a large dataset to find malicious actions through automatic model construction. These approaches allow for a more flexible and distributable way to identify network activity based on limited, incomplete, and nonlinear data sources by identifying adversarial activities [5–9]. Due to these promising capabilities, machine learning-based IDSs have been extensively studied by the research community for many years [10–16]. Network intrusion detection system (NIDS) endeavors to discover unauthorized access to network resources by analyzing the network traffic data and detect the signs of malicious activities which undermine the normal operation of a network [17,18].

However, in real-world operational settings, only misuse detectors are predominantly used in the form of signature systems that scan the network traffic for characteristics byte sequences [19]. The imbalance between the extensive amount of research and the lack of operational deployments of such systems stems in large part from specifics of the problem domain. The high error rate is one of the primary reasons for the lack of success of machine learning-based intrusion detection systems in operational settings. Furthermore, to reduce misclassification errors and minimize false alerts is one of the major challenges in machine learning-based intrusion detection systems [20,21].

To address the challenge of the misclassification errors in the machine learning-based intrusion detection system, this paper introduces a new category to embrace the ambiguity of the decision process and classify the dataset into three categories, benign (confident), malicious (confident), and ambiguous dataset. To categorize the confident and ambiguous datasets, we develop a confidence score system and utilize it for the decision of the classification. The ambiguous dataset is a collection of data that receive mixed decision predictions or unanimously indecisive predictions in the classification process of the model. The proposed system uses an ensemble model for classification and we evaluate our approach with recent real network traffic data. We extract the ambiguous dataset and show that it contains most of the misclassified data in the datasets. In other words, most of the misclassified results in the model, either false alerts or missed attacks, are included in the ambiguous dataset. We re-evaluate the ambiguous dataset to reduce the uncertainty in the decision process. Re-evaluating the ambiguous dataset effectively reduces false predictions with minimal overhead and improves the system performance for intrusion detection. Also, our scheme makes correction decisions on the dataset labeled as "Unknown" attacks which resulted in poor performances previously, and classify them as malicious with high confidence. Our contributions are summarized as follows.

1. The concept of an ambiguous dataset is first introduced to identify a subset of test data that contains the most uncertainty in the decision process of the model for the intrusion detection system.
2. We evaluate our approach with the recent real network traffic data and show that the ambiguous dataset contains 77.2% of misclassified data in our experiment.

3. We show that re-evaluating the ambiguous dataset effectively reduces false predictions and improves the accuracy of the anomaly detection by contributing to classify the full dataset completely into a specific class with almost no ambiguous data.

The rest of the paper is organized as follows. Section 2 describes the motivation of reconstructing classification by embracing the ambiguity in the intrusion detection system. Section 3 presents the structure of the classification and decision model used for intrusion detection. In Sect. 4 we discuss the public datasets available for the evaluation of intrusion detection systems and our model. Section 5 and Sect. 6 include the details of our evaluations and results, respectively. The details of the ambiguous dataset and its impact on our detection model are discussed. Section 7 summarizes related works. We conclude our work with discussion and future works in Sect. 8.

2   Reconstructing Classification by Embracing Ambiguity

While the classification of variable sources and transient events can be obtained using real-time and archival data, the classification will be ambiguous in many cases. Additional data and analysis with other datasets would be needed for the confidence of classification results in the case of interesting events. This poses a challenge of the automated decision-making process for the optimal use of the available, finite computing resources, and limited time constraints. Most machine learning algorithms make the assumption that training data is a random sample drawn from a stationary distribution. A fixed set of features can represent the data when the underlying structure of the data is stationary. When we have more data and especially use optimized feature sets that differentiate malicious activities from benign ones, we can reduce the ambiguity in classification. However, continuous and rapid changes in network usage patterns, as well as the attack patterns, have added another level of challenges [20,21].

Alternatively, instead of maximizing classification accuracy, we consider a scenario where the algorithm chooses a set of data that are most uncertain, determines the follow-up analyses, and improves the accuracy of classification in the subsequent analysis. The goal of the algorithm is to select a set of data that is the most interesting. The subsequent analysis then provides information on how interesting the dataset is. We follow the second approach and select a set of data that are most uncertain, called an ambiguous dataset. The ambiguous dataset is a dataset that is expected to be most informative and can most effectively improve the model in subsequent analysis. The source of the ambiguous dataset is not the intrinsic characteristics of the data but the deficiency of the model used. The selection of the ambiguous dataset thus depends on the balance between efficiency and accuracy of the detection model. There are two parts to this challenge. First, the selected dataset should be the most uncertain sample that is expected to be the most informative and is capable of most improving the model in subsequent analysis. Second, what type of follow-up measurement and/or analysis, given the available set of resources, would yield the maximum information gain in a situation? The subsequent section describes the way to classify the dataset into three classes, malicious, benign, and ambiguous. The definition of the ambiguous dataset and its relation to the misclassified dataset are followed.

2.1 Classify into Three Classes

Algorithm 1 shows the pseudo-code of three-class classification. Firstly, predicted probability is evaluated for each base classifier used in the ensemble model (see lines 1–2). These values are used to evaluate the predicted probability of the ensemble classifier (see lines 3–4). Based on the evaluated predicted probability system classifies data into three classes, malicious (lines 5–6), benign (lines 7–8), and ambiguous (lines 9–10). Base classifiers and ambiguous threshold θ_A are provided as inputs.

Algorithm 1: Three-Class Classification

Inputs:
   classifiers: $\{C_i\}$
   ambiguous threshold θ_A
Output :
   prediction result
1: Calculate the predicted probability from base classifier C_i:
2:    $P_i =$ Predicted Probability (C_i)
3: Take the average of individual predicted probabilities to get the ensemble predicted probability:
4:    $P_{ens} = Avg(P_i)$
5: **if** $P_{ens} > 1 - \theta_A$
6:    return malicious
7: **else if** $P_{ens} < \theta_A$
8:    return benign
9: **else** $(\theta_A < P_{ens} < 1 - \theta_A)$
10:    return ambiguous

For the confident (either benign and malicious) dataset, we take actions based on the type of a decision, benign and malicious, as other traditional intrusion detection systems do. But we take further analysis and evaluation of the ambiguous dataset since most of the false alerts or missed attacks belong to this category and even novel (unknown) attacks can be included in this dataset. Since the ambiguous dataset is a small portion of the full dataset (~10% of the full dataset), the re-evaluation process is light in resource usage and fast in the computing process.

2.2 Ambiguous Dataset

We define the ambiguous dataset as those received mixed decision predictions or unanimously indecisive predictions in the multiple classifier systems. For a system of binary classes, either 1 (malicious) or 0 (benign), each classifier estimates the prediction probability for a specific category (benign or malicious) indicating its decision about the class of the object. The system chooses the class with the highest values of the prediction probability for the object. If most of the classifiers vote for malicious, the prediction probability for the class of the object will be close to 1. Otherwise, the prediction probability will be close to 0 when most of them vote for benign. The ambiguous dataset consists of the data that receive the value near 0.5. When using a probabilistic model for the binary classification, the ambiguous dataset simply queries the instance whose posterior probability of being malicious is near 0.5.

We introduce an ambiguous threshold value, θ_A where $0 < \theta_A < 0.5$, to determine the range of *prediction probability* for an ambiguous dataset. The threshold is the value our model uses for a classification decision to be confident. For binary classification (e.g., malicious and benign), our model classifies to confident "malicious" when *prediction probability* $> 1 - \theta_A$ and confident "benign" when *prediction probability* $< \theta_A$. The ambiguous dataset is defined as those with $\theta_A \leq$ *prediction probability* $\leq 1 - \theta_A$.

Misclassified Dataset. One of the challenges in applying machine learning techniques to intrusion detection systems is the high rate of false alerts. Even though the error rate is very low (1~2%), the number of misclassified data is not negligible with the growing number of data that need to be processed and analyzed. Our analysis in the subsequence section shows that most of the misclassified data – either false alerts or missed attacks – are included in the ambiguous dataset. Figure 5 shows the distribution of the predicted probability in the misclassified dataset. More than 77% of the misclassified dataset are distributed within the window for the ambiguous dataset, $\theta_A \leq$ *prediction probability* $\leq 1 - \theta_A$. This result indicates that most of the misclassified samples distribute near the boundary of two target classes and define the ambiguous dataset.

Evaluation of Ambiguous Dataset. The most uncertain samples are expected to be the most informative and are capable of most improving the model. As we show, the ambiguous dataset contains the majority of the misclassified dataset and is the most uncertain subset in our decision model. The measured performance metrics for the ambiguous dataset show low values compared to those of the confident dataset which excludes the ambiguous dataset from the full test dataset. We re-evaluate the ambiguous dataset to reduce the uncertainty in the decision process. This process concerns not only the uncertainty but also the outcomes and risks of this uncertainty. We build a model for the ambiguous dataset and re-evaluate the performance. The accuracy of detecting malicious activities increases to 90%. The importance of features is re-evaluated for the ambiguous dataset and compared to that of the full dataset.

3   Model Build

In this section, we describe the classification model used in our intrusion detection system. We use an ensemble of classifiers that combines multiple base classification algorithms (Fig. 1). Ensemble classifier systems (also called multiple classifier systems) exploit the mutually complementary decision boundaries produced from individual classifiers to improve the performance of the whole. The goal of an ensemble method is to combine different classifiers into a meta-classifier that has a better generalization performance. Ensemble classifier systems have shown to produce favorable results compared to those of single-expert systems for a broad range of applications and under a variety of scenarios [22]. Many studies have applied the diversity of ensemble methods to the intrusion detection problem [23].

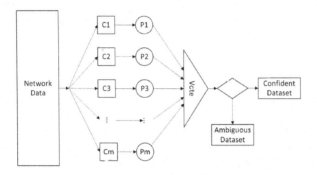

Fig. 1. Design for ensemble classifier system: $C_1, C_2, \cdots C_m$ are base classifiers and $P_1, P_2, \cdots P_m$ are for predicted probability of each individual classifier

We build our ensemble classifier model using base classifiers with different machine learning techniques; Decision Tree [24,25], Gradient Boosted Tree [26, 27], Random Forest [28,29] and Multi-layer Perceptron model [30]. We evaluate individual classifier using Receiver Operator Characteristic (ROC) graphs [31].

3.1   Classification Algorithms

Classification is one of the most frequently encountered decision making processes [32] and used when an object needs to be assigned into a predefined group or class based on a number of observed attributes related to that object. For a classification problem, a set of N training examples of the form (X, Y) is given, where Y is a discrete class label and X is a vector of n attributes. From these examples a model $Y = f(X)$ is inferred and used to predict the class Y of future examples X with high accuracy. Intrusion detection can be approached as a classification problem that classifies audit events as belonging to a benign or malicious class. The learned model labels or predicts new unseen audit data as belonging to one of them [33–35]. An ideal application in intrusion detection would gather sufficient "normal" and "abnormal" audit data for a user or a program to correctly train the classifier and then apply a classification algorithm to make decisions for the (future) audit data as belonging to the normal or abnormal class.

3.2   Confidence of Decision

The general formulation of the design problem of an ensemble system is to generate several individual classifiers and then employ some fusion functions (e.g., majority voting) to combine classifier outputs to achieve high performance. In simple majority voting, a class label is selected when it has been predicted by the majority classifiers, that is, received more than 50% of the votes. For multiclass settings, it can be popularity voting where the class label that received the most votes is selected. In this paper, we use the probability of a predicted class label to make a decision in an ensemble of the classifiers. Each classification algorithm returns the probability of a predicted class label. We calculate the average value of the probability of a predicted class label instead of simply counting the number of votes for a class label. The modified version of the majority vote for predicting class labels from probabilities can be written as follows:

$$\hat{Y} = \arg \max_i \sum_{j=1}^{N} P_{ij} \tag{1}$$

Here, P_{ij} is the predicted probability for a class i by a classifier j.

We are interested in not only the final decision from the ensemble classifiers but also the confidence level of the decision. To formalize the confidence level of the final decision in ensemble classifier, we introduce the "Confidence Score" P which is defined as the ratio of a number of the decision vote (N_D) to the total number of a vote (N) for class label counting:

$$P = \frac{N_D}{N} \tag{2}$$

When the final decision of the classification for a sample is malicious, the number of decision votes is the number of votes for the malicious class. The confidence score for a class label i in the predicted probability approach can be calculated simply by taking the average of the predicted probability of each base classifier:

$$P_i = \frac{1}{N} \sum_{j=1}^{N} P_{ij} \tag{3}$$

where N is the number of base classifiers.

Let's consider simple cases of the decision process for a binary classification problem (e.g., 1 is malicious and 0 is benign) in an ensemble classifier to see the difference from the simple majority voting approach. Five base classifiers are

Table 1. Sample dataset to demonstrate the difference in the calculation of confidence score between majority voting and the prediction using the average value of the probability of a predicted class label. $D_1, D_2, \cdots, D_6$ are different samples. $C_1, C_2, \cdots, C_5$ are different base classifiers. Values in each cell are the predicted probability by each classifier for the "malicious" label. P_1 and P_2 are confidence scores in % for each case using Majority voting and averaging predicted probability, respectively.

	C_1	C_2	C_3	C_4	C_5	$P_1(\%)$	$P_2(\%)$
D_1	0.9	0.9	0.9	0.9	0.9	100	90
D_2	0.6	0.6	0.6	0.6	0.6	100	60
D_3	0.6	0.6	0.6	0.1	0.1	60	40
D_4	0.4	0.4	0.9	0.9	0.4	40	60
D_5	0.4	0.4	0.4	0.4	0.4	0	40
D_6	0.2	0.2	0.2	0.2	0.2	0	20

used and each classifier predicts the probability for the class label to be malicious internally as shown in Table 1 and votes to either malicious or benign based on the predicted probability with equal weights. For example, every base classifier predicts a "malicious" label with a predicted probability of 0.6 for a sample data D_2. Majority vote method will predict malicious with 100% confidence because all classifiers unanimously vote to "malicious". For sample data D_3, the majority vote method will predict malicious with 60% confidence since 3 out of 5 base classifiers vote to "malicious". However, the modified version of the majority vote from predicted probabilities shows different results. For sample data D_2, the modified version predicts the class label as malicious as the same as that of the majority vote method but with lower confidence (60%). More different results come for the sample data D_3 and D_4. Even though more classifiers vote for malicious (benign), final predictions are reversed in the modified version since two of them predict the very low(high) probability for D_3 (D_4).

By using the predicted class probabilities instead of counting the class labels for majority voting, we have more fine-grained confidence levels for the prediction. The same 100% confident prediction can be distributed $50 \sim 100\%$ confidence. Some 0% confidences can have higher confidence scores. Since not only the final decision but also the confidence level of the decision of the individual classifier is taken into account, this approach is accurate when each classifier in the ensemble is well calibrated.

4   Evaluation

We use the recent Kyoto2006+ dataset, which has been accumulated for the year 2015. Kyoto 2006+ datasets have built on the real traffic data which are obtained from diverse types of honeypots [36]. During the observation period, there were

6,581,188 normal sessions and 130,135,437 known attack sessions. Among the attack sessions, 2,770 sessions were related to unknown attacks. All traffic data on honeypots were thoroughly inspected using security software since all traffic data captured from honeypots have been collected as attack data [36]. Among traffic data captured from honeypots, however, there are some sessions that did not trigger any alerts but contained shellcodes. These sessions were labeled as "Unknown" attacks.

We analyze the dataset for the year 2015 month by month and present the result for the January 2015 dataset which has 11,218,206 known attack sessions, 1,186,780 normal sessions, and 553 "Unknown" attack sessions. There are more attack data than normal data, which makes the whole dataset imbalanced. We randomly select from the attack dataset and make the both normal and attack dataset balanced. The data labeled as "Unknown" attacks are collected separately and used own analysis but not used in either training or testing process as shown in Table 2. Results for each month are similar even though there are small differences in details.

Table 2. Summary of the test dataset used in the evaluation

Total	2,374,113
Normal	1,186,780
Known Attack	1,186,780
Unknown Attack	553

4.1 Feature Sets

The Kyoto 2006+ dataset consists of twenty-four statistical features; fourteen features based on features of the KDD Cup 99 dataset and ten additional features [36]. Among the original 41 features of the KDD Cup 99 dataset, insignificant features and content features were excluded in Kyoto 2006+ dataset, because they are not suitable for network-based intrusion detection systems. Fourteen statistical features, which are significant and essential features, were extracted from honeypot data. In addition to the 14 statistical features, additional 10 features were extracted, which allow investigating more effectively what kinds of attacks happened on networks. They also can be utilized for IDS evaluation with the 14 conventional features, and users are able to extract more features using the additional 10 features. In additional ten features, label feature is included. Label feature indicates whether the session was attacked or not; '1' means the session was normal, '−1' means a known attack was observed in the session, and '−2' means an unknown attack was observed in the session.

4.2   Preprocessing

In our evaluation, we don't include IDS, Malware, Ashula detection, and IP address and port number for both source and destination features. For Start Time (indicates when the session was started) data, we divide it into day parting period, "Overnight", "Morning", "Midday", "Afternoon" and "Evenings". There are four categorical features: Service (the connection's service type, e.g., DNS, SSH, etc.) Start Time, Flags (the state of the connection at the time the connection was written), Protocols (TCP, ICMP, etc.). Each categorical feature expressing m possible categorical values is transformed to a value in R^m using a function e that maps the jth value of the feature to the jth component of an m-dimensional vector:

$$e(x_i) = \underbrace{(0, \cdots, 1, \cdots, 0)}_{1 \ at \ position \ j} \text{ if } x_i = j \qquad (4)$$

The set of features presented in Kyoto 2006+ dataset contains categorical and numerical features of diffcrent source and scales. Both the numerical and the categorical features are scaled with respect to each feature's mean μ and standard deviation σ:

$$n(x_i) = \frac{x_i - \mu}{\sigma} \qquad (5)$$

After encoding all categorical features and excluding irrelevant features, there are 47 feature sets used in the experiment. The importance of the features in Kyoto 2006+ data sets are evaluated. Using the Random Forest algorithm, we can measure the importance of a feature as the averaged impurity decrease computed from all decision trees in the forest without making any assumptions whether data is linearly separable or not. For the evaluation of the importance of features, we train a forest of 1,000 trees on the Kyoto2006+ dataset and rank the features by their respective importance measures. In Fig. 2 we plot the ranks of features in the Kyoto 2006+ dataset by their relative importance; note that the feature importance is normalized so that they sum up to 1.0. First, 10 features among 47 features take 81% of importance.

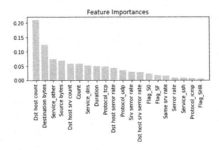

Fig. 2. Relative importance of feature in 2015 data set from Kyoto 2006+ dataset. The feature importances are normalized so that they sum up to 1.0.

In importance feature sets, there are features related to destination charac-teristics, as shown in the paper [36]. In Table 3, the first 10 features are listed in order of importance ("Full Dataset"). Four out of ten most important features are related to destination characteristics, such as Dst host count, Destination bytes, Dst host srv count, and Dst host serror rate. Two of them are service types, Service other and Service DNS. Source bytes, Count, Duration, and Pro-tocol TCP are also listed in the ten most important features.

Table 3. The importance of features for the whole and ambiguous dataset. The first 10 important features are listed in order of importance.

	Full dataset	Ambiguous dataset
1	Dst host count	Destination bytes
2	Destination bytes	Duration
3	Service other	Dst host count
4	Source bytes	Source bytes
5	Dst host srv count	Count
6	Count	Dst host srv count
7	Service dns	Srv serror rate
8	Duration	Dst host srv serror rate
9	Protocol tcp	Period Midday
10	Dst host serror rate	Service dns

4.3   Results: Performance of Base Classifiers

The ROC graphs for individual classification algorithms are evaluated on the data and results are shown in Fig. 3. The ensemble classifiers with Random Forest and Gradient Boost Tree classifier show the best results which attain 99% and 89% True Positive rate, respectively, at 2% False Positive rate. Decision Tree algorithm and MLP show relatively low performance.

Based on the ROC curve, we compute the area under the curve (AUC) to characterize the performance of a classification model. The 10-fold cross-validations were used to calculate ROC-AUC in the training phase and average values (mean) are obtained with standard deviation values (std). Test datasets are used to evaluate the model in the separated dataset to measure its capabil-ity to generalize the predictions to unseen data. Table 4 shows the summary of results. Results for the test dataset are consistent with those for train datasets within errors and show that there is no indication of over-fittings in the trained models.

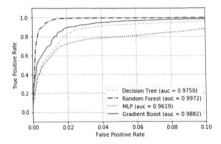

Fig. 3. ROC-curves for classifiers evaluated

Table 4. ROC-AUC for classifiers. Columns "mean" and "std" are results calculated for the train dataset with 10-fold cross-validations and column "test" are for the test dataset

Classifier	mean	std	test
Decision Tree	0.9749 ± 0.0006		0.9753
Random Forest	0.9972 ± 0.0001		0.9973
MLP	0.9624 ± 0.0003		0.9622
Gradient Boost	0.9880 ± 0.0009		0.9873

4.4 Results: Performance of Ensemble Classifier

We evaluate our model using performance metrics, such as accuracy (ACC), precision (PRE), recall (REC), and F1 score (F1). Accuracy provides general information about how many samples are classified correctly and is calculated as the sum of correct predictions divided by the total number of predictions. Precision and recall are performance metrics that are related to a true positive rate that is especially useful for imbalanced class problems. Precision is the ratio of the true positives to the total predicted positives and recall are the ratio of the true positives to the actual positives that are the sum of true positive and false negative predictions. In practice, often F1 score which is a combination of precision and recall is used. These performance metrics are used to quantify the performance of a model in general.

Results are summarized in Table 5 (Full) with 96.7% accuracy, 96.2% precision, 97.1% recall and 96.6% F1 score. Relatively low value of precision compared to that of recall indicates that there are more false positives (false alerts) than false negatives (missed attacks).

For the decision process, we use the probability of a predicted class label, predicted probability P, in our model. Figure 4 shows the distribution of the probability for predicted malicious in the full dataset. 1 means confident malicious (attack) and 0 means confident benign (normal) class. Most of the sessions are classified either as confident malicious (1) or as confident benign (0).

Table 5. Comparison of performance metrics among dataset with all (whole), dataset excluding ambiguous dataset (confidence), and only ambiguous (ambiguous) dataset

Dataset	ACC	PRE	REC	F1
Full	0.9665	0.9618	0.9711	0.9664
Confidence	0.9915	0.9958	0.9871	0.9914
Ambiguous	0.7477	0.7030	0.8267	0.7598

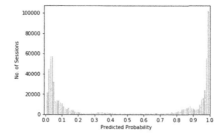

Fig. 4. Distribution of the probability of predicted values for malicious in the full dataset: 1 means malicious (attack) and 0 means benign (normal).

4.5   Results: Misclassified Dataset

In our evaluation, 3.4% of sessions in the test dataset are incorrectly classified. We collect those misclassified sessions, called misclassified dataset, and analyze them. Figure 5 shows the prediction probability distribution of sessions in the misclassified dataset. There are two bands where predicted probabilities of misclassified datasets are distributed. One narrow band is at predicted probability ~1.0 and the other band is rather broad and distributed between 0.2~0.8. The misclassified dataset with predicted probability ~1.0 can be false alerts in our model or missed attacks in the test dataset. We need more investigation for these misclassified sessions and reserve it for future work. Other misclassified dataset is distributed around the boundary of the malicious and benign dataset and rather broadly distributed with predicted probabilities 0.2~0.8.

We define the ambiguous dataset as those have predicted probability in a range close to the boundary between malicious and benign dataset ($P \approx 0.5$). Since misclassified datasets are distributed around the boundary, most of them will belong to ambiguous datasets. When we select a wider range of ambiguous datasets, more datasets are categorized as ambiguous and more misclassified datasets belong to. Figure 6 presents the ratio of the ambiguous dataset to the total dataset and in the misclassified dataset with different selections of the predicted probability range. The ratio of the ambiguous dataset to the total dataset (red graph) increases rapidly when the predicted probability range is after [0.2~0.8]. But the increase of the ratio in misclassified datasets is saturated after [0.25~0.75].

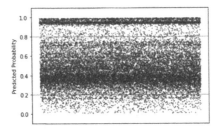

Fig. 5. Distribution of predicted values for misclassified datasets: 1 means attack and 0 means normal. Two horizontal lines (0.2 and 0.8) indicate the window for the ambiguous dataset

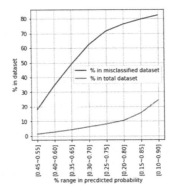

Fig. 6. The portion of ambiguous dataset in total dataset and in misclassified dataset with different selections of the predicted probability

We use the ambiguous threshold, θ_A where $|\theta_A| < 0.5$, to determine the range of *prediction probability* for the ambiguous dataset. The ambiguous threshold value, θ_A, is optimized to maximize the ratio of the ambiguous dataset to the misclassified dataset and to minimize the portion of the ambiguous dataset in the entire dataset. Let the ratio of the ambiguous dataset to the misclassified dataset as a function of the ambiguous threshold $f_1(\theta_A)$ and the portion of the ambiguous dataset in the entire dataset as $f_2(\theta_A)$. The ambiguous threshold θ_A is determined by maximizing

$$f(\theta_A) = f_1(\theta_A) + (1 - f_2(\theta_A)) \tag{6}$$

Figure 7 presents the $f_1(\theta_A) - f_2(\theta_A)$ obtained in our experiments as a function of θ_A. It shows the maximum is reached at $\theta_A = 0.2$. We set $\theta_A = 0.2$ and the range for ambiguous dataset as $0.2 < P < 0.8$ based on this observation. With this selection, the ambiguous dataset contains 77.2% of the misclassified dataset but is only 10.24% of the total dataset.

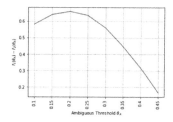

Fig. 7. The dependency of $f_1(\theta_A) - f_2(\theta_A)$ on ambiguous threshold θ_A.

We regroup the test dataset into "Confident" (either malicious or benign) and "Ambiguous" and re-evaluate our model with the confident and ambiguous dataset separately. Results are summarized in Table 5 as Confident and Ambiguous, respectively. The accuracy of the confident dataset is improved by 2.5% to 99.2%. On the other hand, it is decreased for the ambiguous dataset to 74.8%. The same changes can be seen in other performance metrics. This result shows that the ambiguous dataset contains the most uncertain samples. In Sect. 4.7, we re-train the ambiguous dataset alone and resolve these misclassified sessions.

4.6   Results: Unknown Datasets

In our test dataset, there are 553 "Unknown" attacks which are not included in the training phase of the model. We use our model and classify these "Unknown" datasets. Figure 8 shows the distribution of the predicted probabilities. We can see two interesting results for the dataset labeled "Unknown". First, our results show that all of the unknown datasets are classified as attacks in our model (prediction probability > 0.5). Second, most of them are categorized as a malicious dataset with high confidence prediction probability > 0.8. Thus, any novel attacks which are not filtered by the existing intrusion detection systems used in Kyoto 2006 + dataset are classified as malicious and detected in our model.

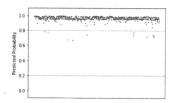

Fig. 8. Distribution of predicted values for unknown datasets: 1 means attack and 0 means normal. Two horizontal lines (0.2 and 0.8) indicate the window for ambiguous dataset

4.7   Results: Re-evaluation of Ambiguous Dataset

In this section, we show that the performance of intrusion detection can be improved by re-evaluating ambiguous datasets with minimum overhead. Since the number of ambiguous datasets is much less than that of the full datasets (10% of the full dataset in our case), the re-evaluation process is light in resource usage and fast in the computing process. We first review the importance of features for the ambiguous dataset. Table 3 compares the first 10 important features in two datasets, full and ambiguous dataset. Three different features are included in the 10 important features for the ambiguous dataset and the order in the importance of features also gets changed. This difference indicates that a separate model has to be learned (trained) for the optimal classification of the ambiguous dataset.

We re-train the ambiguous dataset and rebuild a model. Table 6 shows the performance metrics of retraining results for the ambiguous dataset and compare to previous values. In re-evaluation, the accuracy (ACC), precision (PRE), recall (REC), and F1 scores (F1) are improved by 15%, 20%, 9%, and 15% respectively. We can improve performance and resolve many misclassified samples in the re-training process.

Table 6. Comparison of performance metrics for ambiguous datasets between before and after re-evaluation.

	ACC	PRE	REC	F1
Before	0.7477	0.7030	0.8267	0.7598
After	0.9029	0.9077	0.9194	0.9135

5   Related Works

Machine learning and data mining approaches for intrusion detection derive associative rules from available sample data and use statistical techniques to discover subtle relationships between data items and to find consistent and useful patterns that describe programs and user behavior. There are many survey papers [11–13,16,37] which summarize achievements, current trends, challenges, even limitations in various machine learning-based approaches. Because of simplicity, high detection accuracy, and fast adaptation, many supervised learning algorithms have been adopted in intrusion detection systems. Decision Trees are one of the most commonly used supervised learning algorithms in IDS [38]. The advantages of a decision tree are intuitive knowledge representation, high classification accuracy, and simple implementation. However, the larger the tree, the less intuitive the knowledge representation is because it is difficult to extract the rules for deeper and wider trees. Large trees often have high classification accuracy, but not a high generalization. Kruegel and Toth [33] used decision trees in Snort's misuse detection engine [9]. Zhang et al. [35] applied a Random Forest classifier to anomaly detection where an anomaly detector was used to feed the second intrusion classifier. Sahu et al. used Decision Tree (J48) algorithm to classify the network packet in Kyoto 2006+ data set that can be used for NIDS [39].

The Naive Bayes classifier is a well-known machine learning technique and is also used for machine learning-based IDS. However, because Naive Bayes assumes conditional independence of data capabilities, the correlated features of network data for intrusion detection can degrade performance. Amor et al. [40] and Panda et al. [34] have used the Naive Bayes classifier and applied it to the KDD 1999 dataset for training and testing. In [41], authors present a method that automatically extracts only unknown attacks from anomaly-based intrusion detection system alerts. They modified the existing feature extraction method with new features; duration, source bytes, and destination bytes, and applied one-class SVM to them. Authors in [19] found, however, that machine learning-based intrusion detection system is rarely used in operational "real world" settings despite extensive academic research compared to other intrusion detection methods. This indicates that finding attacks might be fundamentally different from tasks in other applications, making it much more difficult for the intrusion detection community to adopt machine learning effectively. There are many types of ensembles proposed in the machine learning literature. With respect to architecture, individual classifiers can, in general, be structured in forms of parallel (e.g., bagging), sequential (e.g., boosting), or hybrid [42]. For making a decision, the composer of classifiers can apply various mechanisms such as majority voting, Bayesian combination, distribution summation, entropy weighting, and so on [23,42].

6 Conclusion

In this paper, we propose a method to improve the performance of machine learning-based intrusion detection systems and reduce the rate of false alerts. Our focus is the ambiguity of the classification model which leads to misclassification and false alerts. We look for a practical approach to reduce these ambiguities in the domain-specific environment where usage patterns, as well as attack patterns, are continuously and rapidly changed. We take the strategy to choose a set of data that are the most uncertain and thus most informative and improve the accuracy of classification in the subsequent analysis. Those uncertain data are collected as an ambiguous dataset. The goal is to extract the most uncertain dataset and re-evaluate them to reduce the ambiguity and improve the performance of the model. We show that the ambiguous dataset contains 77.2% of misclassified data in our model. We can resolve many misclassified data in the re-training process. We also evaluate the "Unknown" attacks in collected Kyoto 2006+ network traffic data. Our model predicts those data as malicious with high confidence. In future work, we will continue to advance the proposed framework using advanced techniques, such as data stream mining for real-time processing, secure adversarial machine learning, and timely and intelligent response systems.

Acknowledgment. This research was supported in part by Colorado State Bill 18-086.

References

1. Lane, T., Brodley, C.E.: An application of machine learning to anomaly detection. In: Proceedings of the 20th National Information Systems Security Conference, vol. 377, pp. 366–380. Baltimore, USA (1997)
2. Ghosh, A.K., Wanken, J., Charron, F.: Detecting anomalous and unknown intrusions against programs. In: 14th Annual Computer Security Applications Conference: Proceedings, pp. 259–267. IEEE (1998)
3. Cannady, J.: Artificial neural networks for misuse detection. In: National Information Systems Security Conference, pp. 368–381 (1998)
4. Sinclair, C., Pierce, L., Matzner, S.: An application of machine learning to network intrusion detection. In: Computer Security Applications Conference (ACSAC 1999) Proceedings. 15th Annual, pp. 371–377. IEEE (1999)
5. Kumar, S., Spafford, E.H.: A software architecture to support misuse intrusion detection (1995)
6. Ilgun, K., Kemmerer, R.A., Porras, P.A.: State transition analysis: a rule-based intrusion detection approach. IEEE Trans. Softw. Eng. **21**(3), 181–199 (1995)
7. Lunt, T.F., Tamaru, A., Gillham, F.: A Real-Time Intrusion-Detection Expert System (IDES). SRI International, Computer Science Laboratory (1992)
8. Paxson, V.: Bro: a system for detecting network intruders in real-time. Comput. Netw. **31**(23), 2435–2463 (1999)
9. Roesch, M., et al.: Snort: lightweight intrusion detection for networks. Lisa **99**(1), 229–238 (1999)
10. Mukkamala, S., Sung, A., Abraham, A.: Cyber security challenges: designing efficient intrusion detection systems and antivirus tools. Vemuri, V. Rao, Enhancing Computer Security with Smart Technology. (Auerbach, 2006), pp. 125–163 (2005)
11. Nguyen, T.T., Armitage, G.: A survey of techniques for internet traffic classification using machine learning. IEEE Commun. Surv. Tutorials **10**(4), 56–76 (2008)
12. Garcia-Teodoro, P., Diaz-Verdejo, J., Maciá-Fernández, G., Vázquez, E.: Anomaly-based network intrusion detection: techniques, systems and challenges. Comput. Secur. **28**(1), 18–28 (2009)
13. Wu, S.X., Banzhaf, W.: The use of computational intelligence in intrusion detection systems: a review. Appl. Soft Comput. **10**(1), 1–35 (2010)
14. Bhuyan, M.H., Bhattacharyya, D.K., Kalita, J.K.: Network anomaly detection: methods, systems and tools. IEEE Commun. Surv. Tutorials **16**(1), 303–336 (2014)
15. Dua, S., Du, X.: Data Mining and Machine Learning in Cybersecurity. CRC Press (2016)
16. Buczak, A.L., Guven, E.: A survey of data mining and machine learning methods for cyber security intrusion detection. IEEE Commun. Surv. Tutorials **18**(2), 1153–1176 (2016)
17. Denning, D.E.: An intrusion-detection model. IEEE Trans. Softw. Eng. **2**, 222–232 (1987)
18. Mukherjee, B., Heberlein, L.T., Levitt, K.N.: Network intrusion detection. IEEE Netw. **8**(3), 26–41 (1994)
19. Sommer, R., Paxson, V.: Outside the closed world: on using machine learning for network intrusion detection. In: IEEE Symposium on Security and Privacy (SP), pp. 305–316. IEEE (2010)
20. Widmer, G., Kubat, M.: Learning in the presence of concept drift and hidden contexts. Mach. Learn. **23**(1), 69–101 (1996)

21. Lane, T., Brodley, C.E.: Approaches to online learning and concept drift for user identification in computer security. In: KDD, pp. 259–263 (1998)
22. Polikar, R.: Ensemble based systems in decision making. IEEE Circuits Syst. Mag. **6**(3), 21–45 (2006)
23. Giacinto, G., Roli, F., Didaci, L.: Fusion of multiple classifiers for intrusion detection in computer networks. Pattern Recogn. Lett. **24**(12), 1795–1803 (2003)
24. Quinlan, J.R.: Induction of decision trees. Mach. Learn. **1**(1), 81–106 (1986)
25. Quinlan, J.R.: C4. 5: programs for machine learning. Elsevier (2014)
26. Friedman, J.H.: Greedy function approximation: a gradient boosting machine. Ann. Stat. 1189–1232 (2001)
27. Friedman, J.H.: Stochastic gradient boosting. Comput. Stat. Data Anal. **38**(4), 367–378 (2002)
28. Breiman, L.: Random forests. Mach. Learn. **45**(1), 5–32 (2001)
29. Breiman, L.: Out-of-bag estimation (1996)
30. Goodfellow, I., Bengio, Y., Courville, A.: Deep Learning. MIT Press, Cambridge (2016)
31. Bradley, A.P.: The use of the area under the roc curve in the evaluation of machine learning algorithms. Pattern Recogn. **30**(7), 1145–1159 (1997)
32. Mitchell, T.M.: Machine learning and data mining. Commun. ACM **42**(11), 30–36 (1999)
33. Kruegel, C., Toth, T.: Using decision trees to improve signature-based intrusion detection. In: Vigna, G., Kruegel, C., Jonsson, E. (eds.) RAID 2003. LNCS, vol. 2820, pp. 173–191. Springer, Heidelberg (2003). https://doi.org/10.1007/978-3-540-45248-5_10
34. Panda, M., Patra, M.R.: Network intrusion detection using Naive Bayes. Int. J. Comput. Sci. Netw. Secur. **7**(12), 258–263 (2007)
35. Zhang, J., Zulkernine, M., Haque, A.: Random-forests-based network intrusion detection systems. IEEE Trans. Syst. Man Cybern. Part C (Appl. Rev.) **38**(5), 649–659 (2008)
36. Song, J., Takakura, H., Okabe, Y., Eto, M., Inoue, D., Nakao, K.: Statistical analysis of honeypot data and building of kyoto 2006+ dataset for nids evaluation. In: Proceedings of the First Workshop on Building Analysis Datasets and Gathering Experience Returns for Security, pp. 29–36. ACM (2011)
37. Sperotto, A., Schaffrath, G., Sadre, R., Morariu, C., Pras, A., Stiller, B.: An overview of ip flow-based intrusion detection. IEEE Commun. Surv. Tutorials **12**(3), 343–356 (2010)
38. Lee, J.-H., Lee, J.-H., Sohn, S.-G., Ryu, J.-H., Chung, T.-M.: Effective value of decision tree with kdd 99 intrusion detection datasets for intrusion detection system. In: 10th International Conference on Advanced Communication Technology, ICACT 2008, vol. 2, pp. 1170–1175. IEEE (2008)
39. Sahu, S., Mehtre, B.M.: Network intrusion detection system using j48 decision tree. In: 2015 International Conference on Advances in Computing, Communications and Informatics (ICACCI), pp. 2023–2026. IEEE (2015)
40. Amor, N.B., Benferhat, S., Elouedi, Z.: Naive bayes vs decision trees in intrusion detection systems. In: Proceedings of the 2004 ACM Symposium on Applied Computing, pp. 420–424. ACM (2004)
41. Sato, M., Yamaki, H., Takakura, H.: Unknown attacks detection using feature extraction from anomaly-based ids alerts. In: IEEE/IPSJ 12th International Symposium on Applications and the Internet (SAINT), pp. 273–277. IEEE (2012)
42. Rokach, L.: Ensemble-based classifiers. Artif. Intell. Rev. **33**(1), 1–39 (2010)

A Systematic Approach to Building Autoencoders for Intrusion Detection

Youngrok Song[1]($\boxtimes$) (ID), Sangwon Hyun[2] (ID), and Yun-Gyung Cheong[1] (ID)

[1] Sungkyunkwan University, Suwon, South Korea
{id4thomas,aimecca}@skku.edu
[2] Myongji University, Yongin, South Korea
shyun@mju.ac.kr

Abstract. Network Intrusion Detection Systems (NIDS) have been the most effective defense mechanism against various network attacks. As attack patterns have been intelligently and dynamically evolving, the deep learning-based NIDSs have been widely adopted to improve intrusion detection accuracy. Autoencoders, one of the unsupervised neural networks, are generative deep learning models that learn to represent the data as compressed vectors without class labels. Recently, various autoencoder–generative deep learning models–have been used for NIDS in order to efficiently alleviate the laborious labeling and to effectively detect unknown types of attacks (i.e. zero-day attacks). In spite of the effectiveness of autoencoders in detecting intrusions, it requires tremendous effort to identify the optimal model architecture of the autoencoders that results in the best performance, which is an obstacle for practical applications. To address this challenge, this paper rigorously studies autoencoders with two important factors using real network data. We investigate how the size of a latent layer and the size of the model influence the detection performance. We evaluate our autoencoder model using the IDS benchmark data sets and present the experimental findings.

Keywords: IDS · Dimension reduction · Autoencoder · PCA · Semi-supervised machine learning algorithm · (One-class) unsupervised learning algorithm · Deep learning algorithm

1 Introduction

Advanced network intrusion detection systems (NIDS) using machine learning or deep learning techniques have gained a lot of attention in intelligently monitoring network traffic for highly accurate detection [7,18]. Everyday network attacks dramatically evolve into new patterns using different attack techniques [13]. Due to unpredictable attack fashions, a traditional signature-based IDS cannot detect such sophisticated attacks in real-time [17]. However, the intelligent NIDS based on machine learning and deep learning (simply called ML-NIDS) enables us to

© Springer Nature Switzerland AG 2021
Y. Park et al. (Eds.): SVCC 2020, CCIS 1383, pp. 188–204, 2021.
https://doi.org/10.1007/978-3-030-72725-3_14

quickly detect and respond against unknown attack patterns for stable network operation while reducing human intervention [5,8,11].

ML-NIDS has been actively researched both in academic and industry settings to develop an effective and intelligent IDS using various machine/deep learning algorithms [2,3,6,12,19–21,23]. These methods learn the intrusion patterns using supervised learning algorithms [21,23], such as SVM [3,6] and Decision Tree [19]. Alom et al. [2] proposed a deep belief network (DBN) composed of a stack of Restricted Boltzmann Machines (RBMs). [20] proposed a hybrid model that combines a RBM-based DBN dimension reduction and SVM classifier. Kim et al. [12] proposed an IDS based on LSTM (Long Short-Term Memory) networks.

Although this supervised learning approach is known to be effective in achieving a high detection rate, it has several limitations. First, it is difficult to detect new types of attacks, whose patterns do not belong to any of the pre-trained attack classes. Second, the labeling process for the train data generally needs tremendous human efforts.

To address these problems, several groups of researchers recently proposed an IDS using *autoencoders*, a generative deep learning model consisting of an encoder and a decoder [4,16,26]. Given an input of M-dimensional vector, the encoder compresses it into a latent vector represented as a N-dimensional vector where $M > N$, and the decoder subsequently reconstructs the compressed latent vector back to the M-dimensional vector. An autoencoder-based IDS trained with only normal traffic data is expected to recover any input as close as possible to the learned normal patterns. Therefore, an input instance is predicted as an attack if the reconstruction error is larger than a pre-defined threshold; otherwise, the instance is predicted as normal. This operational principle makes autoencoders suitable for unsupervised anomaly detections. An autoencoder-based IDS is capable of detecting unknown types of attacks when their patterns deviate from the learned normal patterns.

The detection performance of an autoencoder-based IDS is very sensitive to the architecture and hyperparameter settings of the underlying autoencoder model. Thus it is critical to find the optimal configurations of autoencoders to obtain the best performing IDS. Even more difficult is that the optimal model configurations may vary depending on the type of data used. Most of the previous papers have reported manually obtained best models by conducting numerous experiments with particular data sets.

However, such manual processes generally take tremendous time and effort and also has to be repeated as data changes. This results in considerable delays in the development of IDS and consequently degrades the practical applicability of autoencoders.

To address this problem, we suggest a systematic approach to designing an autoencoder model architecture.

The contributions that this paper makes are:

- to suggest statistical dimension reduction techniques to determine the optimal latent dimension that represents the latent patterns of a given data

- to investigate the impact of model size on the performance of intrusion detection
- to suggest the use of a validation data set and a standardized Z-score for threshold selection
- to implement and report the experimental results that test the efficacy of our approach

This paper is organized as follows. First, we reviews the related works. Section 3 details our proposed method. Section 4 describes the data used in our evaluation. Section 5 presents our experiments and results followed by discussions. We conclude with suggestions for future work.

2   Related Work

This section reviews two ways of using the autoencoder algorithms for IDS. First, autoencoders can be used for feature extraction to enhance the classification performance. Secondly, the autoencoder model can serve as a classifier for anomaly detection.

2.1   Autoencoders for Feature Reduction

Autoencoder models have been used for reducing the feature dimension for efficient computation. For instance, Javaid et al. [10] developed a network IDS using a combination of sparse autoencoder and soft-max regression (SMR) method. Through evaluations using the NSL-KDD data set, the authors confirmed that using an autoencoder as a feature extraction method can improve IDS performance.

Li et al. [14] proposed an IDS based on a combination of an autoencoder for dimension reduction and a DBN as a classifier. The proposed model was evaluated with the KDD Cup 99 data set, and the results showed that combining an autoencoder and DBN can achieve better detection accuracy than working with DBN alone.

Tao et al. [24] proposed a data fusion approach based on the Fisher score and deep autoencoder whose major objective is to reduce the dimensionality of data. Using the KDD Cup 99 data set, it was confirmed that integrating the deep autoencoder as a feature extraction method can improve the accuracy of classification algorithms.

Zhang et al. [27] proposed a deep learning approach using sparse stacked autoencoders and binary tree ensemble method for network intrusion detection and evaluated its performance with the NSL-KDD data set. The evaluation results showed that the proposed approach achieved a F1-score of 91.97%.

2.2   Autoencoders for Anomaly Detection

Mirsky et al. [16] developed a Network IDS model named Kitsune using a deep learning technique based on an ensemble of autoencoders, to detect malicious traffic in online and unsupervised manners. The proposed model first maps the features of a given network packet into an ensemble of autoencoders, and then each autoencoder tries to reconstruct the packet features and evaluates a root mean squared error (RMSE) as the reconstruction error. The model finally summarizes the RSMEs from each autoencoder and checks whether the final result exceeds the threshold of anomaly. They studied especially on how to distribute the entire set of data features to each autoencoder and how to derive the final decision by collecting and analyzing the results from each authencoder. Their work was applied to online intrusion data which are not publicly accessible for comparative evaluation.

Lopez-Martin et al. [15] proposed a classification model using conditional variational autoencoders to detect and classify the five types of labels (normal, DOS, R2L, PROBE, U2R) in the NSL-KDD data. In particular, given a labeled training data set, the decoding network of the proposed model is additionally trained with the class labels associated with the trained data logs so that the decoding network could estimate the class label associated with reconstructed data features. When reconstructing from a compressed vector, the decoding network predicts the class label associated with the reconstructed data features. Thus this approach requires pre-labeled data for training, unlike our approach which is unsupervised. The task of classifying normal and the rest achieved an F1-score of 0.83.

Aygun and Yavuz [4] constructed autoencoders and denoising autoencoders with one hidden layer consisting of 30 nodes that uses the sum of squared errors (SSE). In order to classify given data as either normal or abnormal, they leverage stochastically selecting a threshold, and this work is complementary to ours. Their evaluation applied to the NSL-KDD data yields an F1-score of 0.895.

As described above, various autoencoder models have been used for intrusion detection. However, it was not clearly disclosed how the particular model architecture and their hyper-parameters were designed. In this article, we propose a systematic approach to tackle these practical issues.

3   Our Approach

3.1   An Overview

Figure 1 illustrates the approach for intrusion detection using autoencoders. The first step is to pre-process the input data to convert the feature values into numerical vectors. In the model training phase, only normal logs (represented as vectors) are used to train the dimension reduction and reconstruction models. In the test phase, an input vector is given to the network to generate an output via compression and reconstruction.

Then, it computes the reconstruction error using L2 norm (i.e., Euclidean distance) between the input and its output. At this point, it is expected that the autoencoder model trained with normal logs will attempt to recover any input log as close as possible to the learned normal log patterns. Therefore, if a given input does in fact belong to an attack class, it is likely that the recovered output would be significantly different from the input. Accordingly, the final step determines the class of the input sample based on the difference; if the difference is greater than a set threshold, it is classified as an attack. Otherwise, it belongs to the normal class.

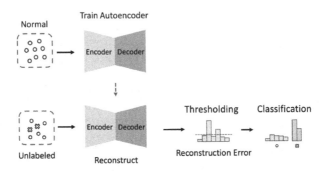

Fig. 1. The overall process of intrusion detection when using dimension reduction and reconstruction methods

3.2   Model Design

As Sect. 2 summarizes, various autoencoder models are used as (one class) unsupervised machine learning algorithms for anomaly detection. However, engineering issues that may arise during the application of these techniques have often been ignored. When designing an autoencoder model, a data scientist or a system administrator are faced with the following decisions:

– How many neurons for each layer and how many hidden layers in total are necessary? How do we design the structure of the hidden layers? The size of each hidden layer can gradually decrease up to the latent layer and then increase to the output layer. Or, some of the layers can be larger than their previous layers, as illustrated in Fig. 2.
– Does the size of the autoencoder model matter for intrusion detection accuracy? Is the bigger model better for IDS?
– What dimension of the latent layer is appropriate to represent the data? For instance, the model may not represent the data well if its latent layer has only one neuron. In that case, the latent layer is likely to be too generic to characterize the data. On the other hand, the model would not benefit the advantage of generalization that occurs during the compression/reconstruction process if its latent layer contains an excessive number of neurons.
– How many options should we investigate to set the hyper parameters, such as batch size, activation function, loss function, and the number of epochs for training?

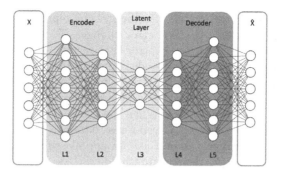

Fig. 2. An autoencoder model where the size of the hidden layer (L1) is greater than the size of the input layer and gradually decreases to the size of the latent layer (L3). X is the model's input and $\hat{X}$ is the reconstructed sample.

These design decisions are interrelated; once the number of hidden layers is set, one needs to decide on the size for each layer. The number of choices which can be made is combinatorial, and thus becomes very large. Hence, it is challenging to determine the optimal combination to achieve the best performance of a given model.

We present a systematic approach to address some of the questions described above. In our approach, we use PCA (Principal Component Analysis) to determine the size of the latent layer. We first analyze the cumulative explained variance ratio of the training data using the PCA algorithm. Then, we use the number of components which can maintain the data distribution at a set of predefined ratios (e.g., 90%, 95%, 99.9%) as the candidate latent sizes. Once we obtain the performance for each candidate latent size, we can further explore the most probable latent size to find the optimal setting. In addition, we investigate if the model size, in terms of the number of parameters, matters for the detection performance.

3.3 Threshold Selection

Since a threshold divides the normal and abnormal (i.e., intrusion in our case) classes, the selection of a threshold has tremendous impact on the performance of IDS. In previous research work, an optimal threshold (as well as the model parameters) was found through experiments on the test data.

However, in real-world scenarios of IDS, the labels of the test data are not known. Therefore, in reality, it is infeasible to set the threshold on the test data. In order to perform a fair evaluation of an IDS, we need to create a validation data set. We measure the performance metrics (e.g., accuracy, F1-score) on the validation data set varying the threshold. Then, the reconstruction error that results in the best performance can be used as the threshold. We then use the set threshold to evaluate the test data.

In addition, we use the Z-score of standard normal distribution as the threshold metric to determine whether a given sample is an attack or not. By using the

Z-score as the threshold metric, the classifier can be reproduced effectively even when the value of the reconstruction error changes. To set the threshold in Z-score, we first find the reconstruction error that results in the best performance on the validation set via the procedure described in the above paragraph. Then we convert the found reconstruction error into a Z-score by standardizing it. The mean and variance values used for standardization are calculated with only normal samples in the validation set. When the threshold is set on the validation data, we convert it into a Z-score. Given a test data, we compute the Z-score of the reconstruction error observed on the data and classify the data as an attack if its Z-score exceeds the pre-defined threshold.

4   Dataset

Several data sets are available for evaluating intrusion detection systems. The most widely known data set is the KDD Cup '99 data set [1]. However, the set contains duplicate records in training and test sets, making it inadequate for testing IDS [23]. Hence, the NSL-KDD [25] data were created by removing redundancies in the training and test sets of the KDD set.

While these datasets are often used as the benchmark data for evaluating an IDS [21,23], it has been two decades since the data were collected, which makes it difficult to evaluate the efficacy of an IDS on recent network attack traffic. Therefore, this paper employs the CIC-IDS 2017 data set as the primary benchmark data for evaluating our approach. In addition, we report the evaluation result of the NSL-KDD data set for comparison purpose. The following sections describe how to preprocess the data in detail.

4.1   CIC-IDS 2017 Data

Dataset Preparation. The CIC-IDS 2017 [22] data are comprised of network traffic which were collected from Monday, July 3, 2017 to Friday, July 7, 2017. The set contains most common modern attack types based on the 2016 McAfee report [22]. The attack types include Brute Force FTP, Brute Force SSH, DoS, Heartbleed, Web Attack, Infiltration, Botnet and DDoS. Table 1 presents the number of samples captured per day and their attack types. There are 2,800,801 normal samples and 556,556 attack samples in total, excluding samples with NaN or missing feature values.

We use the data obtained on Monday as the training set since they contain only normal samples. We use the data collected from Tuesday to Friday and split them 1:9 into a validation set and a test set. When the data are not balanced, the evaluation measures cannot properly represent the system performance. For instance, accuracy is not the best metric when the majority of the data belongs to a particular class. Hence, we construct the final validation and test set in 1:9 ratio with equal number of normal samples and attack samples (see Table 2).

Table 1. CIC-IDS 2017 data count for each attack type

Attack type	Number of instances	Date
Benign (Normal)	**2,271,320**	–
SSH-Patator	5,897	Tuesday
FTP-Patator	7,935	Tuesday
DoS Hulk	230,124	Wednesday
DoS GoldenEye	10,293	Wednesday
DoS Slowhttptest	5,499	Wednesday
DoS slowloris	5,796	Wednesday
Web Attack-Brute Force	1,507	Thursday
Web Attack-XSS	652	Thursday
Bot	1,956	Friday
PortScan	158,804	Friday
DDoS	128,025	Friday
All attack types	**556,556**	–

Preprocessing. The data set consists of generated network flow in both packet format and extracted features format. For data analysis, we use the extracted features represented as 79 feature values. The preprocessing step converts the 78 numerical feature values into [0,1] range using MinMax Normalization. There is a single categorical feature–*Destination Port*, which can be divided into three categories (0–1023), registered port (1024 - 49151), and dynamic port (>49152) and is encoded as a one-hot 3 dimensional vector. After the preprocessing step, the data are represented as 80-dimensional vectors.

4.2   NSL-KDD Data

Dataset Preparation. The original NSL-KDD data consists of the train data and the test data. In order to create the validation set, we randomly split the original NSL-KDD train data into 1:9 ratio of the validation set and the train set. In other words, 10% of the NSL-KDD train data is used for creating our validation set. Then, we filter the train set so that it includes only normal samples for building the autoencoder model. Unlike in the CIC-IDS 2017 data, we split the train data to create our validation set, because the NSL-KDD dataset are often used as the IDS benchmark dataset. Therefore, to compare our evaluation result with that of previous work, we split the NSL-KDD train data instead of its test data. To make the test set balanced, we randomly under-sampled the normal class of the validation set since it contains more normal samples than the attack samples. For the test set, we under-sampled the attacks since the test set contains more attack samples than normal ones. The number of samples for each set is listed in Table 2.

Table 2. Data count

	Normal	Attack
Train	529,481	0
Validation	55,519	55,519
Test	501,037	501,037

(a) CIC-IDS 2017 Data Count

	Normal	Attack
Train	60,592	0
Validation	5,847	5,847
Test	9,711	9,711

(b) NSL-KDD Data Count

Preprocessing. The preprocessing step converts non-numerical data into numerical data in order to build an input to the autoencoder. *Protocol Service,* and *Flag* are categorical data. *Protocol* denotes a network protocol of which value can be *tcp, udp,* or *icmp.* When using one-hot encoding, the *Protocol* feature is represented as a 3 dimensional vector. The *Service* feature contains 86 distinct values, and thus is represented as a 86 dimensional vector. *Flag* has 13 kinds of values and is represented as a 13 dimensional vector. The *Source_port_number* and *Destination_port_number* range from 0 to 65535, and we represent it as a 3-vector, dividing the number into well-known port (0–1023), registered port (1024–49151), and dynamic port (49152–65536).

For numeric categorical data, we normalize the numerical values between 0 and 1. The *Duration, Source_bytes, and Destination_bytes* features and the features suffixed with *count* (e.g., *Dst_host_count, Dst_host_srv_count*) are normalized using the MinMax scaling, after statistical outliers are eliminated. The feature values suffixed with *rate* (e.g., *Serror_rate, Dst_host_serror_rate*) are between 0 and 1, and thus are used as-is, without conversion.

Finally, the data are represented as 114 dimensional vectors by combining 12 general features and 112 one-hot encoded categorical features.

5   Evaluation

We report the major performance metrics that are often used for IDS evaluation: AuC (Area Under Curve), $F1$-score, and accuracy. We can measure the model's overall performance in AuC without using the threshold. $F1$-score and accuracy represent the best performance that the model can achieve when the threshold is set.

5.1   PCA Analysis

First, we analyze the cumulative explained variances of the data for testing the impact of the latent vector size. Table 3 shows the selected sizes and their corresponding cumulative explained variance ratios for the CIC-IDS 2017 and the NSL-KDD data.

We particularly look into the cases where the number of components achieves the variance coverage of less than 50% and approximately 50%, 80%, 90%, 95%,

Table 3. PCA cumulative variance ratio

CIC-IDS 2017

Size	Variance coverage	Cumulative variance
1	<50%	38.9%
2	≈50%	56.48%
5	≈80%	81.96%
8	≈90%	91.97%
10	≈95%	95.37%
27	≈99.9%	99.91%

Size means the number of components.

NSL-KDD

Size	Variance coverage	Cumulative variance
1	<50%	34.47%
2	≈50%	52.81%
6	≈80%	80.07%
10	≈90%	90.10%
16	≈95%	95.60%
37	≈99.9%	99.90%

Size means the number of components.

and 99.9%. As in the table, the selected sizes are 1,2,5,8,10, and 27 for the CIC-IDS 2017 data and 1,2,6,10,16, and 37 for the NSL-KDD data. For instance, in the case of the CIC-IDS 2017 data, representing the latent layer as an 8D vector can explain approximately 91.97% of its variance.

5.2   Experiment 1: CIC-IDS 2017 Data

This section shows the results of our evaluation on the CIC-IDS 2017 Data for evaluating the performance of the model's intrusion detection.

Experiment Configuration. We design a simple autoencoder consisting of *input–2 hidden layers–latent layer–2 hidden layers–output* as shown in Fig. 2. We created two versions of the same model which only differ in the number of parameters for testing the impact of model size. Let us call the model as Autoencoder-128, in which the first and the second hidden layers of the encoder network contain 128 and 64 nodes, respectively, In the Autoencoder-256 model, the first and the second hidden layers of the encoder network contain 256 and 128 nodes, respectively. The decoder network is symmetrical to the encoder network. The size of the latent layer varies for both of the models in the experiments.

The autoencoder model is trained for 30 epochs with a batch size of 256. While training, we compute the model's AuC using the data's validation set and save the model's weights for every 100 iterations. Then, the model which results in the highest AuC value is chosen for evaluation.

To standardize the reconstruction error for threshold selection, the mean and variance of the normal samples from the validation set are used. Then, we select the threshold in Z-score that produces the best $F1$-score when classifying the validation set. We report the average of 5 runs.

Latent Dimension. In this experiment, we test the performance of the autoencoder's intrusion detection when the size of the latent vector alternates. As in Table 4a, we obtained the best performance for Autoencoder-128 when the latent size was 27, which achieved the cumulative explained variance ratio of 99.91%. Its AuC was 0.878, and the $F1$-score was 0.848 when Z-score was 0.447. It is noted that its recall (0.945) was higher than its precision (0.770). The best AuC of 0.884 was achieved when the latent size was 10, and the best accuracy was obtained when the latent size was 8.

In the case of Autoencoder-256 (see Table 4b), the best performance of $F1$-score (0.844) was achieved when the latent size was 8. The best AuC was 0.886, and the best accuracy was 82.82%. In both models, we observe that the performance tends to enhance as the dimension grows up to a certain point and then decreases.

By using the candidate latent sizes, we can approximate the optimal latent size. Once we narrow down the search space of latent sizes, we can further explore the most probable size to find the optimal size. For instance, we look into the latent sizes of 5 to 10 selectively to test if a better performance can be obtained when using Autoencoder-256 which shows a stable performance across different metrics (in terms of latent size). Table 5 shows that the optimal latent size of 9 was found, achieving the AuC of 0.889, the accuracy of 82.91%, and $F1$-score of 0.848.

Furthermore, we look into the classification result of each attack type when Autoencoder-128 was used. In this analysis, the attack types having less than 100 test samples (i.e., Heartbleed, Web Attack-SQL Injection, Infiltration) were excluded. For each attack type, its test set consists of the 1:1 ratio of randomly selected normal samples and attack samples of that type which were present in the entire test set to make a balance.

The results in Table 7 indicate that there are significant differences in performance depending on the attack types. Some attacks such as DoS Hulk and DDoS are easily identifiable and some attacks (e.g., SSH-Patator, FTP-Patator) are not. Like the overall performance, there is a tendency that the performance increases up to a certain latent size and decreases as the size grows.

Model Size. We analyze the results in terms of model size. Table 6 shows that the number of trainable parameters of Autoencoder-256 is roughly 2.8 times of that of Autoencoder-128. Despite the difference in size, both models produced similar results in terms of AuC, $F1$-score, and accuracy (see Table 4a and b). This suggests that the performance does not depend on the model size.

However, we discover that the latent sizes which result in the best performance were different. Autoencoder-256 appears to be more stable as the latent sizes leading to the best AuC, $F1$-score, and accuracy are identical. When using Autoencoder-128, on the other hand, the best latent sizes were different, 8, 10, and 27 for accuracy, AuC, and $F1$-score, respectively.

Threshold Selection. To evaluate the IDS formally, we need to create a validation set to determine the threshold and use Z-score for adaptability to the

Table 4. Classification performance of various latent sizes on the CIC-IDS 2017 data. We created two autoencoder models that differ in size. The best performance is in bold.

(a) Autoencoder-128 (layers of *input-128-64-Latent-64-128-output*)

Size	AuC	Z-score	Precision	Recall	F1	Accuracy
1	0.851	0.177	0.742	0.928	0.821	79.65%
2	0.864	0.238	0.749	0.945	0.834	81.14%
5	0.873	0.388	0.759	0.939	0.838	81.88%
8	0.880	0.492	0.779	0.930	0.847	**83.21%**
10	**0.884**	0.552	0.777	0.932	0.847	83.03%
27	0.878	0.447	0.770	0.945	**0.848**	83.05%
32	0.877	0.478	0.772	0.940	0.846	82.81%

Size means the autoencoder's latent size.

(b) Autoencoder-256 (layers of *input-256-128-Latent-128-256-output*)

Size	AuC	Z-score	Precision	Recall	F1	Accuracy
1	0.849	0.493	0.767	0.883	0.818	80.22%
2	0.853	0.290	0.747	0.937	0.830	80.74%
5	0.872	0.410	0.775	0.916	0.839	82.47%
8	**0.886**	0.468	0.776	0.926	**0.844**	**82.82%**
10	0.864	0.343	0.761	0.943	0.842	82.23%
27	0.867	0.438	0.755	0.954	0.842	82.11%
32	0.874	0.38	0.755	0.946	0.839	81.83%

Size means the autoencoder's latent size.

Table 5. Classification performance of Autoencoder-256 from the latent size of 5 to 10. Size means the dimension of the autoencoder's latent layer.

Size	AuC	Z-score	Precision	Recall	F1	Accuracy
5	0.872	0.410	0.775	0.916	0.839	82.47%
6	0.883	0.350	0.760	0.940	0.840	82.00%
7	0.873	0.464	0.771	0.925	0.841	82.48%
8	0.886	0.468	0.776	0.926	0.844	82.82%
9	**0.889**	0.5	0.786	0.925	**0.848**	**82.91%**
10	0.864	0.343	0.761	0.943	0.842	82.23%

new data set. The histogram in Fig. 3a illustrates the distribution of the CIC-IDS 2017 validation data on the standardized Z-score. The dotted line denotes the optimal threshold that best divides the normal and attack samples.

Table 6. Number of the trainable parameters of the autoencoder models when the size of the latent dimension varies.

Latent Dimension	Autoencoder-128	Autoencoder-256
1	37,457	107,601
2	37,586	107,858
5	37,973	108,629
8	38,360	109,400
10	38,618	109,914
27	40,811	114,283

Table 7. Classification results of the CIC-IDS 2017 data in $F1$-score for each attack type and different dimensions when Autoencoder-128 is used. The results for the SSH-Patator and FTP-Patator attacks are eliminated as their performances are too low for analysis.

Attack type	Latent dimension							Support
	1	2	5	8	10	27	32	
DoS Hulk	0.8405	0.8538	0.8682	**0.8743**	0.8712	0.8716	0.8706	207,058
DoS GoldenEye	0.7389	**0.7743**	0.7492	0.7681	0.7340	0.7668	0.7643	9,297
DoS Slowhttptest	0.6508	0.6367	0.7469	0.7537	**0.8636**	0.8099	0.8118	4,906
DoS slowloris	0.6574	**0.7816**	0.7449	0.7770	0.7198	0.7495	0.8014	5,237
Web Attack-Brute Force	0.4912	0.7016	0.5937	0.5023	0.5110	**0.7167**	0.6044	1,350
Web Attack-XSS	0.4479	0.7195	0.5911	0.4800	04878	**0.7382**	0.6144	584
Bot	0.7321	0.7560	**0.7966**	0.7563	0.7039	0.7382	0.7762	1,759
PortScan	0.8243	0.8353	0.8224	0.8316	0.8387	**0.8421**	0.8356	142,991
DDoS	0.8493	0.8621	0.8691	**0.8823**	0.8787	0.8755	0.8356	115,331
All Types	0.8214	0.8343	0.8384	0.8471	0.8465	**0.8480**	0.8460	501,037

Figure 3b illustrates the distribution of the CIC-IDS 2017 test data. An input that produces a distance between the input and its reconstructed output greater than the (dotted) threshold is classified as *attack*. Otherwise, it is classified as *normal*.

In both data sets, the majority of normal samples are located in the left side of the threshold. Likewise, most attack samples are located in its far right side. Not surprisingly, there are overlapped regions in the center of the distribution, which makes it difficult to classify them when the classification depends only on the reconstruction error.

5.3 Experiment: NSL-KDD Data

This section presents the evaluation results when the NSL-KDD data are employed. The autoencoder model is structured similar to Autoencoder-128 that

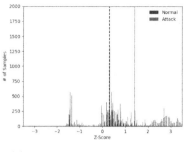

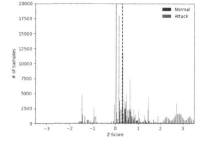

(a) CIC-IDS 2017 Validation data   (b) CIC-IDS 2017 Test data

Fig. 3. Histograms of the standardized reconstruction error using the CIC-IDS 2017 data. The dotted line denotes the threshold in Z-score.

Table 8. Classification performance of various latent sizes on the NSL-KDD data. The best performances in AuC and $F1$-score are in bold.

Size	AuC	Z-score	Precision	Recall	$F1$	Accuracy
1	**0.968**	2.35	0.932	0.809	0.866	87.47%
2	0.962	1.21	0.884	0.889	0.882	88.25%
6	0.962	0.04	0.873	0.958	**0.913**	**90.92%**
10	0.956	0.02	0.886	0.916	0.901	89.90%
16	0.953	0.03	0.889	0.893	0.891	89.07%
37	0.951	0.05	0.893	0.869	0.881	88.25%

Size means the autoencoder's latent size.

was used for the CIC-IDS 2017 data. The network consists of the layers of *input–2 hidden layers–latent layer–2 hidden layers–output*, where the first hidden layer contains 128 nodes and the second hidden layer contains 64 nodes. We trained the model for 50 epochs with a batch size of 512.

As in Table 8, we obtained the best AuC performance with the latent size of 1 which corresponds with the number of components that covers 34.47% of variance. On the other hand, the best $F1$-score of 0.913 was achieved when the latent size was 6 (cumulative explained variance ratio of 80.07%).

It is noted that the best latent sizes for AuC and $F1$-score were different. In other words, the best performing model in terms of AuC does not lead to the best performing model in $F1$-score. In addition, the difference between precision and recall is marginal.

5.4   Discussions

We measured the performance of intrusion detection varying the latent size. In both data sets, we observed that the overall classification performance tends to enhance as the dimension grows up to a certain point and then decreases. When using the CIC-IDS 2017 data, the autoencoder achieved the best AuC of

0.89, F1-score of 0.85, and accuracy of 82.91%. With the NSL-KDD data, the autoencoder achieved the best AuC of 0.97, F1-score of 0.91, and accuracy of 90.92%.

We compare our results with the previous work [9] that uses their proposed autoencoder model on the NSL-KDD data set. Their reported accuracy 88.28% was slightly lower than our best accuracy of 90.92%. This is surprising considering that we employed a simple architecture, aiming at testing the effect of the latent size and the model size, rather than finding the optimal model architecture. This result indicates that finding the optimal size of the latent layer is essential for designing the autoencoder models for IDS.

We also tested if the model size matters for intrusion detection. We expected that a larger model in terms of the number of parameters will result in a better performance. Unlike our expectation, the results indicate that there is no significant difference in performance between Autoencoder-128 and Autoencoder-256.

6   Conclusion

Unsupervised deep-learning algorithms such as autoencoders have been actively researched for IDS since it can alleviate the labor in labeling [4,16]. While various autoencoder models have shown to be effective in detecting intrusions, identifying the optimal model architecture to provide the best detection performance requires tremendous effort that hinder its practical application to an IDS. Unfortunately, few existing works investigate this engineering issue.

This paper presents a systematic method to designing the autoencoder model and determining the parameters. First, we employed the PCA algorithm to determine the optimal size of the autoencoder's latent vector efficiently. Our evaluation results show that the proposed method is efficient for finding the optimal latent size for intrusion detection when using the IDS benchmark data sets. Second, our evaluation results indicate that there is little difference in performance between the different sized models. We will evaluate the proposed method in diverse models and extend the systematic approach to cover other aspects of model design and evaluation.

Acknowledgement. This work was supported by Institute of Information & communications Technology Planning & Evaluation (IITP) grant funded by the Korea government(MSIT) (No.2020-0-00952, Development of 5G Edge Security Technology for Ensuring 5G+ Service Stability and Availability).

References

1. 99 K.C.: KDD Cup 1999 Data (2007). http://kdd.ics.uci.edu/databases/kddcu p99/kddcup99.html. Accessed Mar 2019
2. Alom, M.Z., Bontupalli, V., Taha, T.: Intrusion detection using deep belief networks. In: 2015 National Aerospace and Electronics Conference (NAECON), pp. 339–344 (2015)

3. Ambusaidi, M.A., He, X., Nanda, P., Tan, Z.: Building an intrusion detection system using a filter-based feature selection algorithm. IEEE Trans. Comput. **65**(10), 2986–2998 (2016)
4. Aygun, R.C., Yavuz, A.G.: Network anomaly detection with stochastically improved autoencoder based models. In: 2017 IEEE 4th International Conference on Cyber Security and Cloud Computing (CSCloud), pp. 193–198. IEEE (2017)
5. Buczak, A.L., Guven, E.: A survey of data mining and machine learning methods for cyber security intrusion detection. IEEE Commun. Surv. Tutor. **18**(2), 1153–1176 (2015)
6. Chitrakar, R., Huang, C.: Selection of candidate support vectors in incremental SVM for network intrusion detection. Comput. Secur. **45**, 231–241 (2014)
7. Cyphort: Cyphort Data Sheet (2017). http://go.cyphort.com/rs/181-NTN-682/images/CYPHORT_DataSheet.pdf. Accessed Mar 2019
8. Garcia-Teodoro, P., Diaz-Verdejo, J., Maciá-Fernández, G., Vázquez, E.: Anomaly-based network intrusion detection: techniques, systems and challenges. Comput. Secur. **28**(1–2), 18–28 (2009)
9. Gharib, M., Mohammadi, B., Dastgerdi, S.H., Sabokrou, M.: AutoIDS: autoencoder based method for intrusion detection system. arXiv abs/1911.03306 (2019)
10. Javaid, A., Niyaz, Q., Sun, W., Alam, M.: A deep learning approach for network intrusion detection system. In: Proceedings of the 9th EAI International Conference on Bio-inspired Information and Communications Technologies (Formerly BIONETICS), BICT 2015, ICST (Institute for Computer Sciences, Social-Informatics and Telecommunications Engineering), ICST, Brussels, Belgium, pp. 21–26 (2016). https://doi.org/10.4108/eai.3-12-2015.2262516
11. Kaur, H., Singh, G., Minhas, J.: A review of machine learning based anomaly detection techniques. arXiv preprint arXiv:1307.7286 (2013)
12. Kim, J., Kim, J., Thu, H.L.T., Kim, H.: Long short term memory recurrent neural network classifier for intrusion detection. In: 2016 International Conference on Platform Technology and Service (PlatCon), pp. 1–5. IEEE (2016)
13. Kuypers, M.A., Maillart, T., Paté-Cornell, E.: An empirical analysis of cyber security incidents at a large organization. Department of Management Science and Engineering, Stanford University, School of Information, UC Berkeley (2016). http://fsi.stanford.edu/sites/default/files/kuypersweis_v7.pdf. Accessed 30 July 2020
14. Li, Y., Ma, R., Jiao, R.: A hybrid malicious code detection method based on deep learning. Int. J. Softw. Eng. Appl. **9**(5), 205–216 (2015)
15. Martín, M.L., Carro, B., Sánchez-Esguevillas, A., Lloret, J.: Conditional variational autoencoder for prediction and feature recovery applied to intrusion detection in IoT. Sensors (Basel, Switzerland) **17**, 1967 (2017)
16. Mirsky, Y., Doitshman, T., Elovici, Y., Shabtai, A.: Kitsune: an ensemble of autoencoders for online network intrusion detection. In: 25th Annual Network and Distributed System Security Symposium, NDSS 2018, San Diego, California, USA, 18–21 February 2018. The Internet Society (2018). http://wp.internetsociety.org/ndss/wp-content/uploads/sites/25/2018/02/ndss2018_03A-3_Mirsky_paper.pdf
17. Petersen, R.: Data mining for network intrusion detection: a comparison of data mining algorithms and an analysis of relevant features for detecting cyber-attacks (2015)
18. RSA: RSA Netwitness Logs and Packets (2017). https://www.rsa.com/content/dam/en/data-sheet/rsa-netwitness-logs-and-packets.pdf. Accessed Mar 2019

19. Sahu, S., Mehtre, B.M.: Network intrusion detection system using j48 decision tree. In: 2015 International Conference on Advances in Computing, Communications and Informatics (ICACCI), pp. 2023–2026. IEEE (2015)

20. Salama, M.A., Eid, H.F., Ramadan, R.A., Darwish, A., Hassanien, A.E.: Hybrid intelligent intrusion detection scheme. In: Gaspar-Cunha, A., Takahashi, R., Schaefer, G., Costa, L. (eds.) Soft computing in industrial applications. AINSC, vol. 96, pp. 293–303. Springer, Heidelberg (2011). https://doi.org/10.1007/978-3-642-20505-7_26

21. Sapre, S., Ahmadi, P., Islam, K.R.: A robust comparison of the KDDCup99 and NSL-KDD IoT network intrusion detection datasets through various machine learning algorithms. arXiv abs/1912.13204 (2019)

22. Sharafaldin, I., Lashkari, A., Ghorbani, A.: Toward generating a new intrusion detection dataset and intrusion traffic characterization. In: ICISSP (2018)

23. Siddique, K., Akhtar, Z., Khan, F.A., Kim, Y.: KDD Cup 99 data sets: a perspective on the role of data sets in network intrusion detection research. Computer **52**, 41–51 (2019)

24. Tao, X., Kong, D., Wei, Y., Wang, Y.: A big network traffic data fusion approach based on fisher and deep auto-encoder. Information **7**(2), 20 (2016)

25. Tavallaee, M., Bagheri, E., Lu, W., Ghorbani, A.: A detailed analysis of the KDD CUP 99 data set. 2009 IEEE Symposium on Computational Intelligence for Security and Defense Applications, pp. 1–6 (2009)

26. Zavrak, S., İskefiyeli, M.: Anomaly-based intrusion detection from network flow features using variational autoencoder. IEEE Access **8**, 108346–108358 (2020). https://doi.org/10.1109/ACCESS.2020.3001350

27. Zhang, B., Yu, Y., Li, J.: Network intrusion detection based on stacked sparse autoencoder and binary tree ensemble method. In: 2018 IEEE International Conference on Communications Workshops (ICC Workshops). IEEE (2018)

ConTheModel: Can We Modify Tweets to Confuse Classifier Models?

Aishwarya Ram Vinay⬤, Mohsen Ali Alawami⬤, and Hyoungshick Kim⁽⌧⁾⬤

Department of Electrical and Computer Engineering, Sungkyunkwan University,
Suwon, South Korea
{aishwarya,mohsencomm,hyoung}@skku.edu

Abstract. News on social media can significantly influence users, manipulating them for political or economic reasons. Adversarial manipulations in the text have proven to create vulnerabilities in classifiers, and the current research is towards finding classifier models that are not susceptible to such manipulations. In this paper, we present a novel technique called ConTheModel, which slightly modifies social media news to confuse machine learning (ML)-based classifiers under the black-box setting. ConTheModel replaces a word in the original tweet with its synonym or antonym to generate tweets that confuse classifiers. We evaluate our technique on three different scenarios of the dataset and perform a comparison between five well-known machine learning algorithms, which includes Support Vector Machine (SVM), Naive Bayes (NB), Random Forest (RF), eXtreme Gradient Boosting (XGBoost), and Multilayer Perceptron (MLP) to demonstrate the performance of classifiers on the modifications done by ConTheModel. Our results show that the classifiers are confused after modification with the utmost drop of 16.36%. We additionally conducted a human study with 25 participants to validate the effectiveness of ConTheModel and found that the majority of participants (65%) found it challenging to classify the tweets correctly. We hope our work will help in finding robust ML models against adversarial examples.

Keywords: Machine learning · Social media · Adversarial examples · Tweets

1 Introduction

Various social media platforms are used by a large number of population worldwide for communication as it is easily accessible. Statistics show that in 2020, approximately 3.6 billion people were using social media, and this number would increase by almost another billion by 2025 [6]. All is fine unless otherwise, when what is passed off as "news" on social media is often disinformation. Contrary to real news, fake news develops stories instead of reporting facts. Last October, a new law was passed in Singapore, which bans the spreading of false information. This law does so by allowing the government to instruct popular online social

© Springer Nature Switzerland AG 2021
Y. Park et al. (Eds.): SVCC 2020, CCIS 1383, pp. 205–219, 2021.
https://doi.org/10.1007/978-3-030-72725-3_15

platforms to either remove or rectify the statements that are not in accordance with the general public's welfare [22].

Adversarial manipulations have taken the world by storm. To look at the basic, fake news has created havoc in people's lives since times immemorial, taking an even more serious turn during the 2016 US presidential election. When something as non-trivial as fake news can shake the world, one can imagine the severe impact of perturbations in the text. Even though adversarial learning has helped improve many models' performance, adversarial examples seem to attack state-of-the-art machine learning and deep learning models. The main agenda behind adversarial manipulations (a.k.a maliciously crafted inputs) is to fool the classifiers in producing a wrong output, and these manipulations have found their way into image classification [17,27], speech recognition [4,5], reinforcement learning [2], and natural language classification problems [3,12,30] amongst others. An attacker can arbitrarily create perturbations in the input which are usually unnoticeable to humans but can confuse the classifier by degrading its performance. As adversarial examples are a matter of security, recent research has focused on identifying machine learning classifiers that can be easily fooled and attacked. To contribute to the ongoing research, we propose a new approach called ConTheModel to study the extent to which machine learning classifiers can be confused using the well-designed adversarial examples, which results in the degradation of the models' F1 scores.

Without loss of generality, we develop an algorithm to replace the words with their synonyms or antonyms provided by NLTK corpus's WordNet package [21]. We train the ML models on source tweets collected from Twitter and labeled by professional journalists [31]. During the testing phase, we test the models' performance on (1) original samples (source tweets) and (2) successfully generated adversarial examples that are semantically and syntactically similar to that of the original samples. To show the effectiveness of ConTheModel, we used different categories of machine learning models, including Support Vector Machine (SVM), Naive Bayes (NB), Random Forest (RF), eXtreme Gradient Boosting (XGBoost), and Multilayer Perceptron (MLP) in our experiments. The test results show that the classifiers' performance is degraded after modification, indicating that generated adversarial examples can confuse models without changing the context of tweets. Through our experimental analysis and by considering all scenarios, we found the maximum drops in F1 scores of 13.18%, 16.36%, 12.34%, 12.09%, and 11.18% for RF, XGBoost, MLP, SVM and NB respectively. We also evaluate our approach by conducting a human study to show the modified tweets' effectiveness on human participants.

Our main contributions are as follows:

1. We propose an efficient approach called ConTheModel to investigate the feasibility of confusing classifier-based detection methods on tweets.
2. Our developed ConTheModel approach focuses on considering synonyms or antonyms as a replacement of the target words in tweets to confuse the classifiers.

3. We evaluate the performance of ConTheModel on the PHEME dataset with nine events using five different classifiers, and low results show the validity of our approach at confusing the classifiers under three different scenarios.

The rest of the paper is organized as follows: In Sect. 2, we provide the most recent papers related to our work, then we describe our system overview and algorithm in Sect. 3. The evaluation setup and information about the classifiers used are presented in Sect. 4. The details of the experimental results are shown in Sect. 5. The performance of human evaluation is discussed in Sect. 6. Finally, our conclusions and suggestions for future research are presented in Sect. 7.

2   Related Work

In recent years, adversarial examples have been explored in various domains such as image, video, text classification, and others. The generation of these adversarial examples have been widely studied to bypass the neural networks and many other machine learning classification models. Primarily, it found its way into deep neural networks' classification algorithms exploring into image recognition domain. In this domain, prior work generated examples via optimization techniques by setting in motion unnoticeable changes to the pixel values until the distortion limit was reached [9,18,20,26]. Also, Kurakin et al. [17] showed that machine learning systems could be misclassified if the examples were also constructed in the physical world and perceived through a camera.

Contrary to the image recognition domain, even the smallest change in the natural language domain is noticeable. In the information age, the internet community has become the hotspot for generating fake news due to the ease of creating and spreading this type of news. Consequently, it has garnered researchers' attention in finding efficient mechanisms to detect fake news [13]. Moreover, classifiers are susceptible to attacks where the attacker causes perturbations in the input, resulting in classifiers' misclassification. Adversarial examples have been created in a white-box setting such as the HotFlip method in [7] that performed character editing operations (such as flip, insertion, and deletion) as well as word-level operations against classifiers at both character-level and word-level deep neural network classifier, respectively. Assuming a black-box setting, Alzantot et al. [1] developed a gradient-free optimization algorithm to generate adversarial examples inspired by the natural selection process. They minimized the number of changes in the sentence and performed the attack on the IMDB dataset (Sentiment analysis task) and SNLI (Textual entailment task). In contrast to our work, Jia et al. [11] considered only antonyms from WordNet, and they worked on confusing the models into giving an incorrect answer by inserting sentences to the paragraphs on which questions have been asked. Papernot et al. [24] has shown that by replacing minimal words, an adversary can mislead the categorical and sequential recurrent neural networks without much importance given to grammatically correct adversarial examples. Similar to the generative adversarial network (GAN) [8], Ma et al. [19] proposed an approach where they promote information campaigns via uncertain and conflicting voices in twitter claims. The work in [12] considered a synonym based attack under black-box setting against various target models, including the powerful pre-trained BERT. Vijayaraghavan et al. [29] uses a reinforcement learning frame to generate adversarial examples that operate over characters and words of an input text.

Machine learning algorithms have succeeded in various tasks, amongst which is classification. The relationship between 13 different ML models on new and unseen rumors was investigated, and an ensemble solution of three models, Random Forest, XGBoost, and Multilayer Perceptron were created that overall produced a good F1 score [14]. However, many machine learning classifiers are susceptible to perturbations caused by adversarial attacks and are also vulnerable in various domains. Hu et al. [10] proposed an algorithm based on GAN, which generated adversarial malware examples that bypassed the machine learning-based detection models considering it as a black-box. Similarly, the vulnerability of machine learning classifiers in malware detection by generating five applications is shown in [28] that eventually resulted in yielding a higher misclassification rate. The work in [16] addresses the adversarial inputs on tasks such as spam filtering, sentiment analysis, and fake news detection against LSTM, CNN, and Naive Bayes classifiers. However, in our work, we focus on the tweets' modifications and conducted comprehensive experiments under three different scenarios to evaluate the performance of five categories of classifier-based ML models.

3   ConTheModel Overview

In this section, we present the dataset used in our experiments, the architecture of ConTheModel, and our developed algorithm.

3.1   Dataset

In our work, we consider the PHEME dataset, which is publicly available [15] and is associated with nine buzzworthy news events (Charlie Hebdo, Ferguson, Germanwings Crash, Sydney Siege, Putin Missing, Prince Toronto, Ottawa Shooting, Gurlitt, Ebola Essien) on Twitter. With the collected dataset, news events were classified into rumors and non-rumors. Rumors emerged as unverified at the time of posting and were later proven to be true, false, or remained unverified by professional journalists. According to the dataset's annotation, True news: "misinformation: 0, true: 1"; False news: "misinformation: 1, true: 0"; Unverified news: "misinformation: 0, true: 0".

The rumor news that was proven to be false were rumorous tweets, whereas the rumor news that was proven to be true were non-rumorous tweets. For our work, we ignore unverified news as there is not much information in the dataset but consider only verified tweets. Each tweet is a conversation that consists of the source tweet conveying the news and a thread of responses expressing their opinion to this tweet (response tweets). Table 1 shows the number of rumor and non-rumor tweets of the PHEME dataset; as can be seen, except for Gurlitt

Table 1. Distribution of Rumor and Non-Rumor tweets across all the events of PHEME dataset.

Events	Rumors	Non-rumors
Charlie Hebdo	116	1814
Ferguson	8	869
Germanwings Crash	111	325
Sydney Siege	86	1081
Putin Missing	9	112
Prince Toronto	222	4
Ottawa Shooting	72	749
Gurlitt	0	136
Ebola Essien	14	0

event, all the other events have rumor tweets, and except Ebola Essien event, all the other events have non-rumor tweets. We considered source tweets which contain millennial slang words and hashes as the original sentences that need to be modified.

3.2 System Methodology and Algorithm

The architecture of the proposed ConTheModel is shown in Fig. 1. We split the PHEME dataset into two portions where 75% of the dataset is trained, and the rest 25% is tested as both original and modified. To validate our technique, we compared categories of ML models such as Random Forest, perceptron-based (Multilayer Perceptron), statistical learning (Naive Bayes), Support Vector Machine, and eXtreme Gradient Boosting algorithm. From Fig. 1, Original (1) and Modified (2) test sets are predicted by the ML models to observe the difference in score. We explain our developed modification algorithm shown in Algorithm 1 as follows. We consider 25% of original sentences for modification. Acronyms used to explain the algorithm is defined in **lines 1–7**.

In the beginning, every original sample (OS) in the dataset (X) is considered and tokenized into words (OW), and the score of each OW is calculated based on the probability distribution of n-grams in Gutenberg corpus using the smoothing technique of Kneser-Ney [23]. In **lines 11-21**, we find the position of OW in OS to ensure the substitute words are placed in the respective positions. For each OW, we check for its corresponding synsets in WordNet to replace the OW. WordNet is the NLTK corpus's lexical database and includes words from various parts of speech such as nouns, adjectives, verbs, adverbs but ignores prepositions, determiners, and other function words.

Synsets are a set of synonyms and identified by a 3-part name of the form: word.pos.nn. The first part of the 3-part name of synsets (word) is considered and appended to the list of synonyms (SL) by avoiding repetition of words. Similarly, the list of antonyms (AL) is created by finding antonyms for the OW

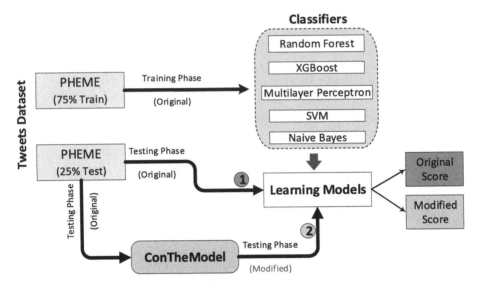

Fig. 1. Overview of ConTheModel.

in WordNet, and these two lists are merged into a dictionary of the form "OW: SL or AL". For example, the word "hold" will have a dictionary of the form, hold: [clasp, grip, carry, give, let_go_of] where "hold" is the key and list on the left are the values. Therefore in our algorithm, the OW is selected for modification provided it has synonyms or antonyms in WordNet.

Furthermore, in **lines 23–25**, considering that there are n OWs in a sentence that can be replaced and each of these OWs consists of m values of variable length, we consider maximum length of m to restrict the number of modified samples (MS) that can be formed. For example, the word "forced" may have a length of m as two, whereas the word "hold" may have a length of five (maximum length). In **lines 26–38**, we replace n OWs in OS with its corresponding m values to form modified samples until maximum length is reached. These MSs are then tokenized, and score is calculated like in OS to ensure that we arrive at a single MS out of all the MSs for each OS. We selected the MS with a minimum score as we found that this showed better performance of our system. In **line 39**, a list of MS is created and are fed to the classifiers to predict the samples as in **line 41**.

For more illustration, Table 2 provides examples of original and modified tweets with multiple word replacements per tweet. As m values are a combination of both SL and AL, the OWs in the OS can be modified using synonym or antonym or union of both. The original words in the original tweets are highlighted in blue (italics), and the modified words in the modified tweets are highlighted in red (italics).

Algorithm 1: Modification of source tweets.

Input : Original test samples(source tweets)
Output: Modified test samples(source tweets)

1 OS: Original test sample
2 MS: Modified test sample
3 X: 25% of the dataset
4 OW: Original word
5 SL: synonym_list
6 AL: antonym_list
7 z: values of both SL and AL

8 **foreach** *OS in X* **do**
9   list_word ← Tokenize OS into words.
10   Calculate the score of each original word.
11   **foreach** *OW in list_word* **do**
12   **foreach** *k in wordnet.synsets(OW)* **do**
13   find the synonym word → build up SL.
14   find the antonym word → buld up AL.
15   **end**
16   **if** *SL and AL not empty* **then**
17   [OW: append(SL and AL)] → dictionary.
18   **else**
19   non empty list → dictionary.
20   **end**
21   **end**
22   max_length = 0.
23   **foreach** *items in dictionary_values* **do**
24   max_length ← Length (longest list of values).
25   **end**
26   **foreach** *i in range(max_length)* **do**
27   **foreach** *OW, z in the dictionary_values* **do**
28   **if** *i < max_length* **then**
29   Replace OW in OS with the values of (SL and AL) to form MS.
30   **end**
31   **end**
32   **if** *OS is not equal to MS* **then**
33   Tokenize MS into words.
34   Calculate the score of MS.
35   Scores←append (score).
36   Get MS sentence with min(Scores).
37   **end**
38   **end**
39   Append MS to list_MS.
40 **end**
41 Provide list_MS to the model to predict.

Table 2. Examples of original tweets and the corresponding modified tweets using ConTheModel.

Relation	Original Tweet	Modified Tweet
Synonym	For those *saying* we don't *yet know* who's responsible for #CharlieHebdo killings, yes, you're right, it *was probably* fundamentalist atheists.	For those *allege* we don't *nevertheless recognize* who's responsible for #CharlieHebdo killings, yes, you're right, it *constitute likely* fundamentalist atheists.
Antonym	JUST IN: Germanwings plane crashes in *southern* France, up to 150 feared *dead* http://t.co/GIZjXnqBU3	JUST IN: Germanwings plane crashes in *northern* France, up to 150 feared *alive* http://t.co/GIZjXnqBU3
Synonym & Antonym	BREAKING a hostage siege in Sydney with a *man* with an IS flag or similar - *live* reports from @bkjabour http://t.co/VWugbceCAR	BREAKING a hostage siege in Sydney with a *civilian* with an IS flag or similar - *dead* reports from @bkjabour http://t.co/VWugbceCAR

4   Evaluation

In this section, we describe the evaluation setup, metric and the classifiers that are used in our work.

4.1   Evaluation Setup

In order to evaluate our technique, 75% of the total dataset is used to train the models and the rest are used to test the performance of the models. We train the models assuming that the attacker has no prior knowledge of the models being targeted. Initially, we gather the performance results of the trained models on original samples, and then we use the modified samples to evaluate the performance using the same trained models. Efficiency of our work is evaluated based on the dissimilarity between the performance results of original and modified samples. During evaluation, we considered PHEME dataset which consists of tweets that were associated with nine buzzworthy news events on Twitter. While exploring the dataset, we observed that the dataset is unbalanced as it contains fewer rumors than non-rumors, as summarized in Table 1. We conducted our experiments on data from different events to investigate our ConTheModel technique's effectiveness in three different scenarios, i.e., *Individual*, *Topics*, and *All Events*. For each scenario, we compared our results between different classifiers such as Random Forest (RF), eXtreme Gradient Boosting (XGBoost), Multilayer Perceptron (MLP), Support Vector Machine (SVM), and

Naive Bayes (NB) which were implemented using the scikit-learn library [25]. The three evaluation scenarios are summarized as follows.

Individual: Since the PHEME dataset consists of nine events, among them seven events (Charlie Hebdo, Ferguson, Germanwings Crash, Sydney Siege, Putin Missing, Prince Toronto, Ottawa Shooting) have both rumour and non-rumour tweets whereas the other two events have either rumour (Ebola Essien) or Non-rumour (Gurlitt) only tweets. Therefore, in this evaluation we consider the seven events which have both rumor and non-rumor tweets.

Topics: The dataset is associated with nine buzzworthy events which are then segregated into five rumor topics [14]; i.e., *Crime* (Charlie Hebdo, Ferguson, Sydney Siege, Ottawa Shooting), Politic (Putin Missing), Entertainment (Prince Toronto), Impact (Germanwings Crash), and *Mixed* (Ebola Essien, Gurlitt). Here, we consider topics with greater than one event.

All Events: In this evaluation scenario, in addition to the seven events considered in *Individual*, we considered Gurlitt and Ebola Essien events as well. So, all the nine events from the PHEME dataset were assessed.

4.2   Evaluation Metrics

We measured the performance of the models on our technique based on F1 score.

Assuming that original samples are labeled as positive and modified samples are labeled as negative, the definitions in the context of our paper can be as follows:

- *True Positive (TP):* If the samples belonging to an actual class (positive) are correctly classified as the positive class.
- *True Negative (TN):* If the samples belonging to an actual class (negative) are correctly classified as the negative class.
- *False Negative (FN):* If the samples belonging to an actual class (positive) are incorrectly classified as the negative class.
- *False Positive (FP):* If the samples belonging to an actual class (negative) are incorrectly classified as the positive class.

So F1 score is calculated as follows:

- *Precision:* The ratio of true positive samples and all tested samples.
- *Recall:* The ratio of true positive samples and all predicted samples.
- *F1 score:* The weighted average of the above two metrics.

4.3   Classifiers

In this section, we explain the classifiers used in our experiments.

Support Vector Machines (SVM). Support Vector Networks are advanced supervised learning algorithm that is used for classification and regression. The basic idea of SVM is of a margin (termed "hyperplane") where either side of the hyperplane form two different classes, and a newly observed object is classified into a class depending on which side of the hyperplane the object lies on.

Naive Bayes (NB). Naive Bayes is a collection of supervised learning classification techniques based on the probability of the Bayesian theorem. NB classifiers work with a strong assumption that given the class variable, the particular feature's value is independent of any other feature's value.

Multilayer Perceptron (MLP). Multilayer Perceptron (MLP) is a perceptron based technique that utilizes the supervised learning algorithm called backpropagation for training. MLP classifier can be viewed as a logistic regression classifier but differs from it so that MLP has at least one hidden layer between the input and the output layer.

Random Forest (RF). Random Forest is also a supervised learning algorithm that applies the bagging technique, which combines several base learners with low correlation to improve the overall result compared to an individual model. Random forest is an ensemble of decision trees where each decision tree is allowed to grow to its maximum extent, and each tree outputs a class, and the class with the maximum count becomes the model's output.

eXtreme Gradient Boosting (XGBoost). The eXtreme Gradient Boosting algorithm (XGBoost) is an ensemble learning method that applies the boosting technique. Boosting is one of the ensemble learners in which trees are built sequentially so that the succeeding tree in the sequence learns from the preceding trees.

5   Classification Results

As presented in Sect. 4, we used different categories of ML classifiers from the scikit-learn library that classify original samples and samples modified by our ConTheModel technique. The classification results provide insights into the performance of our modification technique. We noticed that our dataset is mostly comprised of tweets with a single sentence and has millennial words/lingos, hashes, and links, as a result of which it is hard to find a replacement when compared to most of the other works which attempt to modify more than a single sentence or contains non-millennial words.

We evaluate the efficiency of our work by considering our technique's performance on samples from different events of the dataset under three evaluation scenarios (as mentioned in Sect. 4.1). The samples (column "Sentence") in all scenarios have been classified as *original* and *modified* with F1 score as the metric to measure the performance of the models.

For the first evaluation scenario, we consider events with both rumor and non-rumor tweets (seven events) as shown in Table 1 and report the performance results for individual events in Table 3 on the classifiers. The classifiers' performance is low for samples modified by our ConTheModel technique compared

Table 3. Adversarial evaluation on the classifiers for individual events.

Classifiers	Sentence	Charlie Hebdo	Ferguson	Germanwings Crash	Sydney Siege	Putin Missing	Prince Toronto	Ottawa Shooting
RF	Original	75.10	59.81	90.38	62.00	47.45	78.86	78.68
	Modified	**64.38**	59.50	79.65	59.49	47.42	74.62	65.50
XGBoost	Original	73.19	56.47	85.23	65.52	47.62	59.18	76.79
	Modified	63.41	49.79	**70.59**	61.34	47.42	49.55	**60.43**
MLP	Original	81.70	54.74	87.72	65.08	58.81	49.55	82.17
	Modified	77.42	54.70	75.38	62.24	**53.65**	49.10	73.89
SVM	Original	77.76	49.69	81.16	53.13	48.14	79.73	80.80
	Modified	73.33	49.60	69.07	51.03	48.10	79.63	71.25
NB	Original	49.17	51.31	70.38	54.81	52.23	69.55	67.33
	Modified	41.00	**44.13**	59.68	**46.42**	51.37	**59.37**	56.15

to original samples across all seven events. In detail, we noticed the maximum drop (highlighted in bold) as follows: 7.18%, 8.39% and 10.18% for NB on three events, 14.64% and 16.36% for XGBoost on two events, whereas the other classifiers, i.e., RF, MLP showed a drop of 10.72% and 5.16% respectively for one event each. Also, we observed that RF had an average drop of 5.96% in F1 score; XGBoost shows an average drop of 8.78%; MLP shows an average drop of 4.77%; SVM had an average drop of 4.05%, and NB has an average drop of 8.09% across all the seven events.

Table 4. Adversarial evaluation on the classifiers for Crime and Mixed topics.

Topic	Sentence	Classifiers				
		RF	XGBoost	MLP	SVM	NB
Crime	Original	60.52	62.16	64.74	56.39	34.85
	Modified	50.75	57.10	56.07	51.25	30.86
Mixed	Original	100	73.61	100	100	100
	Modified	97.41	70.90	100	89.29	91.66

In addition, to evaluate ConTheModel's effectiveness on data from a combination of events, we conducted our experiments on six events, which are grouped as *Crime* and *Mixed* (explained in Sect. 4.1). Since the topics related to Politic, Entertainment, and Impact have one event each and have been already considered in Table 3, we pick topics with greater than one event for this scenario. In Table 4, considering the F1 score for modified samples of *Crime*, RF had the maximum drop of 9.77% whereas NB had the lowest drop of 3.99%, and under *Mixed*, SVM showed the maximum drop of 10.71% with RF classifier having the lowest drop (2.59%) whereas the F1 score remains the same for MLP.

We hypothesize that since the number of tweets in both the events under *Mixed* is small, it can be a reason for no change in the F1 score for MLP. Overall, across all classifiers, there was a drop of 6.52% under *Crime* and a drop of 4.87% under *Mixed*.

Table 5. Adversarial evaluation on the classifiers for all events.

Sentence	Classifiers				
	RF	XGBoost	MLP	SVM	NB
Original	75.47	74.15	76.01	71.60	48.16
Modified	72.76	72.04	73.34	69.65	46.35

Finally, we provide the third evaluation scenario where all the nine events are evaluated, and the results of our system's performance on the classifiers are shown in Table 5. We observed that RF had the maximum drop of 2.71% in F1 score, whereas NB had the lowest drop of 1.81%, and the average drop across all classifiers was 2.25%. We observed that models had a performance drop in their F1 scores when tested with modified tweets. We found that in the: first scenario, XGBoost had the maximum drop of 16.36%; in the second scenario, SVM had the maximum drop of 10.71%, and in the third scenario, RF had a maximum drop of 2.71%.

6   Human Evaluation

We verified our technique's efficiency by conducting a human evaluation with 25 participants in a realistic scenario where we considered participants from various nationalities such as Canada, Ethiopia, India, Pakistan, South Korea, Ukraine, USA, Vietnam, and Yemen. Participants in our evaluation skewed male: male (17; 68%), female (8; 32%) with an age range of 23–45 years. The evaluation was conducted online for a week, and participants were instructed not to refer to any search engines to avoid colluding with our work. The participants were provided with 33 randomly chosen questions (samples/ tweets), a combination of either original or modified samples. Participants were then asked to choose an option on a 5-point Likert scale, ranging from "Surely Original" to "Not sure" to "Surely Modified" according to their perceptions. They were also given an option to choose "Somewhat Original" or "Somewhat Modified" if they were not 100% sure about the questions being original or modified.

We assessed the results of our evaluation by iterating over each question's response by every participant, and we arrived at the number of participants who: "correctly classified" (if the question is actually original and the participant has responded as either "Surely Original" or "Somewhat Original") or "confused" (if the participant has responded as "Not sure") or "wrongly classified" (if the question is actually original and the participant has responded as either "Surely

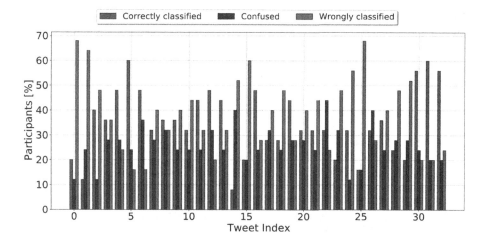

Fig. 2. Human evaluation of each sentence.

Modified" or "Somewhat Modified") each question. As shown in Fig. 2, green represents samples that were correctly classified; red represents samples that were wrongly classified; blue represents samples that were classified as confused. We found that majority of participants: wrongly classified 18 (54.54%) samples, correctly classified 12 (36.36%) samples, confused about two (6.06%) samples, and one (3.04%) was both wrong as well as correctly classified (as in Tweet Index three).

Next, we averaged the response of all 25 participants across each of the 33 questions and found that our human evaluation resulted in 35% of the participants correctly classifying the samples to the original label and 39% of the participants wrongly classifying the samples. However, the remaining 26% were confused as they were not sure about the samples' labels. Our evaluation concluded that majority of the humans (65%) found it difficult to classify the samples correctly and could not detect the modification on tweets.

7   Conclusion

This paper proposed a technique named ConTheModel that generates adversarial examples of tweets to confuse five ML algorithms in three different evaluation scenarios. ConTheModel replaces target words in the original sentence with their respective synonyms or antonyms to form a modified sentence.

Our extensive experiments demonstrate that, on average most of the classifiers were confused in all three evaluation scenarios by showing a drop in performance. Furthermore, our human evaluation justified that humans found it challenging to classify the samples correctly. Our further research will be targeted towards finding other ML classifiers that can be confused by our technique and find robust models that defend against adversarial examples.

Acknowledgments. This work was supported by the ICT R&D Programs (no. 2017-0-00545) and the ITRC Support Program (IITP-2019-2015-0-00403).

References

1. Alzantot, M., Sharma, Y., Elgohary, A., Ho, B.J., Srivastava, M., Chang, K.W.: Generating natural language adversarial examples. arXiv preprint arXiv:1804.07998 (2018)
2. Behzadan, V., Munir, A.: Vulnerability of deep reinforcement learning to policy induction attacks. In: Perner, P. (ed.) MLDM 2017. LNCS (LNAI), vol. 10358, pp. 262–275. Springer, Cham (2017). https://doi.org/10.1007/978-3-319-62416-7_19
3. Biggio, B., et al.: Evasion attacks against machine learning at test time. In: Blockeel, H., Kersting, K., Nijssen, S., Železný, F. (eds.) ECML PKDD 2013. LNCS (LNAI), vol. 8190, pp. 387–402. Springer, Heidelberg (2013). https://doi.org/10.1007/978-3-642-40994-3_25
4. Carlini, N., et al.: Hidden voice commands. In: 25th USENIX Security Symposium (USENIX Security 16), pp. 513–530 (2016)
5. Carlini, N., Wagner, D.: Audio adversarial examples: targeted attacks on speech-to-text. In: 2018 IEEE Security and Privacy Workshops (SPW), pp. 1–7. IEEE (2018)
6. Clement, J.: Number of social network users worldwide from 2017 to 2025 (2020)
7. Ebrahimi, J., Rao, A., Lowd, D., Dou, D.: HotFlip: white-box adversarial examples for text classification. arXiv preprint arXiv:1712.06751 (2017)
8. Goodfellow, I., et al.: Generative adversarial nets. In: Advances in Neural Information Processing Systems, pp. 2672–2680 (2014)
9. Goodfellow, I.J., Shlens, J., Szegedy, C.: Explaining and harnessing adversarial examples. arXiv preprint arXiv:1412.6572 (2014)
10. Hu, W., Tan, Y.: Generating adversarial malware examples for black-box attacks based on GAN. arXiv preprint arXiv:1702.05983 (2017)
11. Jia, R., Liang, P.: Adversarial examples for evaluating reading comprehension systems. arXiv preprint arXiv:1707.07328 (2017)
12. Jin, D., Jin, Z., Zhou, J.T., Szolovits, P.: TextFool: fool your model with natural adversarial text (2019)
13. Kaliyar, R.K., Goswami, A., Narang, P.: Multiclass fake news detection using ensemble machine learning. In: 2019 IEEE 9th International Conference on Advanced Computing (IACC), pp. 103–107. IEEE (2019)
14. Kim, Y., Kim, H.K., Kim, H., Hong, J.B.: Do many models make light work? evaluating ensemble solutions for improved rumor detection. IEEE Access **8**, 150709–150724 (2020)
15. Kochkina, E., Liakata, M., Zubiaga, A.: All-in-one: multi-task learning for rumour verification. arXiv preprint arXiv:1806.03713 (2018)
16. Kuleshov, V., Thakoor, S., Lau, T., Ermon, S.: Adversarial examples for natural language classification problems (2018)
17. Kurakin, A., Goodfellow, I., Bengio, S.: Adversarial examples in the physical world. arXiv preprint arXiv:1607.02533 (2016)
18. Kurakin, A., Goodfellow, I., Bengio, S.: Adversarial machine learning at scale. arXiv preprint arXiv:1611.01236 (2016)
19. Ma, J., Gao, W., Wong, K.F.: Detect rumors on twitter by promoting information campaigns with generative adversarial learning. In: The World Wide Web Conference, pp. 3049–3055 (2019)

20. Madry, A., Makelov, A., Schmidt, L., Tsipras, D., Vladu, A.: Towards deep learning models resistant to adversarial attacks. arXiv preprint arXiv:1706.06083 (2017)
21. Miller, G.A.: Princeton university "about wordnet." (2010). https://wordnet.princeton.edu/
22. BBC News: Facebook bows to Singapore's 'fake news' law with post 'correction', 30 November 2019. https://www.bbc.com/news/world-asia-50613341
23. Ney, H., Essen, U., Kneser, R.: On structuring probabilistic dependences in stochastic language modelling. Comput. Speech Lang. **8**(1), 1–38 (1994)
24. Papernot, N., McDaniel, P., Swami, A., Harang, R.: Crafting adversarial input sequences for recurrent neural networks. In: MILCOM 2016–2016 IEEE Military Communications Conference, pp. 49–54. IEEE (2016)
25. Pedregosa, F., et al.: Scikit-learn: machine learning in Python. J. Mach. Learn. Res. **12**, 2825–2830 (2011)
26. Sharma, Y., Chen, P.Y.: Attacking the madry defense model with l_1-based adversarial examples. arXiv preprint arXiv:1710.10733 (2017)
27. Szegedy, C., et al.: Intriguing properties of neural networks. arXiv preprint arXiv:1312.6199 (2013)
28. Taheri, R., Javidan, R., Shojafar, M., Vinod, P., Conti, M.: Can machine learning model with static features be fooled: an adversarial machine learning approach. Cluster Comput. **23**(4), 3233–3253 (2020). https://doi.org/10.1007/s10586-020-03083-5
29. Vijayaraghavan, P., Roy, D.: Generating black-box adversarial examples for text classifiers using a deep reinforced model. In: Brefeld, U., Fromont, E., Hotho, A., Knobbe, A., Maathuis, M., Robardet, C. (eds.) ECML PKDD 2019. LNCS (LNAI), vol. 11907, pp. 711–726. Springer, Cham (2020). https://doi.org/10.1007/978-3-030-46147-8_43
30. Wang, X., Jin, H., He, K.: Natural language adversarial attacks and defenses in word level. arXiv preprint arXiv:1909.06723 (2019)
31. Zubiaga, A., Liakata, M., Procter, R., Wong Sak Hoi, G., Tolmie, P.: Analysing how people orient to and spread rumours in social media by looking at conversational threads. PloS One **11**(3), e0150989 (2016)

IoT Checker Using Timing Side-Channel and Machine Learning

Kratika Sahu◉, Rasika Kshirsagar◉, Surbhi Vasudeva(✉)◉,
Taghreed Alzahrani◉, and Nima Karimian◉

San Jose State University, One Washington Square, San Jose, CA 95192, USA
{kratika.sahu,rasikaramesh.kshirsagar,surbhi.vasudeva,
taghreed.alzahrani,nima.karimian}@sjsu.edu

Abstract. In the recent era, the adoption of IoT technology can be seen in nearly every other field. However, with its fast growth rate, the IoT brings several advanced security challenges. To alleviate these problems, we propose an inventive framework introduced into the IoT package to gather side-channel information (execution timing) for inconsistency and attack location. We observed that the applications running on the gadget would need more time to execute during the attack as the resources such as memory, I/O, CPU will get drained. This timing information under normal and attack mode will be extracted, processed, and utilized to construct a fingerprint. The support vector machine method will then be used to identify if the device is under attack utilizing the fingerprint.

Keywords: IoT security · Side-channel-attack · Machine learning

1 Introduction

Cybercriminals around the world work continuously to discover new techniques to invade the networks. Specifically, they attempt to find a vulnerable node in the network to quickly get hold of an extensive network. With the advent of the first network-connected smart devices in 1982, IoT now shares a place in almost every network. By 2025, IoT technology is anticipated to touch 6.2 trillion worth [1]. *This rapid growth also brings new security and privacy challenges.* According to numerous investigations carried by M.A.Khan et al. [2], IoT devices are vulnerable to various attacks (Fig. 1).

The IoT ecosystem has four different layers: **sensing, networking, middleware, and application layer** and each layer has a specific function to perform. The sensing layer comprises sensors and actuators, the networking layer is responsible for transmitting the acquired data, the middleware layer is liable for computing and storage, and the application layer takes care of the user inter interfacing capabilities. As each layer has different functionalities, they are susceptible to a different kind of attack illustrated in Fig. 2.

The present security solutions for IoT devices are not entirely successful. Different manufacturers follow various standards, which makes it challenging to

© Springer Nature Switzerland AG 2021
Y. Park et al. (Eds.): SVCC 2020, CCIS 1383, pp. 220–226, 2021.
https://doi.org/10.1007/978-3-030-72725-3_16

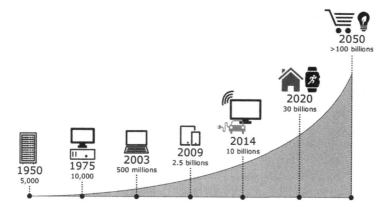

Fig. 1. Expected adoption growth of IoT devices [3]

devise a suitable solution for all ranges of smart objects. The project centers on providing a security solution for IoT devices based on side-channel information and machine learning. It implements a security framework that could recognize a suspicious attack by utilizing the side-channel timing information and machine learning. This recognition is achieved by analyzing side-channel leakage while examining the time variations in process timings and using it as a fingerprint for future comparisons utilizing machine learning algorithms.

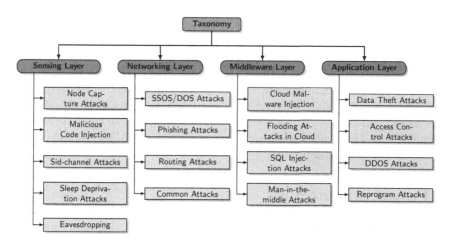

Fig. 2. Simple Taxonomy of attacks at different layers.

2   Literature Review

IoT gadgets are embedded gadgets associated with the web and are outlined to perform a wide variety of functionalities. There is a parcel of energizing and enlightening research working towards the well-known objective of securing IoT gadgets. Vikas Hasija et al. [4] have studied in detail a few issues and challenges found within the security of these gadgets. Additionally, Colakovic et al. [5] have also inspected specific issues commonly experienced within IoT gadgets' security. Moreover, they have talked about issues emerging from the need for standardization amongst IoT gadgets and distinctive advances that can be utilized to furnish security for these gadgets. To address the need for a standard classification of IoT gadgets models, numerous analysts like Kumar and Mallick et al. [6] have thoroughly discussed the diverse sorts of designs and components utilized in IoT gadgets over a long time.

Another essential feature discussed by Hasija et al. [4] is that they have classified different threats on the IoT devices following different IoT devices' layers. As any IoT application can be apportioned into four layers - Application Layer, Middleware Layer, Network Layer, and Sensing Layer, each layer uses a different technology that brings several security issues/threats. Attacks such as Node Capture attacks, Malicious Code Injection, Side Channel attack, Sleep Deprivation layer attack can be seen at the sensing layer. These attacks are feasible due to vulnerabilities and limitations of sensors and actuators appropriated in the sensing layer.

The network layer is responsible for transmitting data from the sensing layer to another layer for computational work. The network layer can be attacked employing Routing attacks, Phishing Site attacks, or DDOS attacks. After the network layer, the middleware layer acts as an abstraction layer for the APIs to associate the network layer to the application layer. This layer is susceptible to attacks like SQL Injection attack, ManInTheMiddle attack, Flooding attack within the cloud, Cloud Malware Injection. The final layer is the application layer, which is responsible for rendering administrations to the end-user. Most of the assaults are particular for a sort of application. Some of the security issues associated with the application layer are information theft, service interruption attacks, and sniffing assaults.

3   Project Architecture

As demonstrated in the project architecture Fig. 3, it comprises two major blocks: Data collection and Machine Learning. The data collection block involves gathering the side-channel timing data. IoT device comprises Raspberry Pi setup as Amazon Alexa and attacking device setup on another Raspberry Pi using Kali Linux. The data is being collected when the IoT device performs the regular operation and also during an attack. The collected data is then fed into the second block, which is the Machine Learning block. Within this block, first of all, the obtained data is prepared, i.e., extraction of features and cleanup.

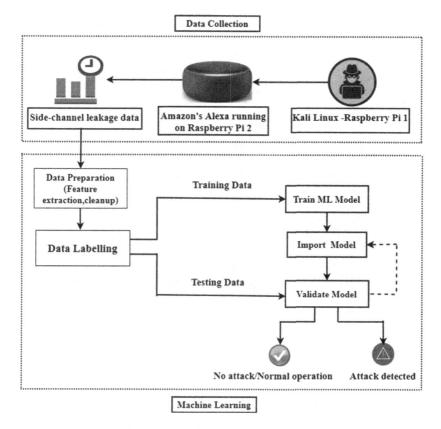

Fig. 3. Proposed project architecture to capture side-channel leakage and implement machine learning algorithm.

The processed data is then labeled to train the machine learning model - Support Vector Machine (SVM). Upon training, the model would be able to identify if the device is under attack.

4 Methodology

4.1 Experimental Setup

For the experiment, we emulated Amazon Alexa as an IoT device on Raspberry-pi 4. Amazon facilitates the Amazon Voice Service Software Development Kit to be configured on the IoT Device. We followed the steps provided in the documentation [7] to configure the emulated IoT device. We attacked the IoT device using Kali Linux version 2020.4 installed on Raspberry-pi 3. Further, we installed "gnomon" to capture timing variations. "gnomon" is a node JavaScript-based tool that can be utilized to get precise timing details. Running the IoT application by piping its output to "gnomon" would enable detailed timing variations (Fig. 4).

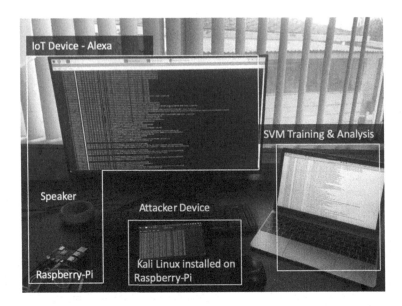

Fig. 4. Hardware Setup for setting up Raspberry Pi as Amazon Alexa - IoT device and attack it using Kali Linux.

4.2   Implementation of Attacks

We performed specific Denial of Service (DoS) attacks using Kali Linux to attack the IoT device. The DoS attack's primary intention is to deprive the attacked device of absolute necessities that it would remain unable to function normally.

Slowloris
Slowloris is a tool that can be utilized to send a huge number of HTTP requests within a concise duration of time, which exhausts the listening device. Once the script is installed on Kali Linux, it can be run as "slowloris IOT_DEVICE'S_IP_ADDRESS". As a result, the HTTP requests were sent to the IoT device, and we observed timing variations using the gnomon tool.

Goldeneye
Once the goldeneye tool is installed on Kali Linux [8], we ran the script using [8], we ran the script using "./goldeneye.py IOT_DEVICE'S_IP_ADDRESS". As a consequence, the IoT device was hit with several HTTP requests. Following this, we collected the timing variation data using the gnomon tool.

Pentmenu
This tool can be utilized to implement various DDOS attacks such as Slowloris, TCP RST Flood, ICMP Blacknurse Flood, TCP SYN Flood, TCP ACK Flood, ICMPEcho Flood, SSL DOS, UDP Flood, and TCP XMAS Flood [9]. Along with providing the Victim's address, the Pentmenu tool enables us to specify the number of connections and the timing duration between each sent request.

For our experimentation, we utilized 15000 connections generated every 5 s for port 80.

For all the attacks, we noted the process timing variations before and during the attack.

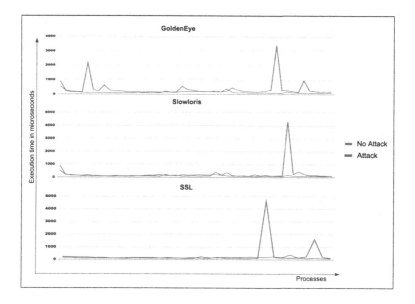

Fig. 5. Time variation for SSL attack.

4.3   Machine Learning Implementation

Since there is a reasonable thought of the anticipated output in this experiment, we have utilized an administered learning technique. Additionally, because we have to discovered if there is an 'attack' or 'no attack,' a classification procedure, the Support Vector Machine(SVM) strategy would be most appropriate for our issue. The SVM calculation takes input from the side-channel leakage of the IoT gadget. The input consists of the title of the processor prepare identifier and the time taken for the method to complete its execution. The dataset comprises of two types of information: 1. The execution time for the processes running on the IoT gadget when the gadget is beneath assault 2. The execution time for the processes running on IoT in case of normal behavior. The SVM will classify the preparing dataset into two classes: 1. Typical behavior class when there is no attack 2. Irregular behavior class when IoT gadget is under attack. Once trained, the SVM would differentiate between the two classes while selecting the hyperplane with the least classification error from multiple generated hyperplanes.

5 Result

Graphs in Fig. 5 demonstrate the side-channel leakage data in the form of a particular process's execution time on the x-axis vs. the process id on the y-axis. Each graph clearly illustrates the difference in execution time when under attack (marked orange) as the time taken is more than the one during normal execution(marked blue). Utilizing the machine learning model for classification, we tried to identify between attack and normal behavior within the first classification with an accuracy of 77.5%. Within multiclass classification, we implemented identification of two different attacks - Goldeneye and slowloris with an accuracy of 68.9%.

6 Conclusion

Utilizing machine learning through this research, we have attempted to control IoT gadgets' security risks. With the simulation of various attacks, we observed the device activity in both standard and abnormal operations. The side-channel timing data is recovered by comparison of both the operations. The collected information set is forwarded to the machine learning computation, which can foresee noxious activity on the gadget. For future work, a more extensive dataset can be utilized for training and testing. Furthermore, the machine learning algorithm can be extended to distinguish more types of attacks.

References

1. Nordrum, A.: Popular internet of things forecast of 50 billion devices by 2020 is outdated. In: IEEE Spectrum: Technology, Engineering, and Science News, 18 August 2016
2. Khan, M.A., et al.: IoT security: review, blockchain solutions, and open challenges. Future Gener. Comput. Syst. **82**, 395–411 (2018)
3. Capra, M., et al.: Edge computing: a survey on the hardware requirements in the internet of things world. Future Internet **11**, 100 (2019)
4. Hassija, V., Chamola, V., Saxena, V., Jain, D., Goyal, P., Sikdar, B.: A survey on IoT security: application areas, security threats, and solution architectures. IEEE Access **7**, 82721–82743 (2019)
5. Čolaković, A., Hadžialić, M.: Internet of things (IoT): a review of enabling technologies, challenges, and open research issues. Comput. Netw. **144**, 17–39 (2018)
6. Kumar, N.M., Mallick, P.K.: The internet of things: insights into the building blocks, component interactions, and architecture layers. Procedia Comput. Sci. **132**, 109–117 (2018)
7. Amazon Web Services. Prototype with the SDK and a Raspberry PI (2019). Accessed 12 Oct 2019
8. jseidl. Goldeneye
9. GinjaChris. pentmenu (2015). Accessed 13 Oct 2020

Author Index

Printed in the United States
by Baker & Taylor Publisher Services